Andrew Brown
and
Cypress Lumbering
In the Old Southwest

Andrew Brown
and
Cypress Lumbering
In the Old Southwest

John Hebron Moore

LOUISIANA STATE UNIVERSITY PRESS

To
Margaret
and
John Hebron, Jr.

Preface

MODERN historians know little about the lumber industry of the
Old South because few firms of that era left records behind.
The manufacturing of building materials below the Mason–Dixon
Line as late as the 1830's was usually undertaken on such a small
scale that elaborate bookkeeping was not essential, and most sawmills
other than export mills at the seaports were still selling their products
directly to local buyers. Under these conditions lumber manufacturers
and their customers exchanged a minimum of correspondence, as did
the various members of any company.

When the scope of lumbering expanded during the 1840's and
1850's, business records became more complex, and department heads
exchanged voluminous communications. Many of these documents,
however, disappeared in the numerous fires which plagued the Southern industry during the nineteenth century. Moreover, lumbermen
were indifferent to the historical value of outdated ledgers, journals,
and correspondence and seldom attempted to preserve them. As a
result, comparatively few collections of documents pertaining to the
lumber industry of the Old South are to be found in libraries and
archives.

Unfortunately, contemporary newspapers and periodicals do not
contain enough information about the antebellum lumber industry to
offset the scarcity of business documents. Although editors displayed
interest in such other industrial establishments as cotton mills, woollen
mills, woodworking factories, iron foundries, and machine shops, they
characteristically ignored the sawmills. They apparently believed
that their subscribers were acquainted with the local lumber yards

and mills and that they were uninterested in similar establishments elsewhere. In holding this view the editors probably were correct, for very few sawmills were constructed or run differently than any others until the 1850's. Sawmilling under normal conditions was a humdrum occupation, becoming newsworthy only when the mills caught fire or were destroyed by boiler explosions. On such occasions local residents witnessed fireworks worth remembering, and the press reported these incidents accordingly. In brief, newspapers seldom recorded information about sawmills aside from their obituaries and paid advertisements.

Letters to editors of newspapers and periodicals are even less fruitful sources of historical information about sawmills. Unlike cotton planters, railroad promoters, textile mill operators, or even plantation overseers, lumbermen almost never published their opinions. As a class, timbermen and lumber manufacturers were poorly educated, and they had little leisure to spend in literary endeavors.

Under such conditions the preservation of the records of a steam sawmill at Natchez is especially fortunate. These documents are valuable historically for many reasons. In the first place, Andrew Brown, the proprietor, was a most unusual lumberman. He was a skilled architect, an amateur scientist, and a cultured gentleman in the best tradition of the Enlightenment. In the second place, Brown was careful and thrifty, traits which caused him to keep remarkably complete records of his business transactions; and he and his successors faithfully safeguarded these documents for three generations. In the third place, the enterprise founded by Brown in 1828 is a splendid example of that evolutionary process by which small lumber mills evolved into complex and sophisticated enterprises. Finally, the Natchez lumber company was one in which slavery was adapted to the requirements of industry, and the records reveal how this was accomplished. Through the Brown company, therefore, one can observe the intimate workings of the lumber industry in the lower Mississippi Valley during the period between 1828 and 1865.

The possibility of writing a history of Brown's enterprise came to light on a hot June afternoon in 1958 in the yard of the R. F. Learned & Son Lumber Company of Natchez. Earlier that day, Andrew Brown Learned, grandson of the founder of the firm, had agreed, upon the recommendation of his grandson, Howard B. Peabody, Jr., to deposit the old records of the company for safekeeping in the Lumber Archives of the University of Mississippi. His decision was not reached easily, for Learned, like his father and grandfather before him, had treasured these family records.

While transferring the bound ledgers and journals from a vault in the office building of the company into the vehicle which was to take them to Oxford, I was delighted to learn from an elderly Negro who had been employed by Learned for many years that other old papers were stored in a nearby corrugated iron tool shed. In due course he unearthed a tin-lined wooden box about the size of a small trunk from beneath a pile of trash. When its lid was pried off, Professor James W. Silver and I saw that the box was packed solidly with bundles of letters which had been compressed in a letter press and bound with tape. Being thus packed, most of the letters were in the same condition as when they were put away. After searching further in the litter of the shed, the workman located still another pile of loose bundles of letters on top of a cabinet crudely constructed of rough boards. Unfortunately, rats and insects had been at work on these papers, and a few of the bundles had been reduced to worthless shreds. The remaining bundles were damaged in varying degrees, but many of the documents they contained were legible in whole or in part.

A cursory examination of these papers, rendered particularly hasty by a swarm of angry wasps who resented our intrusion into their domain, revealed that the old Negro had produced a historical treasure trove such as scholars dream of finding. The loose bundles were largely composed of personal and business correspondence dating from the 1830's to the twentieth century. After unpacking the documents in the library of the University, I discovered that we had acquired the nearly complete business records and correspondence files of an extensive and surprisingly sophisticated business enterprise. Here was a Graniteville of the Southern lumber industry, complete with personalities as attractive as William Gregg himself.[1]

As the bundles were opened, cleaned, and sorted, a most unusual cast of characters came to life. Dominating them all was Andrew Brown of Crail, Scotland, the founder of the business. Probably educated as an architect at the University of Edinburgh, he had emigrated to America and finally settled at Natchez during the 1820's. He pros-

---

[1] Broadus Mitchell, *William Gregg, Factory Master of the Old South* (Chapel Hill, 1928).

pered as a builder in the cotton-rich community, in 1828 buying a saw-mill to supply building materials for his construction projects. Stimu-lated by the depression of 1839–49, he invaded the New Orleans market with his lumber and eventually erected a woodworking factory in that city. While earning two fortunes before the Civil War, Brown, a member of the American Philosophical Society, found time in his busy life to create a famous botanical garden, which he decorated with Italian statuary, and to write a treatise on physics in which he attempted to reconcile the conflicting claims of science and religion.

In important supporting roles were his pious, energetic, and busi-ness-like son, Andrew Brown, Jr., who founded and operated a branch of the business in New Orleans until his death in 1848, and William I. Key, a nephew-in-law and successor to Andrew, Jr., who established and directed the factory in New Orleans. They were assisted by a number of white employees such as Henry S. Solomon, a resourceful sawmill superintendent, and his droll friend "The Apostle," John F. Paul, who was Key's lieutenant in New Orleans.

Aside from Brown himself, easily the most colorful character in the firm was Simon Gray, a hired mulatto slave who served in the capacity of flatboat captain and foreman. Gray, as a minor executive, directed the activities of both whites and Negroes, handled large sums of money, traveled wherever he wished, and in general enjoyed a life more typical of lower middle-class whites than slaves. With the consent of his employer, the riverman carried on minor business ven-tures of his own, amassing enough money to buy his wife and several children by using Brown as a front in the transaction.

The slave labor force of the lumber firm was filled with interesting people in addition to Simon Gray. James Matthews, for example, another mulatto slave, served as foreman in the logging and rafting operations and was in many respects as influential as Gray. Among the workmen were William Thompson, the literate steam engine fire-man, who made his way to freedom in Canada with a pass he had forged; Jacob, the faithful, happy-go-lucky strawboss in the sawmill; and the malcontents, Dan Hunter and John Key, who were habitual runaways.

The firm itself was an interesting example of southern commercial and industrial enterprise. From its beginning as a very small one-saw operation in 1828, it expanded into a commercial empire by 1860. By that date the sawmill had been converted into a modern plant capable of manufacturing three million lineal feet annually; extensive timber lands had been acquired in the Yazoo Valley a hundred miles to the north; a very large wholesale and retail lumber yard had been opened in New Orleans; and the largest woodworking factory in the Crescent City had been erected as a subsidiary of the lumber yard. By the beginning of the Civil War, Brown had emerged as one of the leading industrialists of the lower Mississippi Valley; and his firm, employing slave labor, was probably the largest of its kind in the Old Southwest.

While relating the life and times of Brown's lumber business, I have attempted briefly to trace the evolution of the cypress lumber industry as a whole from its origins in eighteenth-century Louisiana until the late 1820's, when the company came into the picture.

I must acknowledge my great indebtedness to the unusual foresight of Andrew Brown, Rufus F. Learned, and Andrew B. Learned, who preserved the documents upon which this study is based; and to Howard B. Peabody, Jr., who made them available to scholars. Credit for initiating the program of collecting lumber records at the University of Mississippi is due to Elwood R. Maunder, director of the Forest History Society, and to Professor James W. Silver and Vice Chancellor Alton Bryant of the University of Mississippi. I also owe much to my wife, Margaret Deschamps Moore, who has read the manuscript and offered many valuable suggestions.

Most of the illustrations were graciously provided by Dr. Thomas H. Gandy of Natchez from his extensive collection of photographs taken by the professional photographer Henry C. Norman or his son Earl M. Norman. The remainder came from the collection of Howard B. Peabody, Jr.

To the editors of the *Journal of American History* and the *Journal of Mississippi History* I wish to express my appreciation for permission to republish portions of articles which have previously appeared in their publications.

J. H. M.

Contents

Illustrations

Andrew Brown
and
Cypress Lumbering
In the Old Southwest

1

A Lumber Industry
Emerges in the Old Southwest

WHEN Andrew Brown, a Scottish architect, arrived at Natchez during the early 1820's, the lumber industry in the lower Mississippi Valley was already more than a century old. Long before the birth of the Southern cotton and sugar kingdoms, many of the inhabitants of the Old Southwest had earned their livelihoods by manufacturing lumber for sale in the Caribbean possessions of England, France, and Spain. Their commerce with the West Indian sugar islands had originated soon after a colony was established at Biloxi during 1699. The French, immediately after landing, invaded the neighboring pine forests seeking building materials for their houses and fortifications. Later, when their own most urgent requirements had been satisfied, these pioneer lumbermen of French Louisiana began to prepare boards, masts, naval stores, and ship timbers for sale to passing vessels. The Spanish at Pensacola became their regular customers, but most of the lumber sawed by the French settlers was purchased by captains of ships sailing from ports on Martinique and Santo Domingo. In this fashion lumbering became important to the economy of colonial Louisiana early in the history of the province.[1]

Although the colony at Biloxi moved from the Gulf Coast to the banks of the lower Mississippi River during 1718 primarily in search of fertile soils for agricultural purposes, the French settlers continued for scores of years afterward to pay for their imported goods mainly with shipments of lumber.[2] Despite the pleas of colonial authorities

[1] Duclos to Pontchartrain, October 1713, Dunbar Rowland (ed.), *Mississippi Provincial Archives, 1729–1740: French Dominion* (3 vols.; Jackson, Miss., 1927–32), II, 81.
[2] Bienville's Memoir on Louisiana, 1726, *ibid.*, III, 523.

who wished to make a mainland Santo Domingo of Louisiana, the population around New Orleans failed to produce sufficient tropical agricultural products to balance the budget of the colony. Instead of cultivating cotton, indigo, sugar, coffee, or cacao which were highly prized in European markets, the Louisianians raised foodstuffs for local consumption.[3] As farm workers were not needed in the field during late autumn and winter, they were employed in the cypress brakes felling timber and sawing planks for the growing export trade of New Orleans. Indeed, cypress boards and squared timbers were the principal cash products for most of the colonists until the mid-1790's, when sugar culture became profitable in the Mississippi Valley.[4]

Although pine and oak were exported in small quantities for ship-building purposes during the eighteenth century, cypress was the staple commodity of the lumber industry of colonial Louisiana. The French were unacquainted with cypress at the time of their arrival on the Gulf Coast, but they soon discovered that it was exceptionably valuable as a building material.[5] As they became familiar with the wood, engineers and artisans of the colony were especially pleased by its durability. In the course of experiments conducted during 1709, they learned that cypress was not attacked by borers when immersed for long periods in sea water.[6] On the basis of this evidence French provincial authorities recommended that it be used in preference to other woods as pilings and as planking for the hulls of ships.[7] They also reported that cypress was as immune to decay when exposed to fresh water as it was to salt water marine life. This characteristic was discovered by workmen who exhumed long-buried cypress trees while digging foundations. To their astonishment, they saw that the wood was as sound as newly-cut timber.[8] Cypress also passed the acid

[3] *Ibid.*, 524.

[4] *Ibid.*, 520. Refer also to Abstract of the Letters of the Council of Louisiana, August 28, 1725, *ibid.*, II, 494.

[5] Le Page du Pratz, *The History of Louisiana, or of the Western Parts of Virginia and Carolina: Containing a Description of the Countries that Lie on Both Sides of the River Mississippi: With an Account of the Settlements, Inhabitants, Soil, Climate, and Products* (London, 1774), 215, cited hereinafter as Du Pratz, *Louisiana*. Refer also to the Company of the Indies to the Council of Louisiana, Rowland (ed.), *Mississippi Provincial Archives*, II, 225.

[6] Memoir on Louisiana by Mandeville, April 27, 1709, Rowland (ed.), *Mississippi Provincial Archives*, II, 51.

[7] Minutes of the Council: Proposals Made by the Council to the Directors of the Concessions and to the Inhabitants on January 7, 1723, *ibid.*, II, 282.

[8] Du Pratz, *Louisiana*, 215.

test of experience. Builders of the colony concluded after several years that its timbers and planking were less apt to be damaged by the weather than pine, oak, or cedar.[9]

Other qualities besides durability contributed to the popularity of cypress lumber during the colonial era. Pioneer sawyers employing two-man handsaws could manufacture cypress boards easily because the wood was relatively free from resin and was almost as soft as white pine.[10] For the same reasons carpenters found it easier to work with hand tools than other woods of the region.[11] Furthermore cypress boards did not warp when used green, and the straight-grained wood could be split into shingles by wedges without difficulty. Of equal importance was the fact that cypress was much less flammable than yellow pine, its principal competitor. Because of these desirable qualities, cypress lumber gained steadily in popularity throughout the Caribbean area during the 1700's, and the lumbermen of Louisiana gained a burgeoning market for their forest products.[12]

Abandoning an earlier plan to produce tropical products in Louisiana, the colonial authorities at Paris in 1732 assigned the mainland province the task of supplying corn, livestock, and lumber to the French sugar islands. In accordance with their new role, the Louisianians acquired a small fleet of vessels for making regular deliveries of cypress planking and timber to Santo Domingo, Martinique, Guadeloupe, and the lesser islands of the French West Indies. On their return trips these vessels brought back syrup, sugar, rum, and manufactured goods from France. In order to expedite this inter-island commerce, royal officials exempted the inhabitants of the mainland from all customs duties in French Caribbean ports. In this manner Louisiana was integrated during the 1730's into an economically self-sufficient French colonial empire.[13]

[9] *Ibid.*

[10] Minutes of the Council of Louisiana, January 7, 1732, Rowland (ed.), *Mississippi Provincial Archives*, II, 283.

[11] Memoir on Louisiana by Mandeville, April 27, 1709, Rowland (ed.), *Mississippi Provincial Archives*, II, 51.

[12] Du Pratz, *Louisiana*, 179, 215; Simon L. P. de Cubières, *Memoir Sur Le Cypres de la Louisiane* (Versailles, 1809), 22–23; "Census of New Orleans and It's Invirons, Followed by Summary of a Memorial Upon the Land, It's Production, Medicinal Herbs, Grants, Etc., Made by the Inspector General of the Troops in the Province of Louisiana and New Orleans, November 24, 1721," *Louisiana Historical Quarterly*, I (1917), 98.

[13] King of France to Bienville and Salmon, February 2, 1732, Rowland (ed.), *Mississippi Provincial Archives*, III, 573; Bienville and Salmon to Maurepas, May 12, 1733, *ibid.*, III, 603.

The overseas commerce of New Orleans in cypress timber and planking subsequently assumed impressive proportions under the stimulating effects of royal favor and prosperity in the international sugar industry.[14] During 1742 no fewer than twelve merchantmen dropped anchor at the river port laden with wine, flour, and rum to be exchanged for cargoes of rice, beans, and building materials.[15] Two years later the number of arrivals from Santo Domingo alone rose to twenty, and in 1750 more than forty vessels took on cargoes of Louisiana lumber.[16] During the 1750's the value of lumber shipped from New Orleans to the French West Indies almost tripled, rising from 57,000 livres in 1748 to 180,000 half a decade later.[17]

During the Seven Years War (1757–63) the economic progress of Louisiana was checked by a succession of disasters.[18] First, the British navy operating in the Caribbean reduced the flow of lumber from New Orleans to a mere trickle by blockading and capturing French possessions in the West Indies. Then the mainland province was ceded to Spain as part of the peace settlement which ended the conflict.[19] The Spanish colonial officials, in accordance with their traditional policy of mercantilism, during 1768 restricted the trade of Louisiana merchants to designated ports in the Spanish empire.[20] In this fashion the Louisianians were brutally divorced from their former customers on Santo Domingo, Martinique, and the Windward Islands. As there was little need for cypress lumber in these Spanish colonial ports, the overseas commerce of New Orleans virtually dried up in the wake of the Spanish occupation.[21]

Driven by the specter of bankruptcy, the residents of New Orleans

[14] Clarence P. Gould, "Trade Relations Between the Windward Islands and the Continental Colonies of the French Empire, 1638–1763," *Mississippi Valley Historical Review*, XXV (March, 1939), 473–74.

[15] Bienville to Maurepas, February 4, 1743, Rowland (ed.), *Mississippi Provincial Archives*, III, 776.

[16] N. M. Miller Surrey, *The Commerce of Louisiana During the French Regime, 1699–1763* (New York, 1916), 157.

[17] *Ibid.*, 382–87.

[18] François-Xavier Martin, *History of Louisiana from the Earliest Period* (3rd ed.; New Orleans, 1963), 205. Refer also to Charles Gayarré, *History of Louisiana* (3 vols.; New York, 1854), II, 352–53, cited hereinafter as Gayarré, *Louisiana*.

[19] Samuel F. Bemis, *A Diplomatic History of the United States* (New York, 1936), 10–11.

[20] Regulation of Louisiana Commerce, March 23, 1768, Lawrence Kinnaird (ed.), *Spain in the Mississippi Valley, 1764–94* (3 vols.; Washington, D.C., 1946–49), I, 45–49.

[21] Aubry to the Duke of Praslin, November 25, 1768, Gayarré, *Louisiana*, II, 225.

during 1768 rose in revolt against their new masters, only to be subdued by troops from Cuba. Their ill-conceived uprising, however, served a useful purpose by dramatizing the economic crisis.[22] A suddenly alarmed government at Madrid, moving swiftly and wisely for once, undertook far-reaching measures during 1770 to alleviate the economic situation in the newly-acquired colony.[23] All ports of the Spanish empire were opened to Louisiana shipping, and New Orleans merchants were exempted from excise taxes while trading with Havana. When it became evident that the depression had not been relieved by these provisions, Madrid granted permission to the inhabitants of the Mississippi Valley to trade with France and other foreign powers, thus reopening the commerce between Louisiana and the French West Indies.[24] Finally, the Spanish government awarded its French-speaking subjects a lucrative monopoly in the manufacture of wooden packing boxes for the shipment of sugar.[25]

With these fresh economic opportunities available to them, the lumbermen recovered some of their lost prosperity and enjoyed a brisk export trade.[26] The sale of sugar containers was particularly profitable during the 1780's and 1790's. Merchants in Havana purchased about fifty shiploads of the chests annually, paying approximately 100,000 Spanish dollars each year.[27] Because of this specialized industry, sugar planters who operated sawmills as a sideline in the lower Mississippi Valley sometimes earned as much as 30,000 francs a year.[28]

Except for the thriving commerce in sugar boxes, the foreign lumber trade in Louisiana declined during the 1790's because of unfavorable economic developments associated with the French Revolution.[29]

---

[22] O'Reilly to Aurriga, October 17, 1769, Kinnaird (ed.), *Spain in the Mississippi Valley*, I, 103–104.

[23] O'Reilly to Unzaga, April 3, 1770, *ibid.*, I, 166–67.

[24] A. Curtis Wilgus, *Development of Hispanic America* (New York, 1947), 193; Villars and d'Annoy, the French Commissioners, to the Government in Paris, March 30, 1777, quoted in Gayarré, *Louisiana*, III, 106.

[25] Pontalba's Memoir, Gayarré, *Louisiana*, III, 439.

[26] Gayarré, *Louisiana*, III, 71, 73, 154.

[27] Pontalba's Memoir, *ibid.*, 439.

[28] *Ibid.*, 237. Refer also to a document written around 1773 by an unknown author which is published as "A Genuine Account of the Present State of the River Mississippi and the Lands on Its Banks from the Sea to the River Yasons, the N.W. Boundary of the Province of West Florida," Mississippi Historical Society *Publications*, IX (1906), 323–24. A third account written by Caleb Carpenter in 1776 was published in *De Bow's Review*, III (1847), 116.

[29] Gayarré, *Louisiana*, III, 315.

First, emancipation of the slaves in the French possessions during 1793 permanently disrupted sugar production and stifled the market for lumber in the French West Indies. Next, American merchants taking advantage of wartime conditions were able to increase their penetration of the Caribbean lumber markets to the detriment of their Louisiana competitors. Finally, the Spanish colonial authorities transferred the Cuban lumber trade to Mobile and Pensacola after the province of Louisiana was lost from the Spanish empire in 1803. As a result of these successive events, the exportation of lumber from New Orleans dwindled into insignificance around the turn of the nineteenth century.[30]

Fortunately for lumbermen in the lower Mississippi Valley, the decline of their foreign commerce was partially counter-balanced by a simultaneous development of a domestic market within their own area. New Orleans in particular became an important consumer of all kinds of building materials during the difficult transition period. During 1788 and again in 1794 the city was swept by fires which devastated whole districts and consumed unnumbered residences, warehouses, stores, and public buildings. In both instances the subsequent task of reconstruction was immense. While the city was being rebuilt, the construction trades required vast quantities of brick and lumber, especially cypress, which was less of a fire hazard than yellow pine. Even after the burned out sections of the city were restored, and in spite of ordinances against construction of wooden buildings, accelerated growth of the river metropolis under the American flag continued to provide business for the sawmills of the region. In addition, after 1795 many plantations and villages requiring lumber began to spring up along the Mississippi River and its tributaries as new

[30] François Marie Perrin du Lac, *Travel Through the Two Louisianas and Among the Savage Nations of the Missouri; Also in the United States, Along the Ohio and Adjacent Provinces, in 1801, 1802 & 1803* (London, 1807), 89–92, cited hereinafter as Perrin du Lac, *Travels*. Refer also to E. Wilson Lyon (ed.), "Moustiere's Memoir on Louisiana," *Mississippi Valley Historical Review*, XXII (1935–36), 259; to Pontalba's Memoir, Gayarré, *Louisiana*, III, 442–43; to Queries Respecting Louisiana with the Answers, in Clarence Edwin Carter (ed.), *Territorial Papers of the United States* (18 vols.; Washington, D.C., 1934——), IX, 44–45; and to Memorial of the Legislative Council and House of Representatives of the Mississippi Territory to the President, Senate, and House of Representatives of the United States, January 5, 1803, Barbé Marbois, *History of Louisiana, Particularly of the Cession of that Colony to the United States of America; With an Introductory Essay of the Constitution and Government of the United States* (Philadelphia, 1830), 418.

empires of sugar and cotton rose in the Old Southwest. By 1820 economic growth in the lower Mississippi region had increased the domestic consumption of lumber to the point where the loss of foreign markets ceased to be a matter of concern.[31]

While foreign and domestic markets for cypress lumber were developing during the eighteenth and early nineteenth centuries, a simultaneous evolution in the technology of the cypress lumber industry was also in progress. Although the French woodsmen were able to utilize their European lumbering methods in the forests of pine, oak, and cedar along the Gulf Coast, they could not employ the same methods with the cypresses of the Mississippi River. These trees, instead of growing on dry land, were found only in the shallows of lakes, swamps, and streams. Axemen could not fell them in the customary manner because of their aquatic habitat, nor could they chop limbs off partially submerged trunks of fallen trees. After overcoming these obstacles by various expedients, the woodsmen still could not move their logs. Ox teams were unable to work successfully in the boggy cypress brakes, and the heavy sap-filled green logs could not be floated to their destinations. Even when cypress logs were somehow transported out of the swamps to solid ground, loggers still encountered a final frustration. How were they to provide power for the sawmills which were indispensable for large-scale manufacturing of lumber? The lower Mississippi Valley, unlike the coastal plain, was almost devoid of sites for waterwheels. Hence the woodsmen and lumber manufacturers of colonial Louisiana were compelled to devise original methods of logging, rafting, and sawmilling before they could fully utilize the magnificent cypress forests of the Mississippi River, a task requiring more than a century for them to accomplish.[32]

When they moved the scene of their operations to the vicinity of New Orleans, the loggers of the colony virtually abandoned cedar, pine, and oak in order to concentrate upon cypress because nearby brakes offered them by far the most convenient supply of timber. During the early years of the new settlement, axemen working in the cypress swamps preferred to fell trees at low stages of the river so

[31] Gayarré, *Louisiana*, III, 203, 335–36; Perrin du Lac, *Travels*, 89. Refer also to a statement of the mayor in New Orleans *Courier*, March 29, 1813.

[32] Minutes of the Superior Council of Louisiana, September 27, 1724, Rowland (ed.), *Mississippi Provincial Archives*, III, 431; Minutes of Council: Proposals Made by the Council to the Directors of the Concessions and to the Inhabitants on January 7, 1723, *ibid.*, II, 282–84.

that they could work on comparatively firm ground. Having no means at their disposal of moving green timbers overland, the French woodsmen had to cut the logs into planks on the spot with simple two-man handsaws, commonly called pitsaws. Under emergency conditions during periods of high water the axemen sometimes chopped down trees while standing in boats, endeavoring to drop them as close to the shore as possible. Then the woodsmen dragged the giant timbers ashore and rolled them onto dry ground where handsaws could be used.[33]

On those occasions during the early 1700's when engineers of the colony required large timbers for wharves, breakwaters, or fortifications, the logging crews lashed heavy green cypresses to rafts constructed of buoyant woods and ferried them downstream in this manner.[34] Sometimes the green cypress logs were lost in transit when the lashings parted, allowing them to sink to the bottom. In one instance an engineer resorted to transporting large timbers and pilings on the decks of ships in order to assure their safe arrival. By 1725, however, Louisiana woodsmen had solved the lack of bouyancy problem. They simply girdled standing timber sufficiently far in advance of felling to permit the drying of the deadened trees.[35] Cypress treated in this manner floated as well as raftsmen could desire. Utilizing this new procedure, French axemen working in boats or on scaffolds were able to fell the deadened trees into the water, trim the branches off the floating tree trunks, cut the huge boles into saw log lengths, and lash the logs together into rafts, all without once setting foot on land. By making use of this new logging technique, Louisiana woodsmen could dispense with their old handsaws and raft their cypress to sawmills.

Toward the close of the eighteenth century Louisiana cypress loggers worked out an alternate method of harvesting timber. Using this system axemen felled the trees, cut them into ten- and twelve-foot sections during dry seasons, and left them on the ground until the site was flooded by the Mississippi. When the logs floated, they were assembled

---

[33] Minutes of the Superior Council of Louisiana, September 27, 1724, Rowland (ed.), *Mississippi Provincial Archives*, III, 431; Minutes of Council: Proposals Made by the Council to the Directors of the Concessions and to the Inhabitants on January 7, 1723, *ibid.*, II, 282–84.

[34] Minutes of the Superior Council of Louisiana, September 27, 1724, Rowland (ed.), *Mississippi Provincial Archives*, III, 431.

[35] Superior Council of Louisiana to the General Directors of the Company of the Indies, February 27, 1725, Rowland (ed.), *Mississippi Provincial Archives*, II, 403.

into rafts for transportation to mills downstream. With this development, which was widely adopted during the nineteenth century, the logging and rafting of cypress evolved into a complex three-stage process in which months or sometimes years passed between the girdling of a tree and its arrival at a sawmill.[36]

Inasmuch as sawmills were common establishments in seventeenth-century France, it is not surprising that two were erected in Louisiana during 1716 while the principal settlement was still at Biloxi.[37] Yet the French met with failure at a later date when they introduced water-powered sawmills into the vicinity of New Orleans. In the valley, mills did not work effectively because streams were sluggish and proper sites for dams were lacking. As late as 1729 only a single water mill was actually sawing lumber along the lower Mississippi.[38] Temporarily despairing of water power, provincial officials during 1724 began experimenting with mills utilizing animal power.[39] After five years of effort they finally succeeded in perfecting a sawmill worked by two teams of four horses each.[40] Although this arrangement was practical on a limited scale, it could not be put into general use because draft animals were scarce in the colony.[41] Surprisingly enough, no sustained efforts were made to develop windmills in colonial Louisiana.

The French, however, devised an effective method for propelling sawmills with waterwheels before the middle of the century. After constructing levees along the Mississippi near New Orleans,[42] they discovered that these levees served much the same purpose as dams in other regions of America. The plantations of the French settlers protected by the levees were situated on a long, narrow ridge of land forming one bank of the lower Mississippi. Swamps containing cypress brakes were everywhere behind the line of plantations. When the river

[36] For a reference to this system consult Sylvanus Phillips to Samuel C. Roane, July 28, 1822, Carter (ed.), *Territorial Papers*, XIX, 456.

[37] Surrey, *Commerce of Louisiana*, 372.

[38] Messrs. Perier and de la Chaise to the Directors of the Company of the Indies, March 25, 1729, Rowland (ed.), *Mississippi Provincial Archives*, II, 620, 627. Refer also to Perier to Abbé Rouget, August 14, 1728, *ibid.*, II, 587.

[39] De la Chaise to the Directors of the Company of the Indies, March 8, 1724, Rowland (ed.), *Mississippi Provincial Archives*, II, 344.

[40] Messrs. Perier and de la Chaise to the Directors of the Company of the Indies, March 25, 1727, Rowland (ed.), *Mississippi Provincial Archives*, II, 620.

[41] *Ibid.*, 627.

[42] Thomas Hutchins, *A Historical Narrative and Topographical Description of Louisiana and West Florida* (Philadelphia, 1784), 38–39.

rose to flood stage, these swamps filled with water despite the levees and became natural reservoirs. As the water level subsided, the levees slowed the return flow from the swamps and thereby created a difference in water level between river and swamp. Eventually an unsung genius among the settlers conceived a novel plan for utilizing this head of water to drive a sawmill. He dug a ditch from the swamp across the ridge of land, through the levee, into the river, and lined his little canal with boards to prevent the banks from caving in. He then mounted a waterwheel in the ditch and attached it to a sawmill. Swamp water flowing through the ditch turned the wheel and also conveyed sawlogs from the cypress brake to the mill. This simple but ingenious method of sawmilling soon came into general use throughout the lower Mississippi Valley and continued to be employed by small mills until far into the nineteenth century.[43]

Although the water-powered sawmills of Louisiana worked efficiently enough to sustain the colonial commerce in cypress lumber, the system was inherently defective. The essential head of water in the swamp reservoirs was available for relatively brief periods between the cresting of the Mississippi and the emptying of the swamps. Under ordinary conditions such mills could operate for no more than five months in a year.[44] Because of the abbreviated working season for water sawmills, lumber manufacturing in the valley became a part-time adjunct to agriculture. Workers in the mills were farm laborers primarily and consequently had neither incentive nor opportunity to develop specialized skills. By the same token, owners of sawmills were usually planters first and lumber manufacturers second, and they doled out their time and capital proportionately. As a result of these conditions all of the manufacturing units comprising the colonial lumber industry of Louisiana remained very small by standards of the nineteenth century. In fact, significant industrial growth

[43] Donald C. Peattie (ed.), *Audubon's America: The Narratives and Experiences of John James Audubon* (Boston, 1940), 150. On the lowlands of the South Atlantic Coast, water mills worked by the tides were utilized until the middle of the nineteenth century. For a description of a combined rice, grist, and sawmill of this type, refer to the Savannah (Ga.) *Republican*, July 3, 1837. A much rarer wind-driven sawmill was advertised for sale in the Charleston (S.C.) *Courier*, March 24, 1825.

[44] Samuel R. Brown, *The Western Gazeteer, or Emigrant's Directory* (Auburn, N.Y., 1817), 140; Thomas Ashe, *Travels in America, Performed in 1806* (London, 1808), 333.

did not occur in the Old Southwest until steam power made manufacturing operations possible throughout the year.

The introduction of steam engines into the lower Mississippi Valley during the first decade of the nineteenth century revolutionized the cypress lumber industry almost overnight. Credit for this significant economic development is due to Captain James McKeever (or McEver) and Louis Valcourt, a French émigré, who were residents of New Orleans.[45] During 1802 these imaginative business associates drew up a plan to construct and operate a steam-powered river vessel between Natchez and the Crescent City. The following year they ordered a high-pressure steam engine from the inventor, Oliver Evans of Philadelphia, for which they agreed to pay $6,000. Evens, who has been described as the American James Watt, personally supervised the manufacturing of the engine during the autumn of 1803. Valcourt went North to take charge of transporting it to New Orleans, and he received delivery from Evans before the end of the year. During Valcourt's absence from the city, McKeever superintended the construction of their eighty- by eighteen-foot vessel, which was completed before Valcourt arrived by sea with the steam engine. Valcourt brought Mark Stackhouse and Thomas Clark, skilled workmen associated with Evans, with him to New Orleans; and they installed the power plant in the steamboat. When the craft was almost ready for its trial run, however, the Mississippi rose suddenly, breaking the steamboat's moorings and carrying it a half-mile into the swamps, where it was stranded beyond hope of recovery.[46]

The permanent grounding of their steamboat left Valcourt and McKeever in grave trouble. They had invested $15,000 in the craft, much of it borrowed money, and they were on the verge of bankruptcy. At this point William Donaldson, a New Orleans merchant, lumber manufacturer, and director of the Bank of Louisiana, came to their rescue with a proposal. If they would use their Evans engine to drive one of his sawmills, he would lend them enough money to begin manufacturing lumber. McKeever and Valcourt accepted Don-

[45] Oliver Evans to the editor of the Philadelphia *Aurora*, September 12, 1810, *Agricultural Museum*, I (May 22, 1811), 360–64. Refer also to Greville and Dorothy Bathe, *Oliver Evans: A Chronicle of Early American Engineering* (Philadelphia, 1935), 77–78. This work in which much of Evans' correspondence is published will be cited hereinafter as Bathe, *Evans*.

[46] Oliver Evans to the editor of the Philadelphia *Aurora*, September 12, 1810, *Agricultural Museum*, I (May 22, 1811), 360–61; Bathe, *Evans*, 76.

aldson's offer gratefully and dismantled their useless steamboat. Thus a promising pioneer venture into steamboating on the Mississippi ended, and a new era in the history of cypress lumbering began.[47]

With Donaldson's assistance Valcourt and McKeever put up a sawmill during 1803 which had the capacity to produce 3,000 lineal feet of lumber in twelve hours. The partners employed Stackhouse and Clark, the workmen from Philadelphia, to operate their new establishment for them. At the close of the first year Stackhouse, the engineer, reported to Evans that the steam-powered mill had not stopped during this period for as long as an hour because of engine trouble.[48] Because lumber at this time was selling in New Orleans at prices ranging from $50 to $60 per thousand lineal feet, the lumbermen expected to repair their fortunes quickly. This, however, was not to be. Late in 1806 the establishment caught fire, and all the machinery was destroyed except the steam engine. Valcourt and McKeever attributed their latest mishap to the work of arsonists, but the fire probably resulted from careless operation of the steam engine by relatively inexperienced crewmen. Because the engine had not been damaged, McKeever purchased another sawmill, only to fall ill and die while it was being constructed. Although the subsequent history of this steam mill is unknown, it probably went into production under another proprietor.[49]

Having witnessed the success of the Valcourt and McKeever steam sawmill, William Donaldson decided to expand his own lumber manufacturing facilities. He accordingly placed an order with Evans for a more powerful engine incorporating the inventor's latest improvements, and it was delivered to New Orleans several days after the fire in the Valcourt and McKeever plant. Donaldson installed his new twenty-horsepower engine in a sawmill at Manchac on the shores of Lake Maurepas and used it to drive a gang mill incorporating four

[47] Oliver Evans to the editor of the Philadelphia *Aurora*, September 12, 1810, *Agricultural Museum*, I (May 22, 1811), 360–61; Oliver Evans to Thomas Jefferson, December 9, 1808, Bathe, *Evans*, 155. Refer also to Bathe, *Evans*, 132. For additional references to William Donaldson consult Carter (ed.), *Territorial* Papers, IX, 277, 281, 368, 632, and 674; and John Francis McDermott (ed.), *Western Journals of Dr. George Hunter 1795–1805* (Philadelphia, 1963), 65, 116–18.

[48] Bathe, *Evans*, 77–78.

[49] Oliver Evans to the editor of the Philadelphia *Aurora*, September 12, 1810, *Agricultural Museum*, I (May 22, 1811), 360–61.

saws.[50] During January, 1807, he began manufacturing lumber with steam power, using only three saws. In place of the fourth, he substituted a grist mill. This latest Evans engine proved to be as reliable as the older model, and it operated continuously for more than a year without mechanical failure. By November, 1808, Donaldson had cleared approximately $20,000 above his operating expenses, a sum greater than his total investment in the engine and sawmill machinery. Three and a half years after beginning operation, the sawmill had earned Donaldson no less than $70,000, according to Oliver Evans. The production of the mill was so large that it reduced the price of lumber at New Orleans from $50 to $40 per thousand during this interval. Thus the steam sawmill on Lake Maurepas was a spectacular technical and financial success.[51]

A competing sawmill at Baton Rouge, upriver from New Orleans, established quite a different record during these same years. Samuel Harries imported an expensive, low-pressure twenty-horsepower steam engine from England, which by coincidence arrived in New Orleans on the same day as Donaldson's Evans engine. Harries' engineers had great difficulty in erecting the English engine, and the sawmill at Baton Rouge did not go into production until many months after the one at Manchac. As a result Donaldson was able to boast to Evans that he had sawed 386,500 feet of lumber (worth $15,400) before his competitor cut up his first log. Furthermore, Harries' Boulton and Watt type engine required frequent repairs which materially reduced the output of his sawmill. Because of these factors, the Baton Rouge mill was an unprofitable investment. During the period between 1807 and 1811 in which Donaldson's mill cleared $70,000, Harries' plant operated in the red to the amount of $60,000.[52]

[50] A gang mill was essentially a sash mill equipped with two or more saw blades. The frame which held the saws was called the sash because it rose and fell between guide posts exactly as a window sash is raised and lowered. A gang saw was capable of reducing logs to planks with a single forward motion of the carriage. In the vernacular of nineteenth-century Southern lumbermen, sash saws generally had only a single blade and gang saws had several.

[51] Oliver Evans to the editor of the Philadelphia *Aurora*, September 12, 1810, *Agricultural Museum*, I (May 22, 1811), 360–61; Oliver Evans to Thomas Jefferson, December 9, 1808, Bathe, *Evans*, 155; Oliver Evans to Chancellor Livingston, November 20, 1808, Bathe, *Evans*, 150; Bathe, *Evans*, 132; Arlan K. Gilbert, "Oliver Evans' Memoir 'On the Origin of Steam Boats and Steam Wagons,' " *Delaware History*, VII (September, 1956), 165.

[52] Bathe, *Evans*, 132; Richard Claiborne to Oliver Evans, July 12, 1807, *ibid.*, 134.

The successful application of steam power to sawmills in the vicinity of New Orleans apparently attracted much attention, especially from the wealthy cotton planters of the old Natchez District. William Dunbar, for example, was told during 1804 about the achievements of Oliver Evans by Dr. George Hunter of Philadelphia, who was a friend of the inventor. Dr. Hunter, a manufacturer of chemicals and a scientist of note, had come to Natchez to participate with Dunbar in an exploring expedition which they were undertaking on behalf of President Thomas Jefferson. Interested in the possibilities of the Evans engine as described by Hunter, Dunbar instructed his agent in Philadelphia to ascertain what the inventor's price would be for an engine powerful enough to propel a sawmill and a cotton gin. When informed that such engines sold for $6,000, Dunbar abandoned the project as unfeasible.[53] Shortly afterwards, however, planters of this area learned that steam engines were obtainable from Evans' competitors at much lower prices. In August, 1807, Richard Claiborne of New Orleans informed Evans that several planters living near Bayou Sara, on the river between Baton Rouge and Natchez, had ordered steam engines from manufacturers in Kentucky.[54] These engines cost only five hundred dollars each and were distinctively inferior to Evans' products in power and quality. Nevertheless, they were adequate for driving cotton gins or one-saw mills which could manufacture eight hundred feet of plank per day. Responding to Claiborne's warning that they were unwise to sacrifice durability and power for cheapness, the planters replied that cost was their major consideration when selecting an engine. Although Evans subsequently reduced his charges, he still was unable to deliver engines in the lower Mississippi Valley at competitive prices. He therefore lost the valuable market he had opened in the Old Southwest to manufacturers in St. Louis, Cincinnati, and other cities of the upper Mississippi Valley.[55]

Despite the comparatively high cost of Evans' steam engines, two of them were used to power sawmills near Natchez before 1815. Between 1808 and 1814, William Herrins utilized one of these in his Montesano Steam Engine and Saw Mill, located on the river bank close to that port. Herrins' eight-horsepower Evans engine was prob-

[53] Eron Rowland, *Life, Letters, and Papers of William Dunbar of Elgin, Morayshire, Scotland, and Natchez, Mississippi: Pioneer Scientist of the Southern United States* (Jackson, Miss., 1930), cited hereinafter as Rowland, *Dunbar*.
[54] Richard Claiborne to Oliver Evans, August 24, 1807, in Bathe, *Evans*, 135.
[55] Bathe, *Evans*, 139.

ably the same as that employed earlier by Valcourt and McKeever.[56] The Natchez lumbermen used this engine to drag sawlogs up the river bank to the mill in addition to propelling the sawmill machinery proper. The log carriage of the Montesano gangmill was sufficiently long to handle timbers up to thirty feet in length. In this establishment Herrins manufacured cypress and white oak planking, which he floated to New Orleans on rafts.[57]

The other Evans engine, which was rated at twenty horsepower like that of William Donaldson, was erected across the Mississippi River from Natchez in 1812 by Reuben Nichols. On April 4, 1812, Nichols wrote Evans that he was completely satisfied with the "wonderful performance of our engine. We are driving at present three saws and mill-stones with great ease, and it does not appear to me that we use half its power." Engines of this kind were selling at this time for $6,000. Evans, at about this time began to offer purchasers an option. For $10,000 he guaranteed the engines to saw "5,000 feet of boards in twelve hours," and to "work four years without repair." In addition the Philadelphia manufacturer would assure his customers that no competitor would put up an Evans engine in his district.[58]

A large steam sawmill in New Orleans which did not use an Evans engine was destroyed during 1810 soon after it was erected. This establishment belonged to the firm of Bellechasse and Delarue and was believed to have been deliberately set afire. The acting governor of the Territory of Orleans offered a reward of $1,000 for information leading to the conviction of the culprits, as well as pardon to any of them who would identify the planner of the crime. The owners offered an additional reward of $600 per year for a period of five years.[59]

During the second decade of the nineteenth century the use of steam power spread rapidly throughout the lumber industry of the Old Southwest. In 1820 there were eight steam sawmills in the state of Louisiana, six of which were in the vicinity of New Orleans.[60] Three of this number, owned respectively by Saulet, Gaien, and

---

[56] Oliver Evans, "A Trip Made by a Small Man in a Wrestle with a Very Great Man: Answer to the Baltimore Miller's Memorial, and Thomas Jefferson's Letter," *Niles Register*, V (1813–14), 2nd addenda, 10–11.

[57] Natchez *Chronicle*, April 12, 1809.

[58] Reuben Nichols to Oliver Evans, April 4, 1812, *Niles Register*, III (1812), 111; and Oliver Evans to Reuben Nichols, March 12, 1812, *ibid*.

[59] New Orleans *Courier*, August 20, 1810.

[60] *U. S. Census* (1820): *Manufactures*, 24.

Hunter and Bryant, were located on the batture in front of the city.[61] Two others were built on the boat landing at Natchez during 1818 by Samuel Clements and Peter Little.[62] The latter mill was eventually purchased by Andrew Brown. In addition, sugar planters along the lower Mississippi also began to power their operations by steam about this time.[63]

Hunter and Bryant's Steam Saw and Grist Mill, located on the batture in the New Orleans suburb of Saulet, was partly owned by Dr. George Hunter. The chemical manufacturer had moved from Philadelphia to New Orleans around 1815 in order to engage in lumber manufacturing as well as in the preparation of commercial chemicals.[64] When his estate was settled after his death in 1823, his holdings in the city revealed his continuing interest in steam power. In addition to his half interest in the steam sawmill, Hunter owned a second twenty-horsepower engine that he used in his chemical shop. It powered machines for rolling sheets of lead, copper, and iron; a boring machine; a mill for grinding white lead and other paints; and a mill for reducing Peruvian bark to powder.[65]

The largest steam sawmill in the Old Southwest during this period was erected on Sawmill Creek, nine miles above the point where that stream empties into Mobile Bay.[66] This steam-powered establishment was designed to cut yellow pine lumber for the export trade of Mobile, and it was probably the first of its kind on the Gulf Coast. The original equipment of the plant included a gang of five saws and a log carriage which could receive timbers as long as sixty feet.[67] During 1820 Henry Gunnison sold more than a million lineal feet of lumber from his mill, of which three-fourths went to foreign customers.[68] Following a disastrous fire in 1823, he rebuilt his mill on a greatly enlarged scale. His new machinery featured two sets of gangsaws containing four saws each, and regular operation of the mill was

[61] New Orleans *Courier*, August 6, 1821, and January 2, 1824; Mary Ann Hunter to Mrs. C. Y. McAllister, July 30, 1815, McDermott (ed.), *Western Journals of Dr. George Hunter, 1795–1805,* 17.

[62] Natchez *Republican*, March 5, 1818. For an advertisement of a steam sawmill at Baton Rouge, see Baton Rouge *Republic*, May 14, 1822.

[63] New Orleans *Courier*, August 7 and October 11, 1822, January 31, 1824.

[64] McDermott (ed.), *Western Journals of Dr. George Hunter,* 5–18.

[65] New Orleans *Courier*, January 2, 1824.

[66] Mobile *Register*, December 17, 1821.

[67] *Ibid.*, March 6, 1823.

[68] *Ibid.*, December 17, 1821.

resumed in October, 1824. A carefully conducted test determined that each gang was capable of cutting a thousand lineal feet per hour, corresponding to a combined output of 24,000 feet of lumber during the usual twelve-hour working day.[69] An ordinary water-powered sawmill employing two saws by contrast would cut less than 2,500 feet during the same period of time. In one other respect beside its large size the Gunnison yellow pine sawmill was noteworthy. With the exception of the sawyers, most of the workers in this establishment were Negro slaves.[70]

The technical success of Gunnison's steam-driven sawmill inspired the erection during 1823 of a similar plant within the city limits of Mobile. This convenient location, according to the editor of the Mobile *Register*, offered local construction firms an opportunity to purchase lumber "sawed to the dimensions wanted, unsoiled by mud or water." [71] The Mobile mill prospered with the subsequent growth of the Gulf Coast port and under the management of John J. Deshon was still in business as late as 1838, also using Negro crews.[72]

While cypress lumber manufacturers of the Mississippi Valley were adopting steam power for their mills, a parallel development was occurring on the South Atlantic Coast. In June, 1802, William Longstreet, the builder of the first steamboat on the Savannah River, successfully coupled a sawmill and a steam engine.[73] The yellow pine lumbermen of Georgia were slow in following his lead, however, because the water mills of the up-country and the tidal mills of the lowlands were relatively efficient. As a result the early steam sawmills were situated in or near the ports. The Chatham Steam Saw Mill of Savannah, Georgia, was typical of these establishments. Built during 1817, the mill was powered by a sixteen-horsepower steam engine. The machinery included two sets of gangsaws and carriages which could handle logs sixty feet in length. The Chatham mill was located on a riverfront wharf so that ships could be loaded with lumber fresh from the saws. During the 1820's other similar mills were constructed near the city in the neighboring village of Yamacraw and

[69] *Ibid.*, March 30 and October 22, 1824.
[70] *Ibid.*, February 5 and March 6, 1823, September 14, 1824, June 6, 1826, and January 1, 1828.
[71] *Ibid.*, February 5, 1823.
[72] *Ibid.*, June 26, 1834; September 1 and 23, and May 4, 1835; January 11 and July 2, 1838.
[73] Thomas L. Stokes, *The Savannah* (New York, 1951), 238.

on Hutchinson's Island and Fig Island in the Savannah River. Two other steam sawmills were located at Darien, Georgia, a small port at the mouth of the Altamaha River.[74]

In the lower Mississippi Valley during the 1820's sawmill operators did not find it necessary to carry on logging operations in conjunction with lumber manufacturing. In this period ample quantities of logs were being offered for sale at their landings by a hardy breed of raftsmen.[75] These rivermen earned their living, like their predecessors for generations past, by cutting cypress timber on public lands without regard for the niceties of ownership and then rafting the logs to mills along the lower Mississippi.[76] Their services did not become inadequate to sustain the river sawmills until the mid-1830's when high cotton prices generated a great landrush into the Old Southwest. Not until then did the sawmill operators commonly resort to employing their own timber crews in order to assure a steady supply of logs for their mills.[77]

When Andrew Brown accepted employment from Peter Little in his steam sawmill at Natchez during the early 1820's, the lumber industry of the lower Mississippi Valley was hardly larger than it had been in the colonial era. The sawmills which dotted the banks of the Mississippi between Vicksburg and New Orleans were generally of the smallest type, and they were cutting lumber almost exclusively for customers in the immediate vicinity. Little's sawmill was typical

[74] Savannah (Ga.) *Republican*, June 25, 1818, March 20, 1819, March 8 and September 14, 1820, and April 29, 1828; Savannah *Georgian*, January 1, February 26, and November 24, 1827.

[75] *American State Papers: Commerce and Navigation*, II, 745; Natchez *Weekly Chronicle*, April 12, 1809; Natchez *Southern Galaxy*, April 9, 1829; Walter Pritchard, Fred B. Kniffen, and Clair A. Brown (eds.), "Southern Louisiana and Southern Alabama in 1819: The Journal of James Leander Cathcart," *Louisiana Historical Quarterly*, XXVIII (July, 1945), 26.

[76] For references to cypress logging on public lands in the Mississippi Valley consult the following: Samuel Brown to Governor Holmes, June 24, 1811, Carter (ed.), *Territorial Papers*, VI, 206–207; Thomas Freeman to the Secretary of the Treasury, July 9, 1811, *ibid.*, 205–206; Governor Holmes to Mr. Taylor, September 17, 1811, *ibid.*, 224; Samuel C. Roane to Stephen Pleasanton, April 24, 1822, *ibid.*, XIX, 428; Sylvanus Phillips to Samuel C. Roane, July 28, 1822, *ibid.*, 456; Thomas Mathers to Bernard Smith and Benjamin Desha, October 13, 1824, *ibid.*, 710.

[77] After taking possession of the Little sawmill during 1828, Brown was able to purchase all of his logs from raftsmen as late as 1835. See Andrew Brown Journal (1835), Rufus F. Learned Collection, University of Mississippi Lumber Archives. All of Andrew Brown's journals cited in this chapter are in the Learned Collection.

of these establishments. Powered by a five-horsepower steam engine to run the single saw, the sash mill produced between two and three thousand lineal feet of lumber a day.[78] The ultimate in lumber manufacturing technology of that period was represented by the Gunnison mill near Mobile, which had a daily output nearly ten times as great as the small Natchez plant.

Regardless of the size of the sawmill, the organization of the lumber manufacturing firm was of the very simplest variety during the 1820's.[79] The owner himself usually worked as superintendent, chief sawyer, and clerk, all at the same time, employing only one or two assistant sawyers. In units of the size of Little's mill, an assistant sawyer was sometimes given a junior partnership in the firm in lieu of a regular wage. Throughout the industry, as had been the case during the 1700's, both whites and Negro slaves were employed indiscriminately in sawmill crews which usually numbered between ten and twenty men.[80] By the 1820's a noticeable change had occurred in lumber manufacturing. Because steam-powered mills could operate continuously during the year, the sawmill crews were employed on a regular basis. As a result the part-time mill hand and farm laborer was evolving into a skilled and specialized industrial worker. Left for the future, however, was the development of separate divisions for logging, transportation, and merchandising of timber products.

[78] Andrew Brown Journal (1829–30); Chicago Lumber World Review, January 10, 1920.
[79] Andrew Brown Journal (1829–30); Baton Rouge Republic, August 13, 1822; Jackson Mississippian, April 28, 1837, and January 10, 1834; Mobile Register, December 19, 1822, November 26, 1823, March 30, 1824, and June 26, 1834; Rodney (Miss.) Telegraph, April 27, 1839; Woodville (Miss.) Republican, October 16, 1830, and December 1, 1838.
[80] Andrew Brown Journal (1829–30); De Bow's Review, XII (1852), 635.

2

A Steam Sawmill
At Natchez-under-the-Hill

A NDREW BROWN, the future lumber manufacturer of Natchez, was
born during 1793 in the ancient Scottish fishing village of Crail,
at no great distance from Edinburgh.[1] Although his father was a
member of the municipal government, the family was not prosperous.
Both Crail and its fishing industry were declining during the late
eighteenth century.[2] However, despite his lack of affluence, "Bailie"
Brown managed to provide better educations for his sons than most
Americans of that era received. Andrew, the eldest son and his father's namesake, probably attended the University of Edinburgh, for
a student of that name was enrolled in that institution from 1807 to
1810. In any event young Brown had studied architecture before his
marriage at the age of twenty-four to Elizabeth Key, a neighbor's
daughter.[3]

During the early 1820's Andrew Brown left his wife and son (who
had been born in 1818) with relatives in Crail and sailed for the United

[1] Brief biographical sketches of Andrew Brown may be found in *Lumber
World Review* (Chicago), January 10, 1920; *Southern Lumberman* (Nashville),
December 15, 1931; and *Biographical and Historical Memoirs of Mississippi*
(2 vols.; Chicago, 1891), II, 1108–1109.

[2] Alfred L. Brown, "Browns of Fife and Their Descendants in America, 1770–
1953: A Family History Prepared from the Best Available Sources" (unpublished
manuscript dated June 10, 1953). Howard Peabody, president of R. F. Learned
& Son of Natchez, Mississippi, has a copy in his possession. This manuscript
will be cited hereinafter as Brown, "Browns of Fife." Refer also to Crail City
Council, *Royal Burgh of Crail: The Official Guide* (London, c. 1960), 10–11.

[3] Christopher Fyfe to John H. Moore, January 31, 1964, in the possession of
the writer. Through the good offices of Professor Joseph O. Baylen of the University of Mississippi, Professor Fyfe of the University of Edinburgh searched
the records of that institution for references to Brown and found that an Andrew
Brown, Jr., was registered from 1807 to 1810.

States. After working for a time in the building trades at Pittsburgh, he took passage to Natchez on a flatboat. Soon after his arrival in Mississippi Brown accepted employment from Peter Little, who was by then an established merchant, building contractor, and sawmill operator. After he gained a favorable local reputation as an architect, Brown left Little's firm and set up his own construction business. In the meanwhile, Elizabeth and Andrew, Jr., arrived from Scotland to join him. In 1828 Brown purchased the steam sawmill from his former employer in order to assure a dependable supply of lumber for his growing contracting business.[4]

The Little sawmill was located on the famous shelf of land below the bluffs called "Natchez-under-the-Hill," about three-fourths of a mile from the "Upper Steamboat Landing." Little had selected this site for his mill because a natural cavity in the river bank provided a current-free expanse of water in which logs could be stored, and he had subsequently improved the log pond by constructing a breakwater of logs and stones in the river proper. The logs were transported from the storage basin across the mud flats to the foot of the embankment by means of a canal, which lumbermen called a logway. They were then loaded on railway cars and hauled up the bank to the mill by a steam-powered funicular railroad, or log stage. When Brown acquired the mill it was equipped with a single-bladed sash saw, and its daily production was hardly as much as three thousand lineal feet of lumber.[5]

Needing an assistant, Brown took Charles Dart into partnership with him. Dart had previously maintained a mercantile establishment in the village of Petit Gulf, but his firm had failed during the depression of the late 1820's.[6] Although Brown knew little about Dart,

[4] *Biographical and Historical Memoirs of Mississippi*, II, 1108–1109. Peter Little, a mechanic, arrived at Natchez during 1798 and found employment under David Greenleaf, a manufacturer of cotton gins and presses. From this humble beginning, Little rose to a position of affluence in the mercantile community. At the time of his death in 1857 he was the owner of valuable riverfront property overlooking Natchez-under-the-Hill. For references to Little consult Benjamin L. C. Wailes Diary No. 6, March 12, 1853, Duke University Library; Natchez *Chronicle*, April 9, 1810; Natchez *Mississippi Republican*, March 19, 1818; Natchez *Newspaper and Public Advertiser*, May 9 and July 4, 1826; Natchez *Mississippi Journal*, April 19 and June 14, 1833; and Natchez *Courier*, December 30, 1857.

[5] *Lumber World Review*, January 10, 1920.

[6] Natchez *Mississippi Statesman*, February 7, 1827; Natchez *Newspaper and Public Advertiser*, October 25, 1826.

he nevertheless signed an agreement on March 1, 1829, which made the former merchant an equal shareholder in his lumber manufacturing and construction company. Under the terms of their agreement, Dart was to manage the sawmill while Brown gave his time to the building trades. Brown soon became dissatisfied with his associate, however, and after a few months took over the management of the sawmill himself. In order to free himself from all connections with Dart, Brown leased his partner's share of the business for a period of four years, paying him the sum of $4,800 in eight semiannual installments.[7]

At this point the firm of Brown and Dart was heavily indebted, owing a substantial sum to Peter Little in addition to varying amounts to loggers for timber purchased on credit.[8] In order to raise urgently needed cash, Brown had shipped several cypress boats to New Orleans where the lumber was sold on short-term credit. Two of these on April 1, 1830, brought $20 per thousand feet, or approximately $1,700. After withdrawing from an active role in the firm, Dart took a shipment of lumber by flatboat to the city on behalf of the company. He collected the money due from this and previous shipments and then absconded with the cash, virtually all of the liquid assets of the business. Brown was left in serious financial straits. To save himself from bankruptcy, he canceled the rental notes he previously had signed over to Dart and took over his dishonest partner's share in the sawmill.[9] An emergency loan from his friend Stephen Duncan, who probably was the wealthiest cotton planter in the Southwest, tided him over the crisis. Subsequently, Duncan became an equal though silent partner in Brown's lumber manufacturing establishment.[10]

[7] A lengthy public statement by Brown was published in the *Nachez*, June 12, 1830. Refer also to Natchez *Southern Galaxy*, April 2, 1829, for an announcement of the Brown and Dart partnership.

[8] Andrew Brown Ledger (1829–36), Rufus F. Learned Collection, University of Mississippi Lumber Archives. Unless otherwise indicated, all of Andrew Brown's ledgers, journals, and day books cited in this chapter are in the Learned Collection.

[9] *Natchez*, June 12, 1830.

[10] Clement Eaton, *Growth of Southern Civilization, 1790–1860* (New York, 1961), 43. For newspaper references to Duncan refer to Natchez *Courier*, January 27, 1837; *ibid.*, January 5 and December 14, 1838; Natchez *Mississippi Journal*, April 19 and May 3, 1833; Yazoo City *American Banner*, October 3, 1856; Yazoo City *Democrat*, February 9, 1847. Additional information is to be found in the Duncan (Stephen and Stephen, Jr.) Papers, Department of Archives and Manuscripts, Louisiana State University. For his relationship with Brown refer to Andrew Brown Ledger (1829–36).

Brown's journal for 1829 and 1830 reflects vividly the difficulties that small sawmills were experiencing during this period. Cypress prices fell to abnormally low levels. Boards of the type which had brought $40 a thousand in 1818 were bringing only half that in June, 1829. These prices almost matched those of the depression of the early 1820's. There was a small advance during the 1830 season, bringing the price to $25 per thousand for the choicest quality of planking. Brown sold his output almost entirely to builders in Natchez. He continued to contract for the erection of houses and small bridges, and in this activity he was his own best customer. He apparently shipped no lumber to plantations downriver from Natchez or to New Orleans for several years after Dart left the firm.[11]

There was no dearth of logs during this early period when Brown was running only one saw. Because of his small consumption of timber, he did not himself engage in logging operations. Brown's journal records the purchase of such items as a single cypress log for three dollars, and a "Cypress and wood raft" for sixty dollars. The most expensive transaction inserted in the journal for 1829 involved a cedar raft costing three hundred dollars. In comparison with purchases made a few years later, each running into thousands of dollars, these transactions were trifling.[12]

In Natchez the economic recovery of the building trades proceeded rapidly after the bottom of the depression was reached in 1829. "Clear" cypress flooring, the highest grade of lumber available in the markets of the Old Southwest, had risen by 1831 to $30 per thousand feet. In 1835 the price was $40, and two years later an all-time high of $65 was being charged for seasoned cypress lumber of the first grade.[13] Furthermore, Natchez lumber prices held firmly at this high level through most of 1839, despite the generally painful effects of the financial panic of 1837 upon the commercial interests of the Old Southwest. In fact, the value of lumber did not begin to decline noticeably until the cotton market collapsed a few months prior to the end of the decade.[14]

[11] Andrew Brown Ledger (1829–36); Natchez *Mississippi Republican*, April 9, 1818.
[12] Andrew Brown Ledger (1829–36); Natchez *Mississippi Republican*, April 9, 1818.
[13] *Ibid.*; Andrew Brown Journal (1835).
[14] Andrew Brown Day Book (1837–40); Andrew Brown Journal (1836–40); Andrew Brown Ledger (1829–36).

Although his lumber business increasingly absorbed his time and attention, Brown continued to operate as a building contractor through 1835. In August of that year, for example, he contracted with the Adams County board of police to build a bridge on the road between Woodville and Natchez for the sum of six hundred dollars. As this was a comparatively small undertaking, the architect guaranteed to complete the structure within two months. Aside from preparing the plans, Brown took no active part in the building. Instead, he assigned the job to a white carpenter and provided him with a crew of four Negro slaves. One of the Negroes, Simon Gray, was destined to rise to a position of considerable importance in Brown's company in subsequent years, and it is likely that he supervised other colored carpenters even at this early date. In keeping with Brown's custom, the bridge was finished on schedule and without incident.[15]

During the first half of the 1830's the sawmill machinery purchased from Little became inadequate to supply the local demand, and Brown completely rebuilt the plant during 1835. In the process of renovation he replaced the single-bladed sash saw with a much more efficient gangsaw of four blades, which raised the productive capacity to approximately ten thousand feet a day.[16]

Although no description of Brown's sawmill has been preserved, indications are that it was much like an early nineteenth-century mill which has been described as follows:

The common saw-mill, which is generally employed in cutting timber into planks, consists of a square wooden frame, in which a number of saws are stretched; this frame rises and falls in another wooden frame, secured to the foundations of the mill in the same manner as a window sash rises and falls. The timber to be cut is placed upon a horizontal bed or carriage, sliding upon the floor of the mill, which being sufficiently narrow to pass through the inside of the vertical or moving saw-frame, will carry the tree through and subject it to the action of the saw. The carriage is provided with a rack, which is engaged by the teeth of a pinion, and thus gives the means of advancing the carriage. The pinion is turned by means of a large ratchet-wheel, with a click moved by levers connected with the saw frame; when the saw frame rises the click slips over a certain number of teeth of the ratchet wheel, and when it descends to make the cut, the click turns the ratchet wheel round, and advances the wood forward just as much as the saw cuts during its descent. The trees are generally dragged up an inclined plane, through a door at one end of the mill, and being placed upon the carriage, they pass through, and are divided by the saw into two or more pieces,

---

[15] Andrew Brown Journal (1835), August 18 and October 31, 1835.
[16] Andrew Brown Journal (1835); Andrew Brown, Jr., to Washington, Jackson & Co., January 29, 1842, Learned Collection.

which are carried forward and passed out at a door on the opposite side of the mill.[17]

Brown's sawmill is known to differ from the one described above only in minor particulars.[18]

Because the greatly enlarged establishment demanded a more numerous crew for efficient operation, Brown purchased an additional five slaves, making a total of seventeen Negroes in the work force of the company. Brown had been so well pleased with the labor of these Negroes that he had gradually reduced the number of white workmen in the lumber manufacturing portion of his business. By the close of 1835, the shift from white laborers to Negro slaves was almost complete. Aside from a white sawyer who was paid from eighty to one hundred dollars a month and a few skilled artisans called in temporarily to repair machinery or perform other specialized services, Negroes manned the sawmill and its lumber yard. From this date Brown and his various associates recruited white manual laborers only when slaves were not available for hire.[19]

Brown's preference for Negro sawmill hands was characteristic of lumber manufacturers in the lower South during the last thirty years of the antebellum period. Large sawmills generally were manned either by hired slaves or by Negroes belonging to the proprietors throughout the plantation regions. This was especially true in the port towns of the Cotton Kingdom. In Vicksburg, for example, all of the sawmills utilized Negroes to some extent; and at Natchez and at Monroe, Louisiana, the mills were worked almost entirely by slaves, as were some of the establishments in New Orleans. Similarly, slave labor predominated in the export sawmills near Mobile, on the Gulf, and at Charleston, Savannah, and Darien on the Atlantic. Indeed, most of the lumber exported from the ports of the lower South was probably manufactured with the aid of slaves.[20]

[17] M. Powis Bale, *Woodworking Machinery: Its Rise, Progress, and Construction, with Hints on the Management of Saw Mills and the Economical Conversion of Timber* (London, 1922), 36–37.

[18] The journals of Andrew Brown of Natchez during the 1830–60 period.

[19] Andrew Brown Journal (1835); *ibid.* (1836–40).

[20] For some references to slave labor in sawmills consult the following sources: Charleston (S.C.) *Courier*, December 9, 1833, and November 23, 1837; Charleston (S.C.) *Mercury*, September 21, 1850, and September 9 and October 9, 1851; Mobile (Ala.) *Register*, January 12, 1829, May 1, 1839, October 28, 1857, and February 3, March 23, July 19, and November 5, 1859; New Orleans *Picayune*, June 12, 1840, December 21, 1846, October 3, 1847, and June 9, 1848;

Although a majority of the Negroes employed in the sawmills of the cotton states were merely manual laborers, it was by no means unusual for slaves to hold responsible positions. The firm of Gibbs & Gant, for instance, employed large numbers of slaves in their mill at Charleston, South Carolina, some of whom served as sawyers.[21] About one of these skilled men, an owner wrote in 1833: "He has had the entire charge of a Steam Saw Mill for 5 years, which he has managed without accident and with great skill and profit to the owner, putting upon it in that time such repairs as it required." In 1839 a similarly skilled workman, "capable of keeping an Engine in good repair," was offered for sale at Mobile. He too had been responsible for operating a saw and grist mill for several years. More often, however, Negroes of superior capabilities were employed as "engineers" than as sawyers. Less skill was required to tend a steam engine than to run the saws, and few white workmen coveted the hot, monotonous, and dangerous job. Brown always used slaves as enginemen but never put a Negro in charge of the sawmill machinery.

While shifting to slave labor during the 1830's, Brown improved his fortune in spectacular fashion. From a position of near bankruptcy, to which his first partner's defalcations had reduced him at the beginning of the decade, he advanced into the ranks of the affluent—no mean achievement in cotton-rich Natchez during the "flush times!" By the close of this period of prosperity, Brown had acquired thirty-five slaves and had erected a "beautiful and splendid villa" costing more than $60,000. When this house was severely damaged by a

---

Savannah *Georgian*, January 4, 1827; Savannah (Ga.) *Republican*, January 27, 1818, February 6, 1826, May 25, 1835, October 5, 1840, February 4, 1842, August 18, 1843, February 10 and July 1, 1848, December 31, 1850, January 9, 1851, January 22, 1852, and July 26, 1858; Vicksburg *Register*, February 22, 1837; Vicksburg *Sentinel*, May 31 and August 3, 1838; Vicksburg *Whig*, February 10, 1846, May 17, 1849, December 25, 1850, February 22, 1853, December 20, 1854, and November 24, 1858.

[21] For references to Negro sawyers, steam engine "engineers," and firemen consult Augusta (Ga.) *Chronicle and Sentinel*, May 28, 1858; Charleston (S.C.) *Courier*, December 9, 1833, June 24 and August 5, 1840, December 13, 1852, and February 2, 1854; Mobile (Ala.) *Register*, October 29, 1835, October 23, 1838, May 1, 1839, and November 5, 1859; Montgomery (Ala.) *Mail*, November 10, 1858; New Orleans *Courier*, April 1, 1833; New Orleans *Delta*, March 23, 1859, and April 6, 1860; New Orleans *Picayune*, August 6, 1840; Savannah (Ga.) *Republican*, February 5, 1835, January 21, 1841, July 4, 1849, March 31, 1851, February 7, August 16, October 12, and November 15, 1852, July 27, 1853, July 7, 1954, January 1 and January 15, 1855, October 8, 1856, and August 30, 1858; Vicksburg *Whig*, November 24, 1855.

tornado on May 7, 1840, the citizens reckoned this loss as among the most serious in the city.[22]

Brown's rapid march toward prosperity and social prominence is mirrored in his business records. Because of economic stagnation in Natchez, his sales of lumber were still very small as late as 1831; but the turning point was then close at hand. Natchez commercial leaders in 1832 resolved to stimulate business by opening a direct cotton trade with Europe, thus by-passing the commission houses of New Orleans. In order to make this feasible, they arranged for steam towboats to pull ocean-going sailing ships up the Mississippi to the landing at Natchez so that cargoes of cotton destined for Liverpool could be loaded directly.[23] To reduce the bulk of baled cotton, a powerful steam press like those used in New Orleans was planned for the Mississippi port town.[24] Hoping to profit from the anticipated increase in trade, an enterprising businessman erected an inclined railroad which ran 560 feet at a forty-five-degree angle from the top of the buff to the steamboat landing. The railroad cars were pulled back to the top by steam power. The space under the framework was boarded up to provide storage space for ten thousand barrels.[25]

While waiting for the direct cotton trade with Europe to materialize, the business folk of Natchez busied themselves with other local enterprises. The Steamboat Hotel located near the landing was opened in November, 1832.[26] Four months later the firm of Samuel A. Plummer and Company completed a large cottonseed oil mill, one of the pioneers of its type in the nation. The plant's building was a story and a half high and measured eighty by eighty-four feet. A steam engine with a piston measuring 2,292 square inches and having a five-foot stroke powered the machinery of the establishment, which consisted of eight hulling machines, five sets of grindstones, a machine for grinding the kernels of the seeds, eight cylinders for beating the meal, a cam press, and seven lever presses for removing oil from the meal. This cottonseed oil mill was so successful that a second was placed

[22] New Orleans *Picayune*, May 13, 1840; U. S. Census (1840), Adams County, Mississippi.

[23] John Hebron Moore, *Agriculture in Antebellum Mississippi* (New York, 1958), 55–56.

[24] *Mississippi Journal and Natchez Advertiser*, April 19, 1833.

[25] *Ibid.*, February 8, 1833; [Joseph H. Ingraham], *The South-west by a Yankee* (2 vols.; New York, 1835), II, 59.

[26] *Mississippi Journal and Natchez Advertiser*, November 23, 1832.

in operation by 1835.[27] Even more promising for the future development of the town was the organization of the Mississippi Rail Road
Company under the leadership of Brown's silent partner, Stephen
Duncan, who was also president of the Bank of the State of Mississippi. This road was designed to connect Natchez with the capital of
the state.[28] In 1833 the new Agricultural Bank opened its recently
completed 3,100-square-foot, one-story brick building, which fronted
on Main Street.[29] And, in the remaining years of the decade, most
of the magnificent houses in the town and on surrounding plantations
were erected to display the wealth and taste of Mississippi cotton
barons. This spectacular outburst of building encouraged the editor
of the *Mississippi Journal and Natchez Advertiser* to comment during
May, 1833, that "mechanics will find employment and good wages
next fall—come as many as may. Let them come by the fiftys, or by
the hundreds,—we shall say *God Speed Them!*"[30]

As a result of either remarkable foresight or extraordinary good luck,
Andrew Brown was the principal manufacturer of lumber at Natchez
in 1832, and he profited from his near monopoly. Because of it, mer-
chandizing his products was a matter of no concern for him until the
depression of 1839–49. Local construction firms rapidly increased
their purchases of lumber after 1832 until they were absorbing the
total output of Brown's mill. New machinery installed during 1835
temporarily eased the shortage, but the sawmill's annual production
of two million feet was soon insufficient to meet the demands of the
community.[31]

The growth of Brown's business in Natchez during the boom years
can be seen in his relations with the prominent firm of contractors,
Neibert and Gemmell, who employed both white and slave carpenters
in much the same fashion as Brown himself.[32] From 1830 through
1833 they bought lumber at a fairly steady rate in which their purchases were approximately $2000 a year. Between August 1, 1834, and
March 14, 1837, however, Brown delivered lumber to them valued
at $29,467.11, and as usual received payment in cash. While erecting

[27] *Ibid.*, May 3, 1833; Ingraham, *South-west by a Yankee*, II, 160.
[28] *Mississippi Journal and Natchez Advertiser*, May 10, 1833.
[29] *Ibid.*, May 19 and July 19, 1833.
[30] *Ibid.*, May 10, 1833.
[31] Andrew Brown Journal (1836–40).
[32] Andrew Brown Ledger (1829–36); Andrew Brown Journal (1836–40), 119–
20; *Mississippi Journal and Natchez Advertiser*, March 15, 1833.

the City Hotel, a three-story building accommodating three hundred guests, the proprietors ran up a record bill of almost $9000 for a single month.[33] Brown's total sales for 1836, the year when "the west end of Main street . . . [was rendered] . . . the most beautiful and magnificent part of our town," were $56,000, representing approximately two million feet of lumber.[34]

When construction began in earnest on the railroad between Natchez and Canton in January, 1837, the Mississippi Rail Road Company became an increasingly important customer for lumber.[35] Brown supplied them with cypress crossties at $30 a thousand feet and furnished various sizes of planking for buildings and bridges at $35.[36] During the first year of construction the railroad company purchased slightly more than $9000 worth of lumber and timber from the Natchez sawmill.[37] Much of this went into the bridge across St. Catherine Creek, three miles east of Natchez. Completed in January, 1838, the bridge was two thousand feet long and was supported by forty-two brick piers. The *Courier* described the structure as "probably the greatest work of the kind in the Southern States." [38]

The following year was one of much greater activity, and the Mississippi Rail Road Company paid Brown $46,000 in cash for deliveries representing approximately 1,300,000 feet of lumber, well over half of the mill's output for 1838.[39] Even though hampered by the onset of the depression, the company nevertheless bought an additional $15,000 worth of lumber during the first ten months of 1839, before construction was stopped by lack of money.[40] Thus, Brown was probably the principal beneficiary of the abortive effort to make Natchez a railroad center.

That portion of Brown's lumber production which the railroad did not absorb was purchased by Natchez building firms for use in commercial construction or on plantation residences. Between December 1, 1837, and June 23, 1838, the Bellevue cotton press, "in constant

[33] Andrew Brown Journal (1836–40), 141; Grand Gulf (Miss.) *Advertiser*, April 14, 1836.
[34] Andrew Brown Ledger (1836–40), 3–27.
[35] Jackson *Mississippian*, January 27, 1837.
[36] Andrew Brown Day Book (1837–40), 3.
[37] Andrew Brown Ledger (1836–40), 216.
[38] Natchez *Courier*, January 19, 1838.
[39] Andrew Brown Ledger (1836–40), 306–307.
[40] *Ibid.*, 320.

operation day and night . . . and . . . probably doing more than any other press in the whole South," received deliveries of planking worth $5,500, for use in building warehouses.[41] "In the erection of elegant and substantial houses it is taking the lead of Vicksburg," the editor of the *Courier* wrote in June, 1838.[42] During 1837 and 1838 most of the stores in the downtown section were replaced with brick structures, and the "burnt district in Natchez opposite the City Hotel" was covered with "beautiful and substantial brick stores." [43] The Methodist and Presbyterian churches were extensively remodeled, and many residences were being improved.[44] Much of this business was to Brown's advantage. Eli Montgomery, for example, purchased lumber to the value of $4,000 to use on his house. Day and Caldwell, a construction firm, ran up bills totaling $2,900 during 1839; and William Yandell during 1838 used lumber on a single job worth $3,530. While maintaining public facilities, the city of Natchez made various purchases from Brown that year which amounted to $2,750.[45]

Although Brown was untroubled by marketing problems during most of the 1830's, he had to give increasingly close attention to the problem of obtaining enough cypress logs to keep his mill in continuous operation, especially after its enlargement in 1835. The original haphazard method of relying on transient rafts for timber was abandoned. As early as 1832, Brown journeyed to the Yazoo Valley, and signed contracts with loggers to supply him with specific amounts of timber delivered at the breakwater of the mill. In that year, John Johnson delivered 664 logs, for which he was paid $1.05 per log; and C. Beard received $1.50 a log for rafts containing 1,115 timbers of larger size. Aside from a few casual purchases, Johnson and Beard supplied all the timber obtained by the mill that season.[46]

Brown made somewhat different arrangements in 1835. At this time he made substantial purchases of logs from logmen in the Yazoo Valley and contracted with John MacIntosh, a professional raftsman, to bring the timber down river to the mill. According to their agreement, Brown paid MacIntosh fifty cents per log for his services in

[41] Natchez *Courier*, December 15, 1837; Andrew Brown Ledger (1836–40).
[42] Natchez *Courier*, June 29, 1838.
[43] *Ibid.*, July 27, 1838.
[44] *Ibid.*
[45] Andrew Brown Ledger (1836–40).
[46] Andrew Brown Ledger (1829–36), August and September, 1832.

transporting 1,734 logs to Natchez. Out of this sum, the raftsman had to pay wages and provide food for his own hands.[47]

Two years later Brown developed a more systematic method of assuring an adequate and even supply of timber. In the fall of 1837 he contracted with James J. Wheless, a professional logger, to furnish him with all the timber that Wheless and his crews could bring out of the Yazoo Valley that season. Brown undertook to finance Wheless' operations so that the logman could employ crews of maximum size on a continuous basis, and the funds he advanced were to be deducted at the time of final settlement. These timbering operations were located on lands bordering Cassidy's Bayou, a tributary of the Yazoo River. Brown owned either the two cypress brakes outright, or a share of them.[48]

Wheless' reports to Brown reveal how the logging business was carried on in the Yazoo Valley during the 1830's. Dikes, or dams, were built around the area in the swamp where the timber was to be felled. Then, while the river was still low, the trees were cut down and their branches and tops removed. The resulting timber was known in the lumber trade as a "stick" or "tier." Its length was recorded in feet and the diameter of the smaller end in inches. In Brown's records, for example, a typical entry about the purchase of logs would read: "10 tier of 30 inch timber 50 feet long at $3.50." In such a case the price would refer to a sawlog, which was a ten-foot section of a tree trunk. Less frequently the price would be given in terms of tiers.[49]

In preparing timber for transportation to the mill, Wheless cut the forty- to seventy-foot tiers into ten-foot sawlogs while the swamp was still dry. Because of their huge size, Wheless made no attempt to move the logs unless they lay on the bank of a stream. Instead, he preferred to wait until rising waters of the Yazoo flooded the swamp and filled the diked-off area where the logs were lying. Once the sawlogs were afloat, Wheless's crews, working from pirogues, assembled them into small rafts, called "cribs," which usually consisted of ten sawlogs each. The logs composing the cribs were spliced together by wooden poles laid across the top of the cribs, through which wooden pins were driven into holes bored in the logs. When the water rose high enough

[47] Andrew Brown Journal (1835).
[48] Andrew Brown Journal (1836–40).
[49] James J. Wheless to Andrew Brown, November 30, 1837, Learned Collection.

to provide a "float," the loggers opened the dams and poled the cribs out into the stream through a "float road," which previously had been cleared of trees and other obstructions. Once in the main channel, the cribs were fastened together into rafts containing from four to five hundred sawlogs. There they were secured to the bank by means of hemp cables and log chains until the current became strong enough to move the rafts easily. Then the men cast off the moorings and maneuvered their cumbersome rafts down the Yazoo into the Mississippi.[50]

During this period the Yazoo River was from a hundred to two hundred yards wide along its lower reaches. Near its mouth, however, it flowed into an oxbow of the Mississippi, formed when that great stream changed course during the earthquake of 1811. Wheless and other Yazoo raftsmen used this natural mile-wide lake, called "Old River," as an assembly point in which small lots of timber were combined into rafts and also as a market place for displaying their logs to buyers from the sawmills below Vicksburg. In years when the Mississippi rose high enough to provide a good float in the Yazoo Valley, Old River would be almost hidden by acres of rafts containing tens of thousands of cypress logs.[51]

Managing the huge rafts on their downward journey was a difficult task. Not infrequently the current would run them ashore despite strenuous efforts at the sweeps by crewmen; and sometimes rafts would break apart, scattering cribs and individual logs on sandbars and along the shore. In both cases Brown was faced with the problem of salvaging as much of his timber as possible, and he frequently had to dispatch crews of Negroes from the mill to round up stray logs, reform them into rafts, and float them to the breakwater at Natchez. In this fashion, some of the sawmill slaves became adept as rivermen. Simon Gray particularly distinguished himself in these activities, and by the close of the decade he was being trusted by Brown with responsibility for managing small salvage crews. During the next decade the depression forced Brown to economize, so he fell into the practice of using Simon Gray, Jim Matthews, and several other slaves regularly as raftsmen and boatmen. Thus, Brown gradually extended slavery into the rafting part of his lumber business without serious problems.[52]

[50] *Ibid.*, April 16 and September 14, 1838.
[51] Jackson *Mississippian*, February 3, 1837.
[52] The journals of Andrew Brown of Natchez for the 1830–50 period.

During the late 1830's Brown continued to buy from other logmen because Wheless was not able to provide all the timber needed by the sawmill at Natchez. In January, 1838, he bought 1,375 logs from Samuel M. Woods at the rate of $3.75 per log; and in March of that same year James C. Dorsey was paid $2,717 for 317 tiers of timber.[53] These prices, however, were higher than those of the previous year. In May, 1837, for instance, Brown had bought 100 logs fifty feet long at $2.25 each and 132 timbers forty feet long for the same price.[54]

In addition to supervising his lumber enterprise, Brown, during the 1830's, also participated in civic affairs. In 1832 he served on an arrangements committee which was preparing a reception for Senator George Poindexter in company with Adam L. Bingaman, Felix Houston, Levin Wailes, P. M. Lapice, and other prominent residents of the area. He became a director of the Mississippi Rail Road Company, in which the city was vitally interested; and he served in a hook and ladder volunteer fire company. Signifying the importance of his newly acquired prominence among the merchants was his election as a selectman of the city of Natchez in 1838. The following year Brown became a member of the "Standing Whig General Committee of Adams County," and during the summer he served on the committee of five which chose the party's nominee for the state house of representatives. He also was active in a movement aimed at preventing the practice of dueling.[55]

The pinnacle of Brown's social career in Natchez was attained on August 8, 1839. The city fathers had invited the volunteer militia companies of Vicksburg to visit their city, and Andrew Brown was included on the committee appointed by the mayor to prepare a welcome for the visitors.[56] For his part of the program Brown planned an elaborate garden party to which the soldiers from Vicksburg and most of the residents of Natchez were invited. Descending from the bluffs to the Upper Steamboat Landing, his guests looked down on "a gorgeous scene of magnificence and beauty," the editor of the *Courier* reported. "The beautiful Vale and Grove in which, near the margin

[53] Andrew Brown Journal (1836–40), 262 and 282.
[54] Andrew Brown Account Book (1836–40), 1837.
[55] Charleston (S.C.) *Courier*, March 9, 1839; Grand Gulf (Miss.) *Advertiser*, May 5, 1836; Natchez *Courier*, January 5, 1838, and July 26 and August 23, 1839; Vicksburg *Advocate and Register*, September 6, 1832; Vicksburg *Register*, December 29, 1836.
[56] Natchez *Courier*, August 3, 1839.

of the noble Mississippi, the residence of Mr. Brown is embosomed, appeared like some fairy-wrought scene in the Arabian nights," the well-fed newspaperman continued. After their arrival the five hundred guests were entertained with music and served "viands and beverages of every description" from tables on the lawn. In the view of the journalist, "the far-famed gardens of northern cities would have appeared tame and lifeless in contrast with this." [57] The volunteers from Vicksburg stated in their letter of appreciation to the mayor that they regarded Brown's party as the most enjoyable part of their visit to Natchez.[58]

By the close of the decade of the 1830's, Brown's lumber manufacturing establishment had developed into a substantial local business. Judged by standards of the time, the yearly production of two million feet at the Natchez mill was moderately large, and the labor force of Negroes was well-trained. Brown had also devised a reasonably satisfactory system for procuring and transporting timber to the mill. He had, however, taken no steps toward developing a merchandising department comparable to his manufacturing or logging operations. While the boom was running its course, no sales organization was needed as customers took care of this problem themselves. But when the cotton market broke during the fall of 1839, a new and gloomier prospect faced the Natchez lumberman, as well as the planters and commission merchants. Having invested heavily in timber, machinery, and slaves, Brown could not shut down his plant without bankrupting himself. Hence he had to seek new markets for the lumber that continued to accumulate in his yards. During the early depression years, with the aid of his son, Andrew, Jr., he found outlets south of Natchez. In so doing, the resourceful and untiring Scot survived the economic crisis and placed his company in a position to profit when times again became normal in the Mississippi Valley.

[57] *Ibid.*, August 16, 1839.
[58] *Ibid.*, August 30, 1839.

3

Andrew Brown and Son,
Of Natchez and New Orleans

THE flush times of the 1830's ended dramatically in Natchez, the little river town which had aspired to become an oceanic cotton shipping port rivaling Mobile and New Orleans. First, fire reduced to ashes a large part of the business section of the city on top of the hill in September, 1838.[1] Next, cotton prices plummeted downward during the autumn of 1839, bringing swift ruin to a host of formerly wealthy but over-extended cotton planters.[2] Then, after completing only twenty-eight miles of track, the Mississippi Rail Road Company, which merchants had counted on to bring the trade of north-central Mississippi to Natchez, was forced to suspend construction because of lack of funds.[3] The Mississippi Shipping Company also closed its doors, selling off the land and machinery of its Bellevue cotton press along with its foundry and steam sawmill.[4] Finally, nature brought down the curtain on the hopes and ambitions of the little commercial center. On May 7, 1840, a tornado struck the landing and then raked a path of destruction across the city on top of the bluffs. At the landing one steamboat, the *Hinds*, was sunk almost immediately with all on board, another was driven aground, and a third was reduced to floating wreckage. At least sixty flatboats went to the bottom of the river in a matter of seconds. The business section under the hill became a "scene of desolation and ruin which sickens the heart and beggars description." On top of the hill, reported the editor, "hundreds of

[1] Natchez *Courier*, September 13, 1839.
[2] Moore, *Agriculture in Antebellum Mississippi*, 69–74.
[3] Natchez *Courier*, February 9 and July 23, 1840, and August 2, 1843.
[4] *Ibid.*, August 6, 1840.

37

houses, yesterday on firm foundations . . . choke up our streets with mingled materials, in a state of utter destruction."[5]

From points as far away as St. Louis and New Orleans came aid to the stricken population of Natchez. A local relief committee was organized to raise money and to help the most badly injured. More than fifteen thousand dollars was collected by the committee with the largest donations being made by Stephen Duncan and David Hunt, each of whom contributed a thousand dollars.[6] Merchants of New Orleans dispatched lumber and building supplies, and carpenters and mechanics came from the Crescent City to offer assistance in rebuilding. Their efforts and those of local workmen restored a semblance of order to the town. On July 1, the editor of the Natchez *Courier* wrote proudly, "We are pleased to see those portions of our city in which business is transacted so far redeemed from the unsightly and melancholy ravages of the storm." Nevertheless, he concluded pessimistically, "there are still too many testimonials of its power in the heaps of ruins around us. . . . Anything like a general rebuilding cannot be expected for perhaps years to come."[7] He was right in his prediction. The Presbyterian congregation was not able to reconstruct the steeple on its church until 1842 because members had to make such extensive repairs to their damaged homes. During the building season of 1842, however, the inhabitants began to shake off their stupor. Many stores were built "adding new life and cheerful appearance to . . . our city."[8]

Andrew Brown shared fully the misfortunes of his fellow citizens. The tornado damaged his sawmill extensively and almost destroyed his imposing and relatively new residence by the river.[9] Repairing the damage turned into more of a problem than it should have because of the depression. Lumber prices had fallen as drastically as cotton prices in the late 1830's; and during 1840, the year of maximum distress, the Brown sawmill sold almost nothing. The largest single transaction negotiated was a purchase of 30,000 feet of plank by A. L.

[5] *Ibid.*, May 7 and 16, 1840.
[6] *Ibid.*, May 16 and August 20, 1840.
[7] *Ibid.*, June 8 and July 1, 1840.
[8] *Ibid.*, January 20 and February 24, 1842.
[9] Andrew Brown Day Book (1837–40), July 3, 1840. Unless otherwise indicated, all of Andrew Brown's day books, journals, ledgers, etc., cited in this chapter are in the Rufus F. Learned Collection. See also the New Orleans *Times Picayune*, May 13, 1840.

Wilson for $915.95. Most other sales involved less than a hundred dollars. No lumber at all went to the Mississippi Rail Road Company, which had been Brown's most lucrative customer during the 1837–39 period, and the directors themselves were trying to raise money by disposing of their stock of fifty slaves. Natchez construction firms which had been Brown's important customers in recent years were barely surviving.[10]

Adding to Brown's woes were repairs which had to be completed before the mill could resume operation. One boiler for the steam engine had to be replaced at a cost of $205.00, and much metal work was needed on the other two.[11] Yet, even during this period of disaster, wages of skilled artisans remained high; Brown had to pay David Toppar, a New Orleans boilermaker, five dollars a day for twenty-eight days' work at the mill in addition to his transportation costs to and from Natchez.[12] Inasmuch as the mill was closed while the work on the boilers was in progress, Brown took advantage of the opportunity to carry out minor repairs to his other machinery. In accordance with his usual custom at that period, he called in Andrew Donnan, a coal dealer and skilled blacksmith of Natchez, to undertake such tasks as repairing the chains which pulled rafts to the entrance of the canal and hauled cars up the log stage. Donnan's bill on this occasion totaled $73.93, a sum which Brown would have considered negligible two years earlier, but which he now was unable to pay until it was many months overdue.[13]

On June 1, 1840, Andrew Brown's only son joined him in the lumber business.[14] Andrew, Jr., was twenty-two years old when he accepted his father's offer of a job at a thousand dollars a year. Having inherited his father's energetic and adventurous nature, young Brown had gone to sea while still a youth and had served for a brief period on a transoceanic sailing vessel, the *Aggressor*—presumably as a cabin boy.[15] Later, in 1839, he persuaded his father and others to purchase a Mississippi River steamboat, the *Hail Columbia*, of which he was

[10] Andrew Brown Journal (1840–43).
[11] *Ibid.*
[12] Andrew Brown Order Book (1837–40), July 3, 1840.
[13] Bill from A. Donnan to Andrew Brown, December 31, 1841, Andrew Brown Bills and Accounts (1840–49).
[14] Brown, "Browns of Fife"; Andrew Brown Journal (1840–43), 218.
[15] Andrew Brown, Jr., to Andrew Brown, July 31, 1846.

master for several months at a salary of $200 per month.[16] During this time several slaves, including the personable Simon Gray, were employed on board as stewards and waiters in the dining room, chambermaids in the cabins, and deck and boiler hands. For a brief while the *Hail Columbia* enjoyed a brisk business in hauling cotton to New Orleans, but like so many others it was caught by the crash of the cotton market before the owners had liquidated debts incurred in her purchase. For years afterwards, Brown and his son were plagued by lawsuits arising from this short foray into the transportation business.[17] So, in 1840 the young man was badly in need of remunerative employment, and his father was in equal need of a dependable and resourceful lumber salesman. Thus father and son from mutual necessity joined forces to combat the depression, and they soon proved a formidable team. The father retained responsibility for the manufacturing end of the business, while the son took over the task of selling lumber and surplus timber.[18]

Although the young lumber salesman diligently sought customers in Natchez during the early 1840's, he secured few orders. Very little new construction was undertaken before 1843, and carpenters competed fiercely among themselves for available repair work. Local purchases, as a result, did not absorb the production of the mill. In fact, the Browns found themselves in such dire need of cash during February, 1841, that they eagerly assumed the task of repairing streets and other like jobs for the city of Natchez, being paid a dollar a day for each of their fifteen slaves.[19]

While this sort of activity was going on under the direction of Andrew Brown, Sr., the son worked desperately to dispose of some of their huge and accumulating stock of lumber. In April, 1841, he took 52,650 feet of planking to New Orleans on a flatboat and managed to sell it on the levee for $1,268.25 in cash, which amounted to approximately $25 per thousand. Not counting the price of the flatboat, the trip cost the company $135.85 in expenses.[20] Similar trips to New Orleans followed this initial venture, at least six being made before the end of 1841. Aside from the obvious merit of getting rid of surplus stocks, these cash transactions on the levee above the Crescent City

[16] Journal of the steamboat *Hail Columbia* (1839–40), Learned Collection.
[17] William I. Key to Andrew Dott, May 11, 1850, Learned Collection.
[18] Andrew Brown Journal (1840–43).
[19] *Ibid.*, 50.
[20] Andrew Brown Cash Book (1838–44), April 30, 1841.

brought into the coffers of the company money which could be used immediately for operating expenses.[21]

Andrew, Jr., soon became discontented with this unsystematic method of peddling lumber in New Orleans. Although he was offered $23.50 per thousand for 150,000 feet of plank which he had brought down with him in two flatboats in December, 1841, he did not accept the proposition. Instead, he canvased the builders of New Orleans for orders. He managed to sell 35,000 feet to a contractor named Lida, who promised to buy the remainder if he closed several contracts then under negotiation. Brown also investigated the possibility of having a portion of their cypress flooring dressed smooth by a local planing shop as he believed that the finished article would command much higher prices than his rough planks.[22]

At this time Brown was encountering strong competition in New Orleans from "a man by the name of Pryne from Louisiana opposite Vicksburg," who had a stock of more than 300,000 lineal feet of cypress in the city and who was receiving almost daily additional loads from his large mill. Happily for the Browns, their own product was recognized by builders as being superior in quality to Pryne's, and the young salesman found that he could outsell his rival. He became so confident, in fact, that he instructed his father to rush additional wide planking and flooring.[23]

Despite his relative success in New Orleans, Andrew, Jr., was not overly optimistic about the future of the family lumber business as a whole. On March 12, 1842, he wrote his boyhood friend A. J. Postlethwaite, who then was employed at the Natchez mill as a clerk: "I will do all I can, you may depend, but the best can't do much these times. The state of things here is awful, as I suppose it also is in Natchez. The Carrolton Hotel is not to be built up at present, so there is an end to that calculation. There is nothing else here that I see to be done." Brown wrote further that "Hundreds of mechanics are now out of employment & the prospect is dark & gloomy." Characteristically the young Presbyterian ended on a note of pious stoicism: "We have got to show a bold front, for it is no use giving way to despondency, & I trust we will reap the fruits of our perseverence

[21] Andrew Brown Journal (1840–43).
[22] Andrew Brown, Jr., to Andrew Brown, December 12, 1841, Learned Collection.
[23] *Ibid.*

some day not far distant, & rise out of the ashes purified & doubly determined to follow a virtuous, energetic & independent course with the full satisfaction that it will be its own reward." [24]

In spite of his apprehensions about the future of the family business, young Brown doggedly continued his work. During 1842 and 1843 he made arrangements to sell his lumber on commission, usually at 5 per cent, through established merchants in the river towns. While conducting negotiations to this end with the New Orleans firm of Washington and Jackson, he assured them that "I will guarantee the general satisfaction of the lumber, as we buy nothing but the best quality Yazoo Cypress timber, and as the mill can cut 8 to 10,000 feet per day, and [flat]boats can be had at all times here to carry it, we are prepared to execute orders to almost any amount on short notice." He informed them, too, that his father could cut lumber to any dimensions not exceeding forty feet in length.[25]

When his busy schedule permitted, Andrew, Jr., personally took flatboat loads of lumber downriver with the intention of peddling small quantities at retail prices to customers along the way; and he welcomed orders of any size from plantation owners who resided near the river. The first of his "coasting" trips was undertaken in June, 1841, at a time when the company was desperately in need of funds. This expedition was moderately successful, for he was able to dispose of 56,000 feet of "common," or medium grade cypress planking for $980 in cash.[26] In an attempt to boost sales along the German Coast, Brown advertised in the New Orleans *Picayune* that his firm was "at all times prepared to fill orders for Cypress Lumber of all dimensions delivered anywhere on the river between Natchez and New Orleans, on the most reasonable terms." [27] Simon Gray accompanied the young Scot on many coasting ventures during the early 1840's, and under his tutelage the Negro eventually developed into an accomplished and enthusiastic retail lumber salesman and boatman.[28]

By the end of 1842 the two Browns concluded that they had won

[24] Andrew Brown, Jr., to A. J. Postlethwaite, March 12, 1842, Learned Collection.
[25] Andrew Brown, Jr., to Washington, Jackson, and Company, January 29, 1842, Learned Collection.
[26] Andrew Brown Journal (1840–43), June, 1841.
[27] New Orleans *Times Picayune*, December 8, 1842.
[28] Andrew Brown, Jr., to Andrew Brown, June 18, 1844, Learned Collection.

their battle against economic disaster. Their sales of lumber that year had totaled $21,000, which meant that they had moved more than a million feet or half the maximum capacity of the mill.[29] With such funds as they were able to collect from their none-too-prosperous customers and with timely assistance from Stephen Duncan, they had met their most pressing obligations. Before the beginning of the new year, they were even able to repay more than $9,000 on the loans which Duncan made them between December, 1841, and January, 1843.[30]

At the beginning of 1843 the outlook for the lumber market was so favorable that Andrew, Jr., asked to buy Duncan's half-interest in his father's lumber partnership. The Natchez financier had a particular liking for the Browns and agreed to sell his portion of the machinery, real estate, timber, and slaves belonging to the mill for $36,239.91. According to the terms of the contract signed on March 1, 1843, the younger Brown was to pay Duncan approximately $5,000 on the first of each January through 1850;[31] and as long as he lived, the young businessman faithfully fulfilled this obligation. After his son's death from yellow fever in October, 1848, Andrew, Sr., assumed Andrew, Jr.'s debts and bought his equity in the business from Elizabeth W. Brown, his daughter-in-law.

When the Browns entered the New Orleans lumber market in 1843, they arranged with the firm belonging to Henry T. Sherman and James Prague, commission merchants, lumber dealers, and personal friends of long standing, to sell their cypress on a commission basis. Although Prague and Sherman maintained a stock of Natchez cypress for them and succeeded in selling a considerable amount of lumber, the Browns were not satisfied with the arrangement. They regarded the 10 per cent commission that Prague and Sherman charged as excessive and believed the two partners were not sufficiently aggressive in seeking orders for lumber. Consequently, the Browns, after giving careful consideration to the complexities of the move, decided to open a lumber yard of their own in New Orleans under the management of Andrew, Jr.[32]

[29] Andrew Brown Journal (1840–43).
[30] Andrew Brown Cash Book (1838–43).
[31] Andrew Brown Journal (1840–43), March 1, 1843.
[32] Prague & Sherman to Andrew Brown, October 25, November 8, and 26, 1843, Learned Collection; Andrew Brown Day Book (1843–48), December 27, 1843; New Orleans *Times Picayune*, December 16, 1843.

Before committing themselves to this new enterprise, Andrew, Jr., at his father's suggestion consulted by mail John McQuewan, of Pittsburgh, Pennsylvania. He and Andrew, Sr., had been friends during that period in the early 1820's when Brown had worked in Pittsburgh before coming to Natchez, and they had continued their pleasant relationship over subsequent years. McQuewan was also a lumberman by profession, and he was accustomed to sending white pine on flatboats to New Orleans by way of the Ohio and Mississippi rivers. Brown occasionally purchased cargoes of white pine from the Pittsburgh firm, McQuewan and Douglas, for resale in Natchez, and McQuewan often acted on Brown's behalf in Pittsburgh when the latter wished to obtain supplies or manufactured articles in that city. McQuewan, being well acquainted with the business possibilities of the Crescent City, advised the Browns definitely to open an outlet there because "I am satisfied that money ought to be made at N. Orleans at the Lumber Business." [33]

While establishing and stocking his yard in New Orleans during May, 1844, Andrew, Jr., encountered an unexpected but not unpleasant difficulty—customers on the levee insisted on buying the lumber before it could be hauled to the yard. On May 28, he wrote his father somewhat ruefully that he was "selling at 22.50 & 23 & some at 25 as fast as I can get it." [34] A. M. Depouilly, who operated a woodworking plant and lumber yard on Carondelet Canal, was snapping up eight- and nine-inch plank as fast as it came ashore. [35]

In New Orleans the depression in the building trades was fading away during the summer of 1844. In July, Andrew, Jr., urged his father to ship every stick of lumber from the Natchez yard to New Orleans as he had already disposed of everything in stock, "rubbish & all." [36] When the requested shipment arrived, the new lumber dealer promptly sold both loads, although a Yazoo River lumberman had arrived at about the same time with a large cargo of cypress flooring. [37] The sawmills in New Orleans were obviously unable to

[33] John McQuewan to Andrew Brown, Jr., May 9, 1844, and McQuewan to Andrew Brown, September 29, 1849, both in Learned Collection; Andrew Brown & Co. Journal (1855–60), 61.

[34] Andrew Brown, Jr., to Andrew Brown, May 28, 1844, Learned Collection.

[35] Ibid.; Mobile Register, April 28, 1841; New Orleans Times Picayune, February 10, 1843, May 3, 1845, and July 18, 1852.

[36] Andrew Brown, Jr., to Andrew Brown, July 23, 1844, Learned Collection.

[37] Ibid., July 30, 1844.

cope with the rising demand. Unfilled orders from construction firms were piling up in their offices, and their supplies of timber were nearly exhausted. Builders in the city were experiencing great difficulty in obtaining seasoned plank and were being compelled by the shortage to complete many new buildings with unsatisfactory green lumber.[38] "There is a great demand for stores & houses here at present," Andrew reported to his father in August; "as soon as the foundation of a building is laid someone rents it. . . . Thus it will be for the next three years to come; or more if [Henry] Clay is elected," the Whig lumber dealer concluded optimistically.[39] His renewed hopefulness was not unjustified for one of his satisfied customers had promised to buy between two and three hundred thousand feet of lumber from him during the next season. Apparently the Browns had established themselves in the river port at a most propitious time.[40]

On the basis of a season's experience in New Orleans, Andrew, Jr., concluded that his father should concentrate on stacking and drying all the lumber the sawmill at Natchez was producing. Contractors in the city were so eager to obtain seasoned plank that they were offering handsome premiums to obtain it, and they would usually buy it in preference to green lumber almost without regard to the price differential. "All the stuff you have had better be stacked so as to dry quick as fast as you cut it; it will pay well to do so even if you have to hire [extra] hands," he warned his father.[41]

Those merchants who were selling Brown's lumber on commission in the various river towns below Natchez were also clamoring for more plank now that the depression had run its course. From Donaldsonville, Louisiana, for example, J. W. Proffetts wrote Andrew Brown, Sr., at Natchez, that he had disposed of all the boards he had on hand and that he could sell an additional flatboat cargo at advanced prices "without the least trouble. . . . I can work and sell in this place 30,000 ft in one year if you can furnish me," he assured the lumberman.[42]

The immediate prospects were so bright in June, 1845, that the younger Brown made arrangements to expand the facilities of his

[38] *Ibid.*, August 20, 1844.
[39] *Ibid.*, August 24, 1844.
[40] *Ibid.*, December 17, 1844.
[41] *Ibid.*, February 8, 1845.
[42] J. W. Proffetts to Andrew Brown, March 9, 1845, Learned Collection.

lumber yard. He rented six adjoining lots on Magazine Street which gave him sufficient space to contain more than a million feet of lumber and was fortunate to strike a bargain with the owner for a rent of only $25 a month.[43]

Lumber prices had risen materially since the Brown lumber yard was established in New Orleans the year before. During June, 1845, better grades of cypress were selling briskly at from $27.50 to $30 a thousand even though they were not well seasoned, and buyers were offering $35 a thousand for good air-dried plank.[44] Andrew, Jr., who was most anxious to establish a permanent clientele, was troubled by his inability to accumulate a sufficiently large stock in his yards to assure his customers constant satisfaction. He reckoned that maintaining a permanent supply of properly seasoned lumber would add to the income of the yard by at least two thousand dollars a year. Providing such a stock was beyond the capability of the Natchez mill, however, for sales were so good that Andrew, Sr., could not transport the lumber from Natchez rapidly enough. In August, the son advised his father that he could easily sell half a million feet of seasoned first-quality lumber within sixty days. "So, to get it here as fast as possible now ought to be the grand object," he said for the dozenth time.[45]

No matter how pressing business affairs became, Andrew, Jr., never let them interfere with his observance of religion. His scientifically-inclined father, on the other hand, was a Presbyterian who had allowed his Scottish Calvinism to be tempered by deism; and he frequently worked on Sunday when the circumstances required it, salving his conscience by paying slaves for this "extra" work. On one such occasion, Andrew, Jr., though hard pressed for lumber at his New Orleans yard, wrote that "I do sincerely hope that this will be the last boat you will start on the Sabbath, *it is not right*, and I can say without fear of contradiction that no business ever did prosper, or ever will, to the good of those engaged in it that intrudes itself on the sacredness of that day!"[46]

The pious son was deeply concerned by his father's rationalism in matters of religion. "You will probably say Knowledge is the way [to happiness]," he wrote in 1844. "I grant it is, properly applied, but

[43] Andrew Brown, Jr., to Andrew Brown, June 21, 1845, *ibid.*
[44] *Ibid.*, June 28, 1845.
[45] *Ibid.*, August 12, 1845.
[46] *Ibid.*, February [no date], 1845.

being wise in the wisdom of this world alone is not the way. Let . . .
[me] then beseech you . . . to change your studies . . . & take up the
revealed will of God to man as set forth in the sacred scriptures. . . .
Imitate the example of a Newton or a Locke or a host of others who
after treading the labyrinth of science & philosophy for years . . .
came at last & threw all their research at the feet of Jesus." [47] Andrew,
Sr., better educated than his son, accepted these sermons with polite
resignation, but without modifying his own views. Thus the Browns
typified two generations of educated Southerners: the older was a
man of the Enlightenment; the younger, of that upsurge of Protestant
Puritanism which overwhelmed the men of the Enlightenment during
the 1830's.

Toward the close of the 1845 building season the available stocks
of lumber in the New Orleans market were practically exhausted. Mills
in the vicinity had sawed up all their logs, as had other lumber manufacturers at Baton Rouge and on the lower Mississippi. The Browns
fortunately had obtained a substantial quantity of cypress logs from
the Yazoo, and as a result Andrew, Jr., could anticipate receiving a
normal supply of lumber from his father's sawmill during the spring
months. He was so resolutely determined to accumulate a stock of
lumber in his yard at this time that he actually refused to fill an order
for fifty thousand feet from one of his regular customers. By this date
he was able to boast, "I could sell more lumber in this place than all
the [other] yards . . . did I [but] have a good assortment of seasoned
[plank]. I believe in the system of having a yard more strongly every
day. Prague & Sherman sell no cypress hardly now, neither would
anyone else could they [but] get it here. The cry will still be More!" [48]

The lumber shortage in New Orleans during 1844 and 1845 caused
lumbermen to erect new mills and remodel old ones. In April, 1845,
for example, Andrew, Jr., informed his father that Labarre, "the only
man here that knows how to cut plank," was tearing down his mill
and intended to replace it with a larger and improved one.[49] Samuel
Russell during the same month advertised in the New Orleans *Times
Picayune* that he had completed extensive repairs on his sawmill
"opposite the city" and was supplying all kinds of cypress at his yard

[47] *Ibid.*, December [no date], 1844.
[48] Andrew Brown, Jr., to Andrew Brown, November 1, 1845, Learned Collection.
[49] *Ibid.*, April 19, 1845.

on the corner of Girod and Magazine streets.[50] F. Gardere, a friend and regular competitor of Andrew, Jr., was building a second saw-mill in the vicinity of New Orleans using machinery taken from a mill formerly owned by Joiner and Dubois which was situated below the cotton press.[51] Theodore Verret completed a steam sawmill in the Third Municipality near the sugar refinery and began sawing under the superintendent, N. Sheldon, in November, 1845.[52] Finally, Margaret Priestly, an unusual businesswoman, put a large and modern steam sawmill into operation in St. James Parish during 1845 and advertised its lumber for sale at Priestly and Bein's Hardware Company on New Levee Street, New Orleans.[53] When the year ended, the lumber manufacturing capacity of the city had been greatly expanded; for the time being, however, the new mills only made the timber shortage more acute.

Early in the 1846 building season Andrew, Jr., began to purchase building materials from other sawmills because he perceived that his trade in New Orleans had exceeded the capacity of the plant at Natchez. In February, for example, he bought a shipment of Pittsburgh white pine lumber from J. B. "Yankee" Morgan, paying the relatively high price of $27.25 per thousand feet for the lumber at wholesale. Yet he had no qualms about the wisdom of the purchase, being confident that he could easily get $35 for white pine plank at retail.[54] Building in New Orleans was continuing at a rapid pace even during this winter month, and boards of all kinds were accordingly in more than usual demand. Young Brown was certain that he could triple his past sales record provided he could obtain a large enough supply of seasoned planking. Having decided to draw upon all sources of lumber within reach in addition to the Natchez saw-mill, Andrew, Jr., further enlarged his yard by renting still another large adjoining lot. "You see," he wrote his father, "I am always crying lumber, lumber. It seems we will never have enough!"[55]

His remarkable success as a New Orleans lumber dealer encouraged

[50] New Orleans *Times Picayune*, September 21, 1844, and April 19, 1845.
[51] Andrew Brown, Jr. to Andrew Brown, March 20, 1845, Learned Collection.
[52] New Orleans *Times Picayune*, November 1, 1845.
[53] *Ibid.*, January 5, 1845.
[54] Andrew Brown, Jr., to Andrew Brown, February 10, 1846, Learned Collection. For another reference to Morgan refer to the New Orleans *Times Picayune*, December 16, 1852.
[55] Andrew Brown, Jr., to Andrew Brown, February 27, 1846, Learned Collection.

Andrew, Jr., to turn his thoughts for a moment to his own domestic situation. In March, 1846, he informed his father that he had decided to marry, build a house in New Orleans, and settle down permanently in that city. Before daring to take the added financial responsibility, however, he sought advice from Stephen Duncan, to whom he still owed a very large sum of money.[56] Duncan, as always, responded with kindness and affection. "I am happy to hear you are about to take unto yourself a helpmate . . .," Duncan replied to Andrew Jr. "I can with truth say that from you and your father I have received evidence enough of an overflowing gratitude to compensate for much of the ill will I have recd. at the hands of others who have partaken more largely in the way of benefit at my hands. . . . In regard to your payments to me," Duncan concluded, "I can only say that they need not interfere with your present or future plans, make yourself comfortable."[57]

Duncan, whose religious views were much like those of the elder Brown, had suffered too from young Andrew's evangelical bent. On this occasion, he responded kindly, tactfully but firmly. "I wish I was like you a consistent professor of religion," he wrote, "but I am so organized that I fear I would do discredit to it, did I make a public confession of it. . . . I must therefore go on as I have done for some years feeling & expressing the most thorough convictions of its truth & importance & the sincere desire for its advancement, and manifesting for the cause on all occasions the truest & highest respect." [58] Upon receiving the above, Andrew, Jr., completely misunderstood the gentle reproof. He sent his father a copy adding, "I consider such a testimonial from such a man as more precious than a crown of diamonds." The prospect of losing young Andrew to New Orleans must have aroused mixed emotions in both Stephen Duncan and his father, for he was, to paraphrase Mark Twain, a good man in the worst sense of the word.[59]

Like all persons who have undertaken to build a house, Andrew, Jr., was not entirely convinced that it was the right step. He did not relish parting with the two thousand dollars in cash it would cost him; yet, he did not approve of renting either, for New Orleans at

[56] *Ibid.*, March 20, 1846.
[57] Stephen Duncan to Andrew Brown, Jr., March 16, 1846, Learned Collection.
[58] *Ibid.*
[59] Andrew Brown, Jr., to Andrew Brown, March 20, 1846, Learned Collection.

all periods was "an awfull expensive place to live, either to rent or to board." [60] His doubts about the virtues of houseowning soon vanished, however, when his bride of a year gave birth to a son, whom they named Hugh.[61]

During the first year of his marriage, the young lumber dealer was kept very busy. Indeed, obtaining enough products to sell was a greater problem for him than the selling itself. The younger Brown cringed whenever he had to tell a prospective customer that he had no lumber of the kind required, and he was hounded by dreams in which people shouted at him, "When is that [lumber] boat to be here?" He therefore resolved to stock the yard somehow before the next building season began and to cease selling lumber on the German Coast or anywhere else except Natchez or New Orleans until his yard was full.[62] At this time New Orleans was developing an apparently insatiable appetite for cypress lumber. A great many buildings were going up during the summer of 1846, and plans were under way for as many more. Although mills at Vicksburg and Opelousas shipped in huge quantities of planking, the demand nevertheless remained stronger than any Andrew, Jr., had previously encountered.[63] He was handling both bricks and coal in addition to lumber during this period, and he reported to his father that New Orleans "is the place after all to sell anything." [64]

In December, 1846, Andrew, Jr., and his bride Betsy were visited by two young relatives, Alexander and Thomas Brown. These teen-aged lads were sons of Alexander Brown, Sr., a younger brother of the Natchez sawmill operator who had settled during the 1830's on a farm near Chicago. Having become old enough to carry out boyish ambitions, they had come South to sample the life their slave-owning uncle was enjoying at "Magnolia Vale," as Brown's house at Natchez-under-the-Hill was called. Their experiences evidently did not square with their earlier concepts, if one can read between the lines of their letters home. Instead of riding to hounds or spending their time at balls, the youngsters were set to work as manual laborers at the saw-mill and on rafts and lumber flatboats. A single piece of evidence that Andrew, Sr., regarded them as members of his family can be

[60] Andrew Brown, Jr., to Andrew Brown, August 11, 1846, Learned Collection.
[61] Ibid., July 27, 1847.
[62] Ibid., August 11, 1846.
[63] Ibid., July 31, August 5 and 20, and September 15, 1846.
[64] Ibid., August 20, 1846.

seen in his uncharacteristic omission of any reference to wages. He may have considered it impolite to discuss such mundane matters as money with kinsmen, but more likely he was waiting to see if the boys could do men's work before setting a price.[65] They must have proved their worth, for they were eventually carried on the records as day laborers at the going wage for strong backs—a dollar a day, and keep.[66]

While attached to a flatboat crew under the command of "Captain" Simon Gray, Alexander spent several days with the Browns in New Orleans and then wrote an account of this experience to his father and mother which might have come from the pen of Huckleberry Finn: "Andrew's house is very fine fitted up," he wrote. "One chair cost 40$, soffys, shower baths, and I don't know what all. . . . Uncle Andrew's house in Natchez is more plain and soots me better as it is more like home. You will perhaps wish to know what kind of provisions they use here. Just about the same as with you except this difference—sweet potatoes and corn dodgers. . . . Andrew's very religious and never misses going to church," the Illinois farm boy concluded, and then added plaintively, "I think I can say the same as long as I stopped [with him] in N. O." [67] To all members of his family, Andrew, Jr., was a bore on the subject of religion; only on the topic of business was he worth listening to, a not uncommon failing among dedicated men of commerce in all times and places.

According to Alexander, lumbering in the lower Mississippi Valley was not all play: "I wish some of the North Branch boys was here that thinks they have to work so hard. Then they would find out what it is to work for a living. Theirs no stopping here for a rainy day nor yet for a rainy week, but as we are all well and harty we do not mind it now. . . ." With a trace of regret he reported that "there is no danger of our falling in bad company here as we work all the week, Sundays too, when on the flatboat." [68]

While young Andrew Brown was developing an outlet in New Orleans for the products of the Natchez plant, his father was conducting the manufacturing end of the business with equal skill. After he completed extensive boiler repairs during 1840, Brown encountered

---

[65] Alexander Brown, Jr., to Alexander Brown, December 30, 1846, Learned Collection.

[66] Andrew Brown Journal (1848–53).

[67] Alexander Brown, Jr., to Alexander Brown, December 30, 1846, Learned Collection.

[68] *Ibid.*

no serious mechanical difficulties in the sawmill until 1844. In the spring and summer of that year there occurred what the contemporary historian John W. Monette described as "one of the most memorable floods ever known upon the Mississippi by civilized man." [69] The rise of waters was so great that the sediment they deposited completely sealed the outlets of all the old river lakes on the eastern side of the Mississippi Valley for a distance of six hundred miles.[70] During the next season, Governor Alexander G. McNutt, of Mississippi, while advertising a Yazoo–Mississippi Delta plantation for sale, wrote that "not withstanding there were no levees near this land, a small portion of it was not covered by the great flood of 1844." [71] This, McNutt believed was convincing proof that his plantation was situated on unusually high ground for that part of the state and that the land was the more valuable for this fact. While the water level did not rise high enough on the landing at Natchez-under-the-Hill to flood Brown's sawmill, the ledge of ground beneath the bluffs was nevertheless converted from solid earth into a dangerously soft mud bank. Brown had to stop the engines of the mill in order to prevent the machinery and supporting foundations from sinking below ground level. Long after the water level had returned to normal, the mud deposited between the mill and the channel remained too soft to allow Brown's workmen to dig a new logway from the river to the mill. In fact, the mill was not able to recommence sawing until the middle of September, an interruption of nearly half a year.[72]

As soon as the ground under the mill became firm again, Brown began to make extensive repairs and some alterations in his plant. His boilers were old and unreliable and had required regular minor repairs over the past several years. Brown junked all three and replaced them with new boilers at a cost of approximately a thousand dollars.[73] The copper pipes and escape valves alone cost $340; and

[69] John W. Monette, "The Mississippi Floods," Mississippi Historical Society Publications, VII (1903), 468.

[70] Robert W. Harrison, Alluvial Empire: A Study of State and Local Efforts toward Land Development in the Alluvial Valley of the Lower Mississippi River (Little Rock, 1961), 67.

[71] Jackson Mississippian, December 3, 1845.

[72] Andrew Brown to Andrew Brown, Jr., September 11, 1844, Learned Collection.

[73] Andrew Brown Journal (1843–48), 61–63; Andrew Brown Cash Book (1838–44), July and September, 1844.

one workman, C. Steenrod, a boilermaker's assistant, was paid for thirty-five days' work at two dollars a day.[74] Brown ordered a complete new set of sash saws from W. Rowland of Philadelphia and was disappointed to learn that his order could not be filled promptly. In the end, he had to turn to a similar firm operated by T. and B. Rowland, nephews of the better-known sawmaker.[75] A foundry bill for making castings used in repairing sawmill machinery submitted by Wilkins, Humason & Company came to $1,283.18.[76]

The capacity of the mill was not materially increased by the alterations made during 1844. When Brown felt an urgent need to step up his output during the New Orleans building boom of 1846, he resorted to the somewhat dangerous expedient of running his machinery around the clock. This not only increased the danger of accidents to workmen in the mill, but also made the ever-present fire hazard much more serious because of the necessity of utilizing oil lamps in highly flammable surroundings.[77] With Brown enforcing extreme precautions, however, white sawyers and Negro workers performed this difficult operation without injuries to themselves or to the plant. Even so, the mill during 1846 was not able to fill the orders Andrew, Jr., sent to Natchez from the New Orleans lumber yard.

Keeping the mill in running order had required the frequent attention of a blacksmith, and the resulting bills for this kind of service had averaged $300 a year. As such regular outlays of cash were most annoying to Andrew, Sr., he determined to add a skilled Negro blacksmith to his force of slaves. Eventually he located a Negro named Spencer who had the requisite qualifications and bought him on behalf of Brown and Son for the sum of $1,020, a comparatively high price during the mid-1840's.[78]

Because the sawmill was no longer able to provide the New Orleans lumber yard with all the cypress lumber his son required, Brown decided in 1847 to modernize his machinery. He began his program

[74] Andrew Brown Journal (1843–48), 66.
[75] F. F. Folger to Andrew Brown, Jr., October 5, 1844, Learned Collection. For a reference to another manufacturer of saws consult New Orleans *Times Picayune*, May 11, 1850.
[76] Wilkins, Humason & Company to Andrew Brown, 1844, Andrew Brown Bills and Accounts (1840–49).
[77] Andrew Brown, Jr., to Andrew Brown, February 3, 1846, Learned Collection.
[78] *Ibid.*, May 1, 1846; Andrew Brown Journal (1843–48), December 31, 1846.

by making extensive modifications in his old sash sawmill. The saw gates were rebuilt to admit logs of greater diameter to the gangsaws, and both the log carriage and its railroad were lengthened. When these changes were completed, the mill could saw logs of more than three feet in diameter and sixty feet in length. Brown also replaced worn parts in the sash mill and repaired the railroad and cars by which logs were carried up the log stage to the sawmill carriage.[79]

By this period southwestern cypress lumbermen were becoming interested in the circular saw.[80] Since a mill at Port Gibson, Mississippi, had installed such a device in 1838, the circular saw had proved itself a practical tool for manufacturing cypress plank. On the other hand, this type of saw was less useful for working white or yellow pine because their resins built up a residue which ruined the cutting edges of the teeth. No such problem was encountered with cypress and hardwoods like walnut or oak, and circular saws possessed certain advantages over the reciprocating gangsaws, whose motion was a simple forward-and-back one. Among these, the most important was the much higher velocity with which they operated. Because of its high speed, a circular saw could cut through a log lengthwise in a fraction of the time required by a gangmill. It could also be set to cut narrower dimensions than conventional upright saws and thus could manufacture much thinner panels than gangsaws could.[81] However, circular saws had disadvantages, too. In the first place circular saws were unable to process the large timbers that gangsaws could because they could not make a cut greater than half their diameter. In the second, their high speed generated great heat and materially increased the danger of fire in the mills employing them. Finally, the blades became dull more quickly than upright saws and had a tendency to warp unless they were run by a highly skilled sawyer.[82] Because of these characteristics—good and bad—circular saws were

[79] Andrew Brown, Jr., to Andrew Brown, July 3 and 31, 1847; Thomas Seaton to Andrew Brown, January 9, 1849, Andrew Brown Bills and Accounts (1840–49).

[80] New Orleans *Times Picayune*, April 29, 1848, and February 19, 1853; Port Gibson (Miss.) *Correspondent*, June 16, 1838; Woodville (Miss.) *Republican*, August 12, 1843. An excellent history of the development of sawmills, including circular sawmills, is contained in Bryan Latham, *Timber, Its Development and Distribution: A Historical Survey* (London, 1957), 206–23.

[81] Key to Dott, August 14, 1849, Learned Collection; Natchez *Free Trader*, March 13, 1857.

[82] Bale, *Woodworking Machinery*, 8–34.

first employed by woodworking shops and were adapted to cypress lumber manufacturing somewhat later. A portable circular sawmill manufactured in various sizes by George Page and Company of Baltimore was introduced into the lower Mississippi Valley during the early 1840's and soon won such universal approval that it became virtually standard for small mills during the late 1840's and 1850's.[83] Other makes, however, were also widely employed.[84]

Intrigued by the possibilities of circular saws, Brown added a complete mill of this type to his Natchez establishment as an essential part of his modernization program. He realized that it would be necessary to use the largest possible size since he seldom bought cypress logs of less than two feet in diameter, and he reckoned that fifty inches was the smallest saw that would serve his purposes. When Andrew, Jr., inquired of New Orleans dealers, however, he found that none larger than thirty-six inches were kept in stock. Through Slark, Day, and Stauffer, the local agents for the great saw manufacturer, R. Hoe and Company of New York, Brown finally ordered a fifty-inch cast steel saw, and in due course it was installed in his new machinery.

[83] For references to the Page circular sawmill refer to Herbert A. Keller (ed.), *Solon Robinson: Pioneer and Agriculturist* (2 vols.; Indianapolis, 1936), I, 277; New Orleans *Times Picayune*, December 23, 1849, May 30 and June 2, 1850, and August 3, 1854; *De Bow's Review*, XXIV (1858), advertisement section. A court decision involving the patent rights of the manufacturer is discussed in Yazoo City (Miss.) *Whig*, June 16, 1854.

[84] Among the many firms manufacturing circular sawmills during the 1840–60 period were Leed's Foundry, Armstrong's Foundry, and W. P. Kelsey & Company Steam Manufactory of New Orleans; Phoenix Foundry, and William Alderson & Company of Mobile, Alabama; Winter Iron Works, and Montgomery Iron Works of Montgomery, Alabama; Nashville Manufacturing Company of Nashville, Tennessee; Ettenger & Edmond, Burger & Boyle's Great Southern Steam Saw Manufactory, P. Rahm's Eagle Machine Works, and the Tredegar Locomotive and Machine Works of Richmond, Virginia; George Page & Company, Baltimore, Maryland; Land & Bodley of Cincinnati, Ohio; New York Steam Saw-Mill and Machine Company, and Albany Iron & Saw Works of Albany, New York.

For references to these manufacturing establishments, see Albany (N.Y.) *Daily Statesman*, March 9, 1858; Atchison City (Kan.) *Freedom's Champion*, February 27, 1858; Chambersburg (Penn.) *Repository Transcript*, March 10, 1858; *De Bow's Review*, XXIV (1858), advertisement section; Mobile *Register*, March 1, 1853, September 8, 1855, October 31, 1857, August 27, 1859, November 1 and 4, 1859, January 20 and February 16, 1860; Mobile *Tribune*, March 5, 1858; Natchez *Courier*, December 30, 1857; New Orleans *Evening True Delta*, March 2, 1858; New Orleans *Times Picayune*, January 14, 1844, October 24, 1848, September 18 and October 13, 1852, June 19 and August 3, 1860; Wayne County (Ill.) *Fairfield Gazette*, April 1, 1858.

The circular sawmill equipped in this fashion was found to have a capacity of more than five thousand feet of lumber a day.[85]

When the alterations to his machinery had been completed, Brown conducted a test to determine the maximum capacity of the plant under nearly ideal conditions. One crew under a Negro foreman named Randall succeeded in sawing six large logs, which produced 12,905 feet of lumber. Another under Jacob, apparently manning the circular saw mill, cut up nine smaller logs and made 11,782 feet. Thus, the extreme capacity was determined to be approximately twenty-five thousand feet a day, although members of the firm continued to regard fifteen thousand feet as a more reliable average.[86]

Brown's mill at this period was described in an article in the Natchez *Free Trader* which was republished in *De Bow's Review.* Brown during 1847, according to the writer, was running his sawmill fourteen hours a day (approximately the hours of daylight during the summer) and employing between forty and fifty workers in milling, logging, rafting, and transporting lumber. The mill was manufacturing about fifteen thousand feet of lumber a day, which was sold during 1847 at an average price of $25 per thousand feet. From Brown the editor had learned that sales for the year had totaled $56,000, and, during the same period, that a backlog of half a million feet of lumber had been accumulated in the yards. According to Brown, $28,000, or half the gross, had been "clear profit over and above all expenses." The books of the Brown company reveal that the retail sales at Natchez had been merely $14,500. During the year, Andrew, Sr. shipped 1,158,000 feet of lumber to the New Orleans yard, and was paid $28,400 at wholesale. On the basis of these statistics, it is clear that the business had attained its pre-depression dimensions and was making an excellent return on an investment of slightly less than $75,000. As the editor of the *Free Trader* remarked, the mill was making more money than any two ordinary cotton plantations in Mississippi.[87]

The Brown sawmill in 1847 was not alone in the lumber trade in Natchez. Brown Cozzens, an architect and contractor, had erected another steam mill at the Middle Landing which was turning out annually slightly more than a million feet. In 1847, Cozzens was

[85] Andrew Brown, Jr., to Andrew Brown, July 27 and 31, 1848, Learned Collection. New Orleans *Times Picayune*, January 1, 1850.

[86] Andrew Brown Day Book (1843–48), 291.

[87] *De Bow's Review*, V (1848), 380; Andrew Brown Journal (1843–48).

employing a crew of ten workmen, whom he worked fifteen hours a day. His product was inferior to Brown's, and the average selling price during the year was $18 a thousand. His gross sales during 1847 totaled somewhat less than $20,000. Cozzens, however, was unable to make a success of this venture, and he offered the mill for sale in October, 1852. As he failed to find a buyer, it was sold by the sheriff for taxes in 1853.[88]

In New Orleans, the younger Brown had firmly resolved that his yard would not start the 1847 season as short of lumber as it had during the previous year. He, therefore, began to buy lumber from other sawmill operators when the flatboats came down from the Yazoo in the spring. In April, for example, he bought two flatboats loaded with cypress lumber which had been sawn by mills at Yazoo City, Mississippi, paying an average price of $17 per thousand in cash for the planks they contained. Even before the first boat was unloaded, a customer purchased fifteen thousand feet from him at a retail price of $30.[89]

The timber famine in New Orleans ended early in 1847 when the Mississippi River rose high enough to make a good float in the swamps bordering its tributaries. By June the levees at Carrolton were almost hidden when viewed from the river by rafts of cypress timber from the Homochitto, Arkansas, Red, and Yazoo rivers; and "good, sound 30 in. timber" was selling for as little as a dollar a log.[90] Now that they were able to buy all the logs they needed, other sawmill operators in the New Orleans area began to compete with Andrew, Jr., again; and he lost the exceptionally favorable position he had enjoyed during the previous season. Toward the end of July, usually a very busy time for the lumber yard, he wrote his father that "I cannot say much for business operations—they are rather slim." Nevertheless, weatherboarding which could be cut from small cypress logs was still selling well, and he advised his father to make up a good supply of this type of planking.[91]

It was during this summer, too, that yellow fever again struck the Crescent City. So Andrew, Jr., sent his wife and two small sons to

[88] *De Bow's Review*, V (1848), 380; Natchez *Courier*, October 27, 1852 and February 3, 1853.
[89] Andrew Brown, Jr., to Andrew Brown, April 24, 1847, Learned Collection.
[90] *Ibid.*, June 11, 1847.
[91] *Ibid.*, July 27, 1847.

Biloxi on the Gulf Coast for safety and visited them whenever he could arrange to be away from his office.[92]

Despite his best efforts Andrew, Jr., was not able to equal the sales record set during 1846. During that prosperous year he had disposed of more than a million and half feet of lumber and had taken in slightly more than $36,000. During 1847, however, his sales totaled no more than $28,000, and a half million feet of sawed lumber had to be carried over into the 1848 building season. Even so, the firm of Brown and Son still managed to earn roughly a 30 per cent profit on its capital investment.[93]

The Browns began the 1848 building season in unusually good condition. Their mill could manufacture half again as much lumber as formerly, their supply of logs was adequate for the coming months, and their lumber yard for once boasted a stock of more than half a million feet of lumber. From the start business was moderately brisk both in Natchez and New Orleans, and by the end of the summer it was apparent that the Browns would realize more money than in 1847.[94] At that juncture disaster struck the family. Andrew, Jr., died of yellow fever on October 24, 1848, leaving behind a young wife, two baby boys, Hugh and Andrew, and a thriving wholesale and retail lumber business in New Orleans.[95]

During his short career of eight years as a lumber dealer, Andrew, Jr., had performed invaluable services for the firm of Andrew Brown and Son, of Natchez and New Orleans. Largely through his efforts, the Natchez sawmill had been able to push its products into the lucrative New Orleans market so that the mill had been able to work to full capacity after 1843, never once stopping through want of sales. With the mill producing at its maximum rate for a period of several years, Andrew and his father had been able to restore their fortunes, which had been more than a little reduced during the early years of the depression. They had even succeeded in acquiring full ownership of the enterprise and had managed to pay off most of the debt owed to Stephen Duncan. When an inventory of the company was taken immediately after Andrew's death, the total assets of father

[92] Andrew Brown, Jr., to Andrew Brown, January 25, 1848; Henry S. Solomon to Andrew Brown, August 29, 1848, both in Learned Collection.
[93] Andrew Brown Journal (1843–48).
[94] Ibid., 259.
[95] New Orleans Times Picayune, October 26, 1848.

and son were valued at $78,442.19, exclusive of slaves and some real estate. The sawmill at Natchez between the first of the year and the date of Andrew's demise had sold $55,000 worth of lumber, of which $36,000 had gone to the New Orleans lumber yard. The company owned 8,800 cypress logs and had 950,000 feet of cypress plank stacked in the yards at Natchez and New Orleans. Andrew, Jr., had personally accumulated a house, several slaves, and an equity of more than $10,000 in the family firm in addition to paying off several thousands in debts from the enterprise connected with *Hail Columbia*. These were indeed remarkable achievements for a young man to accomplish within so short a time.[96]

[96] Andrew Brown Journal (1843–49), 259.

4

Cypress Logging
in the
Yazoo-Mississippi Delta

Pʀᴏᴠɪᴅɪɴɢ a supply of cypress logs for the mill at Natchez was Brown's personal responsibility during the 1840's and 1850's. This somewhat troublesome task was made easier by the seemingly inexhaustible cypress brakes in the Yazoo-Mississippi Delta. Located along the streams and in the marshes of that alluvial plain, these brakes were not far upriver from Natchez, as raftsmen reckoned distances.

The fertile, triangular-shaped expanse of lowland situated between the Yazoo and Mississippi rivers offered almost unparalleled opportunities to cypress loggers during this period. Virtually all of the Delta, which is roughly 250 miles long and 65 miles wide at its broadest expanse, was subject to annual inundation by the rivers delineating its boundaries and had in fact been created from silt deposited over the centuries by these overflows. Very few sites rose much above the highwater mark, but as a general rule the land was more elevated close to the rivers and less so in the interior. Numerous streams of various sizes meandered across the valley before emptying into the Yazoo; and many large lakes, which had once been segments of a river bed, were scattered throughout the region. In addition to these permanent bodies of water, immense acreages of low-lying terrain assumed the aspect of tree-studded lakes during flood periods but were merely vine-tangled woodlands during dry seasons.[1]

The cypress trees which flourished abundantly along the banks of creeks, bayous, and rivers and in lakes and lowlands composed one of the nation's largest remaining stands of this valuable timber. Most

[1] Natchez *Mississippi Journal*, March 29, 1833.

of the cypress brakes in the Delta were reasonably accessible because a network of sloughs and creeks connected them with the Yazoo River; timbermen used these water courses to transport logs to the principal waterway during floats.[2]

In the years between 1830 and 1860, a large number of persons earned their livelihood by felling and rafting cypress logs which they cut in the brakes of the Delta. During the first two of these decades, much of the timber the loggers rafted to market was taken illegally from public lands or stolen from private property. In the closing decade of the antebellum period, however, professional loggers were able to obtain title to the cypress-bearing swamplands at most reasonable prices and apparently preferred to do so rather than run the risk of arrest or litigation.[3] Among the larger operators, some like James A. and C. H. Allen of Warrenton, who logged along the Big Black River, combined the management of cotton plantations with sawmilling and selling lumber and cypress timber. Others, like James J. Wheless, who had been associated with Brown during the 1830's, were connected in some fashion with a sawmill, but concentrated their attention on their logging businesses. Still others bought cypress-bearing swamplands and secured their entire incomes by marketing timber. Finally, some plantation proprietors who owned lands along the Delta water courses supplemented their income from cotton by selling timber rights to professional loggers who cut, rafted, and marketed cypress sawlogs taken from these lands.[4]

In another category was Daniel O. Williams, who owned one cotton plantation near Canton in Hinds County and another on Deer Creek in Issaquena County. He was one of the many planters who valued the cypress trees growing on his Delta lands too highly to sell them to loggers. In reply to his son's suggestion that he dispose of some of the

[2] Benjamin L. C. Wailes, *Report on the Agriculture and Geology of Mississippi, Embracing a Sketch of the Social and Natural History of the State* (Jackson, Miss., 1854), 347–49, cited hereinafter as wailes, *Mississippi*.

[3] During 1850 the Federal government donated the cypress-bearing swamplands of the Mississippi Valley to the states in which they were situated. The states then sold these timberlands to individuals at relatively low prices. John William Wade, "Lands of the Liquidating Levee Board through Litigation and Legislation," Mississippi Historical Society *Publications*, IX (1906), 273–311; Nollie Hickman, *Mississippi Harvest: Lumbering in the Longleaf Pine Belt, 1840–1915* (University, Miss., 1962), 88–93; Harrison, *Alluvial Empire*, 67–85.

[4] Yazoo City (Miss.) *Yazoo Democrat*, December 3, 1844. James Allen to Andrew Brown, April 15, 1854; C. H. Allen to Andrew Brown, April 19, 1855, both in Learned Collection.

timber, Williams characteristically replied: "Under no consideration would I for a moment think of selling a single stick of cypress out of our break. Our plantation will need every stick of it and more too in the course of time." [5]

Because so much cypress lumber was used in cabins for slaves, houses for overseers and owners, gins and other outbuildings, and in fences and bridges, many plantation owners of the Delta operated sawmills along with their other plantation machinery, powering them with the same steam engines which drove their cotton gins. Ordinarily, their lumber was consumed at home, but upon occasion some of these amateur lumber manufacturers disposed of their surplus planks to professional lumbermen who carried them to market in flatboats in conjunction with cargoes of their own manufacture. [6]

After exhausting the more accessible cypress brakes along the lower Yazoo and its larger tributaries during the 1830's and 1840's, some of the professional Delta loggers shifted their operations into the lakes and marshes of the interior during the 1850's. Others moved northward into the upper reaches of the Yazoo River system, where the remaining cypress brakes were smaller. In both cases, loggers found their transportation problems more difficult than in earlier years. Those who worked in the lakes and marshes usually had to fell timber several miles from sizeable streams. They then were compelled to wait for a float before they could move their huge logs into the Yazoo. As high waters of this depth occurred infrequently, loggers sometimes waited several years before bringing their cypress timber to market. [7]

The great flood of 1858 came at the end of a long period during which the Delta escaped extensive inundation. In the interval between floods, loggers in the interior felled tens of thousands of trees which they were unable to move. Then, as the Yazoo and its tributaries rose to almost unprecedented heights during April, 1858, no less than $5,000,000 worth of timber was rafted out of the Yazoo Valley. [8]

The network of levees being constructed along the Mississippi and

[5] Daniel O. Williams to Sampson Williams, July 1, 1858; and Daniel O. Williams to Lacy Williams, August 20, 1858, Sampson Williams Papers, in the possession of the writer. This collection relates to a Delta plantation for the period between 1850 and 1876.

[6] For an example consult the *Yazoo Democrat*, September 24, 1851.

[7] George Powell to Andrew Brown, March 26, 1850, Learned Collection.

[8] Quoted by the Natchez *Courier*, May 1, 1858.

Yazoo rivers during the 1850's, by keeping flood waters out of the interior, benefited cotton planters of the Delta but not cypress loggers. Knowing that woodsmen hated the levees because they made rafting more difficult, planters suspected them of complicity whenever a levee was breached during a period of high water. A typical report published in the Coahoma (Miss.) *Citizen* during April, 1858, clearly revealed the general attitude of the planters in this regard: "The levee at Lewis' Swamp, about thirty miles from Friar's Point, to the lower part of Coahoma county, was cut out a few days since by some unknown scoundrel—supposed to be the work of raftsmen, who did it to run their timber from this swamp." [9] Whether the loggers were actually guilty of such reprehensible activities is now a matter of conjecture. Even at the time landowners were seldom able to verify their surmises.

Not only did loggers wait lengthy periods to move their timbers, they also spent months preparing sizeable quantities of cypress logs for rafting. A report which James J. Wheless submitted to Brown during 1857 gives an indication of the time required to carry out the deadening phase of a logging operation under ordinary circumstances. According to his statement, Wheless had engaged a skilled white woodsman to girdle enough timber in his Roebuck cypress brake to compose a raft. McMurry, the axeman, had agreed to do the job "by the tree," receiving payment from Wheless at the rate of "four bits" a tier. The woodsman estimated that he could deaden the requisite number of trees within a month or six weeks. In accordance with his bargain with Wheless, McMurry was provided with sufficient food and supplies to last him for this period, with the "furnish" to be deducted from his pay at the time of final settlement.[10]

Unless an unusually large party of axemen was employed, the felling of the standing timber, the trimming off of branches and tops, and the division of the forty- to seventy-foot boles into sawlogs were lengthy operations. Apparently, a two-man crew of axemen could chop down from two to four trees, top and trim them, and cut them into sawlogs in a day's time. In all likelihood most of the axemen employed by Delta timbermen were paid by the tree, as McMurry was. During 1840, for example, Brown hired George Hoover, Edward Coles, and L. Gennings to work as "timber cutters" in the swamp, paying the

[9] Republished in the Columbus (Ga.) *Corner Stone*, April 13, 1858.
[10] James J. Wheless to Andrew Brown, June 23, 1857, Learned Collection.

white workmen 62.5 cents per tier of timber.[11] During the 1850's, however, Brown preferred to hire white axemen by the month for wages ranging from twenty to thirty dollars and their rations.[12] Foremen in charge of his logging crews received much higher salaries, which varied from fifty to one hundred dollars per month.[13]

Once the timber for cypress rafts had been cut into sawlogs, logging crews could do nothing more until the brake was flooded deeply enough to float the logs. If they were fortunate, the requisite rise might come during the following winter; but chances were equally good that a float would not occur until another twelve months had passed. J. W. Ward, a logger who operated during 1844 with a crew on the Bogue Phalia, a stream in Washington County, cut 735 tiers of cypress ranging in diameter from twenty-six to forty inches. He was able to move only 135 of these to market during the spring rise. As a result, with the timber cut during the summer of 1845 he was able to offer a thousand tiers to Brown in November, 1845, provided there was a float.[14]

When the timber became water-borne, the cribs which would eventually compose the raft could be assembled by the "splicers" with relative ease. Then, if the water level rose high enough to provide a passage for the cribs through the floatroads to the river, a raft could be put together and readied for its trip downstream. Even at this point, the timbermen were far from certain that the journey to the mill could be completed during that winter season. A moderately strong current was required to propel the heavy cypress, and the Yazoo did not always fall sufficiently rapidly after cresting to speed the logs on their way to the Mississippi. In the event that the desired current failed to materialize, another year's delay was added to the interval between felling and delivering the cypress trees to their ultimate destination.[15] The raft owner also had to pay woodsmen to guard his property from timber thieves and to see that its lashings were secure. In this period watchmen expected thirty dollars a month

[11] Andrew Brown Time Book (1838–40). Unless otherwise noted, all day books, journals, ledgers, etc., of Andrew Brown cited in this chapter are located in the Learned Collection.

[12] Andrew Brown Journal (1848–53), 220.

[13] An excellent description of logging in the lower Mississippi Valley is found in De Bow's Review, XII (1852), 596–603.

[14] J. W. Ward to Andrew Brown, November 18, 1845, Learned Collection.

[15] C. Fraisse to Andrew Brown, June 30, 1850, Learned Collection.

Andrew Brown, a Scottish immigrant, established a sawmill in Natchez which by the end of the Civil War had become one of the most successful in the Lower Mississippi Valley.

Cypress logs, cut from the numerous brakes found in the Yazoo-Mississippi Delta, were rafted down the river to sawmills in Vicksburg, Natchez, and New Orleans. (Both sketches are from *Harper's New Monthly Magazine*.)

Log raft on the Mississippi River near Natchez (top) and the landing at Natchez-under-the-Hill (bottom), showing the Brown sawmill.

An early view of Natchez-under-the-Hill from the top of the bluff.

Steamboat landing (top) and stores (bottom) at Natchez-under-the-Hill (c. 1880).

Rufus F. Learned, Andrew Brown's stepson who bought the latter's sawmill interests in Natchez in 1871, and his wife Elizabeth, Andrew Brown's daughter.

Magnolia Vale, built by Andrew Brown in the 1830's, survived a tornado which severely damaged it in 1840 and stood beneath the bluff in Natchez for another hundred years before fire destroyed it.

Lumber drying at the R. F. Learned Sawmill in Natchez (c. 1920).

for their services.[16] Under ideal conditions, the logmen could cut and raft their timber within the span of a single season; but such conditions were exceptional in the Yazoo-Mississippi Delta during the 1850's.

Because of the uncertain length of time required to market cypress timber, logging operators needed flexible credit arrangements in order to finance their enterprise. If all went well, the money they borrowed to pay and supply their crews could be repaid within a few months; under other circumstances, their debts might go unliquidated for several years. Commission merchants at Vicksburg were understandably reluctant to make large advances of cash and supplies to loggers for indefinite periods, preferring instead to reserve their resources for the more reliable cotton growers. Therefore, big timber suppliers formed associations with large lumber manufacturers who could extend the requisite credit on the security represented by a crop of timber in the swamps and who could afford to wait for several years if necessary before taking delivery of the logs at the mills.[17]

When Yazoo loggers brought rafts of cypress logs for sale into the great timber marketplace in Old River, they preferred to sell their wares to buyers representing Mississippi River sawmills for cash paid in full on the spot. Small transactions usually were handled in this manner, but large purchases were generally made under different rules. In such cases, a logger received a cash downpayment representing a third or a fourth of the total price in the form of a sight draft written on the purchaser's commission merchant in Vicksburg, Natchez, or New Orleans. The remainder of the price was paid to him in installments with notes bearing interest of about 8 per cent, dated thirty, sixty, and ninety days after the date of the transaction.[18]

Throughout the decades of the 1840's and 1850's, Andrew Brown negotiated many purchases of large rafts from the logmen who operated along the Yazoo and Big Black rivers. During 1853, for example, almost all of the timber he acquired was bought in this fashion. His initial purchase, deliverable at the mouth of the Big Black, was made from James Allen at Grand Gulf on May 15, consisting of 322 timbers fifty and sixty feet long. The total price, at the rate of three dollars a sawlog, came to $4,750 and was paid to Allen in two installments.[19]

[16] Andrew Brown Timber Expense Book (1857–60), August 18, 1857.
[17] Daniel Winchell to Andrew Brown, August 11, 1845, Learned Collection.
[18] Many examples can be found in the journals of Andrew Brown of Natchez for the 1840–60 period.
[19] Andrew Brown Receipts (1850–60), May 15, 1853.

Leaving the Big Black after completing this transaction, Brown traveled upriver by steamboat to his landing at Old River where he subsequently bought 468 timbers ranging in length from forty to sixty feet from Dr. William B. Ball, paying the planter and logger $7,558.55 for this raft.[20] A month later the Natchez lumber manufacturer purchased a third lot from D. B. Smith, which contained 201 timbers. These, when measured, were found to be equivalent to 1,030 ten-foot sawlogs, of which one hundred were unusable and not included in the price. Brown paid Smith at a rate of $4.10 per sound sawlog, which meant that the logger was receiving $24.60 for each of his sixty-foot cypress timbers.[21] (The land from which timbers of this kind were cut, incidentally, could be purchased from the state of Mississippi for as little of $1.75 per acre.) A final transaction with Dillon & Co. involving 1,996 sawlogs at $3.50 each completed Brown's major purchases of logs for that season.[22] An inventory of all timber at the mill and in the swamps belonging to the partnership when completed on October 31, revealed that Andrew Brown of Natchez owned 4,600 sawlogs. This stock of timber had been purchased at prices ranging from $3.00 to $5.10 per log and represented an investment of $18,-181.20.[23] As a rule of thumb, Brown expected to double the value of the timber by manufacturing the logs into planks.[24]

The diameter of standard ten-foot sawlogs was one of the more important factors determining the cost of cypress timbers. In one transaction between Colonel Ezekiel M. McNabb, one of the larger of the Yazoo Delta loggers, and Andrew Brown, negotiated during October, 1844, the price of the timber was stipulated as follows: Brown was to pay McNabb "two dollars per [saw] log for 29 in. timber, & 10 cts. for each and every inch over 29 in., or 10 cts. less for each and every inch under."[25] This arrangement, while common in purchases of small lots of timber, was seldom employed so explicitly when buying large rafts of cypress. In such cases, a flat price was usually paid for all logs, with the purchaser adjusting his offer in accordance with his estimate of the average size of the sawlogs, the

[20] Andrew Brown Journal (1853–60), 67; William B. Ball to Andrew Brown, June 8, 1853, Learned Collection.
[21] Andrew Brown Receipts (1850–56), July 9, 1853.
[22] Andrew Brown Journal (1853–60), 67.
[23] Ibid.
[24] Andrew Brown, Jr., to Andrew Brown, August 8, 1846, Learned Collection.
[25] Ezekiel M. McNabb to Andrew Brown, October 10, 1844, ibid.

quality of the timber, and the state of the timber market.[26] In almost all instances, however, a reduction in price was allowed for "pecky" sawlogs. These were sections of the huge cypress timbers that were honeycombed by a fungus infection to the point where saleable lumber could not be manufactured from them.[27]

James Allen of Warrentown, Mississippi, from whom Brown bought timber during 1853, was an enterprising cotton planter who operated a sawmill on his plantation beside the Big Black River in addition to selling timber taken from his cypress brakes. After disposing of his stock of logs to Brown in April, Allen succeeded in felling approximately seven hundred trees during the remainder of the year. The river rose high enough in the early spring of 1854 to give him a "short float," as he described it, which enabled him first to assemble a raft of five hundred selected large timbers in the Big Black, then to move it to the mouth of the stream. The water level dropped, however, before he could splice the remaining two hundred logs of smaller size into cribs, and thus they could not be marketed until after the next rise of the river. This appears to have been a typical crop harvested within a season by cypress timbermen during the late antebellum period, and the five hundred-tier raft would bring approximately $10,000. This was a significant addition to the income from cotton that was obtained by using plantation workers during periods when they were not needed in the fields.[28]

During the years between 1855 and 1860, Brown occasionally purchased large quantities of timber from C. H. Allen, who also marketed timber on the Big Black River. He and Henry Solomon, Brown's able sawmill manager, were warm friends and often engaged in amiable bickering. While writing to inform Brown on one occasion that an accident in his sawmill would prevent him from keeping an appointment at Natchez, Allen remarked jestingly that "Mr. Solomon writes as if I did not have any thing to [do] out here in the Woods. Tell him if he had to do it, I think he would alter his mind. I have the swamp business, plantation & my Mill to attend to." [29] In April, 1855, he informed Brown that he had a thousand cypress timbers ready to "rush out" in the event of a float, and that at the time he was engaged in

[26] For an example refer to Isaac N. Farris to Andrew Brown, August 1, 1845, *ibid.*
[27] *De Bow's Review*, XIX (1855), 611–12.
[28] James Allen to Andrew Brown, April 15, 1854, Learned Collection.
[29] C. H. Allen to Andrew Brown, May 4, 1855, *ibid.*

preparing an additional four hundred trees.[30] Although Brown did not wish to purchase any timber from Allen that season, he did try to buy his crop in 1857. Allen, however, sold his rafts to "a large new Saw Mill now in course of erection at Bouligny for a Spanish firm, Ping Mir & Co." of New Orleans.[31] During June, 1858, Brown bought 3,526 sawlogs from Allen for $7,763.00 In this batch 703 logs were found to be "pecky & hollow," and Brown of course did not pay for them.[32]

The prices of cypress timber purchased by Andrew Brown during the 1840's and 1850's varied considerably as depression turned into prosperity. During the 1840–43 period when the lower Mississippi Valley was reeling from the impact of the 1839–49 depression, cypress sawlogs brought from $0.75 to $1.25 each. With the beginning of recovery from the depths of the panic, in 1844–45, the price ranged between $1.25 and $2.00. In the 1846–49 interval there was further improvement in the price, with better grades of cypress bringing from $2.00 to $2.50 per log. During the final decade of the antebellum period, Brown paid from $2.00 to $4.50 for his timber, buying a larger proportion at the higher rate during 1859 and 1860. At all times, of course, fifty- and sixty-foot cypress tiers brought somewhat higher prices than forty-foot tiers when graded and sold by size. In large transactions involving five hundred to a thousand logs, however, a single price prevailed without regard to length or diameters. Allowance was made only for pecky or otherwise unsound logs.[33]

Brown's purchases of timber gradually increased between 1840 and 1857, reflecting general economic improvement in the lower Mississippi Valley as well as the Natchez sawmill's increasing share of the market in New Orleans. During 1840, a year of minimum activity in the building trades, Brown bought no more than 4,500 sawlogs from six different Delta loggers and paid $8,000 for the lot. Three years later, at a time when the cotton market was at its lowest ebb, he bought 5,500 sawlogs in small quantities from ten logmen at very low prices, paying on an average somewhat less than a dollar a log. With the opening of the retail outlet in New Orleans, however, his timber requirement rose appreciably; and he invested $12,000 each year for

[30] *Ibid.*, April 19, 1855.

[31] Key to Henry S. Solomon, April 25, 1857, Learned Collection.

[32] Andrew Brown Day Book (1856–58), 351.

[33] Purchases of timber were recorded in the journals of Andrew Brown of Natchez for the period 1840–60.

a total of approximately 1,400 logs during 1844 and 1845. Two years later, Brown obtained 10,000 logs from fifteen different timbermen at a cost of $16,000. During 1850, he encountered serious difficulty in procuring the timber supply he needed and was able to buy only 5,000 logs, for which he nevertheless had to pay $11,000 as a result of rising prices. Brown's sawmill consumed more than $14,000 worth of timber that year, 1850, exhausting the supply of logs carried over from the previous season. The following year saw little improvement in the timber supply, but a further rise in price. In all, Brown purchased 8,500 logs during 1851, of which 6,000 were obtained from a single supplier, C. Gillespie, late in December. Despite the small stock of timber involved, the lumberman's investment exceeded $18,-000.[34]

Because of increasing uncertainty about the supply of timber and a rising demand by sawmills of New Orleans, Baton Rouge, and other points along the river, Brown in 1849 began to experiment on an increasing scale with partnerships involving loggers with whom he had previously done business. Two of these early partnership arrangements were made by Brown with James M. Whittier and John H. Wisdom, both of whom were logging and rafting timber in the Yazoo–Mississippi Valley.

When Brown began to purchase timber from Whittier in 1845, the latter was still operating on a small scale with a partner named Wallace. The first transaction concerned only 106 timbers valued at a mere $814.00.[35] A second, occurring two years later and involving Whittier alone, was much larger than the first: 286 timbers containing 1,389 sawlogs and valued at $2,800.[36] In 1849, Brown entered into a logging partnership with Whittier by which the lumberman purchased a half interest in some cypress timber which the logger wished to bring to market. Under the terms of the understanding, Brown, acting in the capacity of customer, advanced Whittier and Brown sufficient funds to cover the expenses of cutting and rafting the timber to Old River. Within the timbering partnership, Brown and Whittier shared the cost of the logging and rafting operation equally between them. For his part, Whittier directed the work of the logging crews in the woods; Brown handled the transportation of the rafts after they were

[34] Andrew Brown Day Book (1843–48); *ibid.* (1848–51).
[35] Andrew Brown Day Book (1843–48), June 29, 1845.
[36] *Ibid.*, July 31, 1847.

assembled in the Yazoo River. By the end of July, 1849, Brown and Whittier delivered 630 cypress timbers containing 2,533 sawlogs to Andrew Brown of Natchez, and received $4,203.50 in payment. This sum was divided between Brown and Whittier, and Brown made a profit of $1,132.37 in this logging venture. For unknown reasons, however, he made no subsequent business arrangements of this kind with Whittier.[37]

During 1850 and 1851 Brown made similar logging agreements with John H. Wisdom from whom he had bought rafts on several previous occasions. In the course of the first year, the new partners succeeded in getting out 1,492 sawlogs which they sold to Andrew Brown of Natchez at a rate of $2.50 per log. The total cost of preparing the timber for rafting and the cost of transporting the logs to the mill at Natchez came to $1,351.50, a figure which approximated a dollar per log. During the following season the remainder of the timber in which Brown held an interest was sold to Andrew Brown of Natchez for $1,455.00, and the partnership was then terminated, though Brown continued to buy rafts from Wisdom under the usual agreements.[38]

In 1857 Brown renewed his association of earlier years with James J. Wheless, forming a partnership with the logger which lasted through the remainder of the antebellum period. With a brisk and rising demand for lumber from the New Orleans construction industry pressing upon him, Brown had to take steps to assure a steady flow of logs for his sawmill. By linking up with a large timberman like Wheless, he obtained first call on all the cypress he brought to market. From their past association the Natchez lumberman knew that Wheless was a resourceful and energetic logger who could be depended upon to get his cypress into the Mississippi if anyone could. Furthermore, Wheless owned large acreages of cypress swampland in the Yazoo Valley and was in the habit of buying more whenever his resources permitted. He, therefore, was in a position to furnish Brown with timber over a period of several years, always subject, of course, to the vagaries of river transportation.

At the outset of the new partnership arrangement Brown bought all of the timber that Wheless had already prepared for rafting—258

[37] Andrew Brown Journal (1848–53), 60; Andrew Brown Day Book (1848–51), July 30, 1849; Settlement with Jas. M. Whittier, 1849, Andrew Brown Bills and Accounts (1840–49).

[38] Andrew Brown Journal (1848–53), 203, 282; Andrew Brown Pocket Day Book (1851), June 12, 1851.

tiers located in the Yazoo River. For this raft Brown paid the logger $3,003.[39] Upon learning that Brown was connecting Wheless's timber business with their own lumber enterprise, William Key, who was Brown's junior partner during the 1850's, expressed his satisfaction in a letter to Solomon. "I am very much pleased," he wrote, "that an opportunity has offered for investing in Timber & I hope that the Old Mill will be kept hard at it all summer. We want a big stock of lumber here. . . ."[40] The investment to which he referred was the purchase of a half interest in a thousand timbers which Wheless had felled in his Cassidy Bayou brake in Tallahatchie County, but which had not yet been assembled into cribs. Brown paid Wheless $2,500 for the part interest in the timber, and in so doing laid claim to almost a year's supply of logs for the Natchez mill.[41] At the same time, the old Scot purchased a half interest in six hundred acres of cypress swamplands situated in Sunflower County as well as half interest in the standing timber on another piece of land in the same section of the Delta, commonly known as the Roebuck brake.[42]

During December, 1858, Brown extended his business connection with Wheless further by buying interests in other cypress brakes belonging to the logger. He purchased a 25 per cent interest in 1,000 tiers of timber which Wheless had felled in his California brake in Sunflower County, a 50 per cent interest in each of 270 tiers in Morehead Bayou and 104 tiers in Turkey Bayou, and a 25 per cent interest in 70 tiers of "Tchula" timber, all of which were to be delivered by Wheless to Brown's landing in Old River.[43] From these transactions the logger realized $2,250 in cash before his logs were removed from the swamp. In this same month Brown and Wheless disposed of a quarter section of land from which they had removed the timber for $2.50 an acre, a price higher than the state was charging for virgin swampland in the Delta.[44] In this case the farmer obviously valued cleared land for agricultural purposes more than acreage with trees still on it. By the end of 1858, Wheless had delivered 1,242 sawlogs to Brown's rafting crews at Old River, with the total logging expenses costing the two partners $4,250. Andrew Brown of Natchez paid them

[39] Andrew Brown Receipt Book (1848–58), May 2, 1857.
[40] Key to Solomon, May 5, 1857, Learned Collection.
[41] Wheless to Andrew Brown, June 13, 1857, *ibid*.
[42] Andrew Brown Journal (1853–60), 335; Andrew Brown Day Book (1856–58), 185.
[43] Andrew Brown Journal (1853–60), 452.
[44] *Ibid*.

$3.50 per log in addition to the operating cost already mentioned.[45] Wheless extended his timber holdings by buying 1,280 acres of land from the Brunswick Land Company for $6,400. He then sold a half interest in the timber on this land for $3,500.[46]

Brown's partnership with Wheless remained in effect during 1859 and 1860, but his rising timber requirements led him to make large additional purchases from other loggers as well. From Colonel Ezekiel McNabb he bought $2,300 worth during 1859; $1,700 worth from Brown and Johnston of Vicksburg; $1,500 worth from Robert Coyle and John Blythe of McNutt, Mississippi; and $993 worth from John Poindexter. He also acquired many small lots of logs costing less than $500 for each raft.[47]

A glimpse into logging conditions on the upper Yazoo at this period was given by a letter to Brown from John Poindexter, dated November 30, 1859. The timberman wrote from Lowry's Landing on the Yazoo, as follows: "I wrote you some time since acknowledging my receipt of your check for four hundred dollars as you requested. I am getting on finely with my Roebuck timber. I have three hundred tier cut and cleaned up and will get from one hundred twenty-five to fifty more. We are having a very pretty rise in the river and I am now puting new splice on the timber I sold you, and, if the water should hold on, will run it at once, as soon as I turn it loose. . . ."[48]

During 1860 Brown engaged William J. Hindman to conduct a logging operation for him on a share arrangement, which was intended to supplement Wheless's timbering on behalf of the Natchez sawmill.[49] According to the contract Hindman was to hire a white logging crew and supervise their labors in the cypress swamps in person as his part of the bargain. Brown, as his contribution, furnished the timberland where Hindman's crews were to work. In addition to his other holdings, the Natchez lumber manufacturer purchased a half interest in California brake from W. N. Scales for the sum of $3,400.[50] Consequently, Brown's logging operations grew during the 1850's roughly in proportion to the expansion of his manufacturing capabilities.

[45] *Ibid.*, 451.
[46] Andrew Brown & Co. Journal (1855–60), 276.
[47] Andrew Brown Cash Book (1855–64); R. M. Coyle to Andrew Brown, November 15, 1859, Learned Collection.
[48] John Poindexter to Andrew Brown, November 30, 1859, Learned Collection.
[49] Andrew Brown Cash Book (1855–64), 260; Manuel Sparling to Andrew Brown, April 30, 1860, Learned Collection.
[50] Andrew Brown Journal (1853–60), 669; *ibid.* (1861–70), 84.

5

Transportation
Of Logs and Lumber

ON August 20, 1853, the Selma (Ala.) *Sentinel* heralded the dawn of a new era in the transportation of logs and lumber. "Another large lot of pine spars have been brought down from Shelby and Bibb counties by the Alabama and Tennessee Railroad," the editor reported. "This is an evidence of the value of railroads. . . . This Timber is brought from a section of the country, four years ago impenetrable, and these trees as they then stood were worthless. When now they can be carried to Mobile at a cost of less than $10, where they will average $100 a-piece."[1] The Sumter (Ala.) *Democrat* also perceived the significance of the transportation revolution with respect to the lumber industry. "There are immense forests of pine, and every species of Oak, which stand in their original integrity in the interior of Alabama and Mississippi, which will soon be made accessible by means of railroad transportation," the readers of the journal were informed.[2] In Mobile, the impact of the steam horse on the lumber trade was visible before the Mobile and Ohio Railroad reached forty miles into the interior. During 1852, according to the editor of the Mobile *Register*, "considerable quantities of cotton have been brought in the present season, in addition to wood, timber, brick, poultry, game, etc."[3]

Each of these journalists correctly inferred that the lumber industry of the Old Southwest would eventually be transformed by the network of railroads then in process of construction. In fact, the radically different lumber industry of the 1880's, which devastated thousands

[1] Quoted by the Mobile *Register*, August 24, 1853.
[2] *Ibid.*, August 30, 1853.
[3] *Ibid.*, November 13, 1852.

of square miles of timberlands in Louisiana, Mississippi, and Alabama, had its genesis in the transportation revolution described in the early 1850's by these editors. Only with the aid of rail transportation could mills operate that were as large and destructive as typical units of the late nineteenth century.

Before the introduction of railroads, the lumber industries of the Gulf Coast and lower Mississippi Valley were cut to simpler and more picturesque patterns by the system of water transportation then in vogue. Sawmills, almost always located on the banks of rivers, received their logs in rafts steered downstream with the current by an adventurous breed of rivermen who enjoyed the solitude and slowly changing scenery on the inland waters. Similarly, lumber sawed by mills above New Orleans and Mobile drifted down to market on rafts or flatboats manned by the same colorful breed of inland sailors. In both cases, logs and lumber traveled at a leisurely pace during seasons of the year chosen by the river. As a result, patience was the cardinal virtue of antebellum lumbermen.

Because the Mississippi was an immensely wide highway, rivermen working on its lower reaches could handle rafts of very great size and yet leave passageways for the host of steamboats that puffed busily up and down the river with their cargoes of cotton and other commerce. One extraordinarily large raft described in the Natchez *Courier* during May, 1858, was 560 feet long and 200 feet wide.[4] Ordinarily, however, rafts from the Red, the Ouachita, the Yazoo and the White rivers contained from fifty to five hundred tiers of timber. Some of these rafts were assembled from ten-foot sawlogs spliced together into cribs, while others were composed of the great uncut cypress timbers similarly secured.[5]

Much of the rafting on the lower Mississippi River was carried on by timbermen who themselves owned the logs they were transporting to market. Many of the "rafters" were like the frontiersmen described by John J. Audubon in 1820 as the "Squatters of the Mississippi." Within a short time after arriving on the shores of the river, according to the artist, immigrants from the East usually learned that a market for timber was available in New Orleans; and, working with

[4] Natchez *Courier*, May 14, 1858.
[5] *De Bow's Review*, IV (1847), 229; *ibid.*, V (1848), 302; *ibid.*, XII (1852), 644. A. de Puy Van Buren, *Jottings of a Year's Sojourn in the South* (Battle Creek, 1859), 51.

axes and crosscut saws, they began to fell cypress for rafts without regard to the ownership of the timberlands where they were working. The new loggers constructed their rafts on the shore and loaded cordwood aboard to sell in the city for fuel. When the water level rose, they moored the buoyant rafts with cables, or grapevines if cables were lacking, until there was a strong current in the river. Then the frontier families boarded their rafts, released the lines, and worked them out into the current with sweeps and skiffs. Crews of such Mississippi rafts as these usually consisted of from six to twelve men who lived on board for weeks at a time, sheltered from the elements by crude cabins or tents.[6]

After selling their timber to one of the sawmills situated along the lower Mississippi, the raftsmen either returned home in their skiffs, which they laboriously rowed upstream, or on steamboats as deck passengers. Thieves and robbers made a trip home even more dangerous than a passage down for the raftsmen, especially during the early years of the nineteenth century. An incident reported in the St. Francisville (La.) *Phoenix* during 1834, was all too typical of the period.[7] According to the editor, five raftsmen from the mouth of the White River recently had stopped near the town on their way back home in a skiff. While they were ashore buying provisions, they told the residents of the area that they had sold their raft to a sawmill at nearby Bayou Sara. Two of the men, who had been the owners of the raft, made the mistake of displaying large rolls of bills. A few days after their departure from St. Francisville, the bodies of both were found on the shore above the town, and no trace of their companions or of their money was ever discovered. Not infrequently, raftsmen, like one in 1857, were found dead on their rafts as "the result of an accident"—or foul play.[8]

Although most of a rafting trip was usually accomplished under relatively placid conditions, there were occasions when raftsmen had to work like galley slaves. Sometimes the Mississippi would appear to delight in running rafts aground and at other times would perversely drift these cumbersome craft into river lakes or backwaters where there was no current. Occasionally the river would break rafts apart,

---

[6] Peattie (ed.), *Audubon's America*, 128; Prichard, Kniffen, and Brown (eds.), "Southern Louisiana and Southern Alabama in 1819," 25.

[7] Quoted by the Jackson *Mississippian*, June 27, 1834.

[8] Natchez *Courier*, January 24, 1857.

causing the rivermen to lose valuable timbers. Accidents like these occurred so frequently that riverside plantation owners came to regard salvaging timber as a source of income. When a runaway portion of a raft was sighted in the river, crews of Negroes were dispatched in boats to bring the timber ashore. If ownership of a raft could be determined, the proprietor would be notified that he could regain possession of his timbers upon paying a salvage charge. In the event that the proper owner could not be identified, however, the one who secured the timbers could sell them as his own property.[9] Professional timbermen guarded against loss of their logs during transit by marking them on the butts with hot branding hammers. Andrew Brown, for example, marked his logs with an "AB," while James Allen used "JA."[10]

An incident occurring during 1849 illustrates several aspects of the timber salvaging problem along the Mississippi. In May of that year the lower Mississippi Valley was covered by a flood which breached the levees and almost submerged the city of New Orleans.[11] The swollen river carried many rafts considerable distances beyond its normal banks, and not a few of them were stranded when the waters subsided. For weeks afterward, timbermen scoured the valley seeking rafts that had broken their moorings and been lost. Brown, in common with many other timber owners, suffered losses during the flood. He subsequently learned that one of his rafts had gone over the bank of the Mississippi near Warrenton and had lodged in a field belonging to John Henderson, a planter. Before Brown's crew reached the scene, however, another person took nineteen cypress timbers from the site. A slave belonging to Henderson had seen Brown's raft cross over the embankment, and he informed his master that the timberman, Turner, had made off with some of Brown's logs. Somewhat later, a second timberman with a crew of five men presented himself to Henderson and laid claim to the same raft, offering to swear before a notary that the logs were his property. In some perplexity, Henderson asked Brown by mail to describe the identifying marks on his timbers. The logs included in a portion of raft lying three hundred yards from the

    [9] Natchez *Statesman and Gazette*, August 7, 1828; New Orleans *Courier*, May 21, 1831; New Orleans *Times Picayune*, February 9, 1841; Joshua James to Andrew Brown, July 11, 1859, Learned Collection.
    [10] James Allen to Andrew Brown, April 15, 1854, Learned Collection.
    [11] William I. Key to Andrew Dott, May 12, 1849, *ibid.*

river were branded with the letters "TN," Henderson informed Brown, while those in the raft which he believed to be the property of the Natchez sawmill owner were marked with the letter "A." [12]

Maneuvering a raft of cypress logs ashore was a difficult task for rivermen, roughly equivalent to landing an aircraft without power, for the crew had no chance to correct an error. If rivermen allowed a raft to pass beyond the intended landing place, for example, they had no practical method of bringing it back upstream.[13] To be sure, steamboats and steam tugboats could pull small rafts against the current and were sometimes utilized to tow timber to the mills.[14] As the cost of this service was excessive, however, rivermen and sawmill owners resorted to employing towboats only in emergencies. On a voyage downstream, raftsmen could guide the cumbersome rafts within narrow limits by means of long sweeps, and they customarily worked the raft close to the bank in this fashion in preparation for a landing. Then strong cables or chains fastened to the raft at one end were carried ashore in rowboats by the rivermen and secured to large trees in order to check the forward progress of the crude river craft. When properly executed, this method caused the raft to be pushed ashore by the current, where it could then be secured by additional cables.[15] Sometimes, when crews wished to moor a raft for an indefinite period, they would resort to the easier method of steering the raft into shallow water until it went aground; but this was seldom, if ever, possible at a sawmill.

On those not infrequent occasions when rafts ran beyond their destinations, the crews had no option but to continue their voyage downstream in hopes of selling the timber to mills along the way. Andrew Brown considered himself fortunate when a season passed without his losing a runaway raft. He lost one raft in this manner during January, 1841; another in July, 1845; a third during May, 1846; a fourth in April, 1849; and still others during 1854, 1856, 1857, and 1858.[16] Accidents of this nature were serious nuisances to a sawmill

[12] John Henderson to Andrew Brown, September 28, 1849, *ibid.*

[13] Alexander Brown, Jr., to Alexander Brown, December 30, 1846, *ibid.*

[14] Andrew Brown Cash Book (1848–55), February 1, 1853. Unless otherwise specified, all cash books, ledgers, journals, etc., cited in this chapter are located in the Learned Collection.

[15] Andrew Brown, Jr., to Andrew Brown, May 4, 1842; Alexander Brown, Jr., to Alexander Brown, December 30, 1846, both in Learned Collection.

[16] Andrew Brown Journal (1840–43), January 15, 1841; *ibid.* (1853–60),

operator in that they deprived him of the use of timber. As a rule, however, runaway rafts did not often cause an owner serious financial losses because the timber could be sold to sawmills located between Baton Rouge and New Orleans. Brown, for example, disposed of a raft which passed his mill in 1854 to the firm of Henderson and Peake, who operated a large sawmill at Baton Rouge, for the sum of $1,200.[17] During the 1840's, Andrew Brown, Jr., sold several rafts to mills at New Orleans after failing to interest sawmill operators below Baton Rouge. In the event that purchasers for the timber could not be found, as in 1858, the timber owner could have his cypress logs sawn into plank by one of the New Orleans mills, paying for this service with a share of the boards or in cash. On one occasion, William Key paid the Bobbs sawmill six hundred dollars for cutting up a cypress raft rather than accept an offer of five hundred dollars for his logs.[18] Again, during 1859, the lumberman had a raft sawn up by the same mill, this time at a cost of $1,300.00.[19]

Although lumber was sometimes stacked aboard rafts of logs bound for the timber market at New Orleans, cargoes of planking ordinarily were shipped from the sawmills on the Yazoo and Mississippi rivers to the Crescent City in large flatboats. These craft were constructed on the Ohio and the upper Mississippi rivers to carry coal, iron, corn, flour, pork, and other products from the Old Northwest to river ports in the South. At Vicksburg and Natchez, lumbermen purchased empty vessels from merchants to whom they were originally consigned, at prices ranging from forty to one hundred dollars. They then repaired them and loaded them with lumber destined for the New Orleans building industry. Upon completion of their second voyage southward, the flatboats, after their cargoes were discharged, were sold to "breakers" who salvaged the rough, used lumber from their hulls. These craft usually brought about as high a price in New Orleans as the lumbermen had paid in Vicksburg or Natchez.[20]

122, 127. Andrew Brown, Jr., to Andrew Brown, July 18, 1845, and May 26, 1846; Key to Dott, April 14, 1849; John F. Paul to Henry S. Solomon, March 11, 1856, and January 12, 1858; Key to Solomon, June 11, 1857, all correspondence in Learned Collection.

[17] Andrew Brown Journal (1853–60), 127.

[18] Paul to Solomon, January 12, 1858, Learned Collection.

[19] Andrew Brown & Co. Journal (1855–60), 421.

[20] Andrew Brown Jr., to Andrew Brown, April 11, 1845, Learned Collection; De Bow's Review, IV (1847), 556.

Mississippi River flatboats were no more than rectangular, covered wooden boxes, "a covered shed five or six feet high with a bottom . . . impervious to water," as a correspondent of the Natchez *Courier* decribed them.[21] The roof of a typical flatboat was fashioned by bending two layers of boards over a ridgepole running from end to end of the shed so that there was enough curvature to shed water. Having neither sails nor engines and being designed to float with the current, the "flats" required neither keel, rudder, nor pointed bow or stern. They were controlled by means of a long wooden sweep resting on a pivot at the stern and maneuvered by crews of five or six men working additional sweeps through oarlocks along the sides. Most of the flatboats used by lumbermen were equipped with simple capstans or windlasses, which permitted crewmen to pull the vessels upstream by winding in cables fastened to trees along the river bank. Many flats were winched up the Yazoo River to the sawmills between Yazoo City and Greenwood, but some were towed to their destinations by steamboats at a cost of approximately $150.[22]

Flatboats used to transport lumber on the lower Mississippi River measured from eighteen to twenty-five feet wide by seventy-five to 170 feet in length. These river craft, because of their box-like shape, were able to stow away loads of cypress plank almost equal to the volume of their hulls. During the 1840's the smallest variety in common use carried approximately 60,000 feet, which was equal to the cargo capacity of large Caribbean lumber schooners. Much larger flats employed during the 1840's and 1850's, however, transported more than a quarter-million feet each.[23]

Though slow, the transportation of lumber by means of flatboats was inexpensive. The vessels hardly constituted an expense worth reckoning; hence, the total cost of hauling a cargo of lumber from Natchez to New Orleans was limited virtually to the wages of the crew, the cost of their rations, and the price of their steamboat transportation back to the sawmill. As a trip from Natchez to the Crescent City usually took about two weeks, the expense of transporting a load of lumber ranged between $80 and $150. In fact, the cost of loading and discharging cargoes were larger items in the ledgers of the lumber

[21] Natchez *Courier*, May 5, 1837.
[22] Andrew Brown Cash Book (1855–64), 246.
[23] Andrew Brown Journal (1843–48), 134.

companies than the actual bills for moving cargoes of lumber by water.[24]

The crews of lumber flatboats, like raftsmen, often were subjected to great discomfort from exposure to inclement weather; and they contracted their share of malaria in summer and fall and respiratory ailments during winter and spring. They ran less risk of fatal accidents than steamboat crews, however, because their primitive craft possessed no boilers to explode nor thin hulls to be ripped open at high speeds by snags. Furthermore, tightly-packed cargoes of buoyant cypress lumber rendered flats almost unsinkable; thus, even large leaks were only annoyances rather than serious threats to the safety of the rivermen. "Sunk boats" reached the wharfs at New Orleans as surely as their more water-tight fellows, although their crews had to labor more strenuously at the sweeps and the passage was somewhat slowed by the weight of water they were carrying. Nevertheless, water-filled lumber flatboats were quite safe craft, and their cargoes aside from discoloration were not damaged by immersion. These sunken boats were more difficult to discharge than those afloat, of course; and before removing the cargo, the usual practice was to pump them dry while tied to a wharf.[25]

Despite the reliability of flatboats, the crews who manned them could at times encounter real danger on the river. During high water stages, the mighty Mississippi lived up to its reputation. Its powerful currents generated giant whirlpools or eddies which could overturn a flat, and crevasses in the levees sometimes sucked unfortunate river craft into their maws. One such incident happened during the flood of 1859 when two coal-laden flatboats were swept into a crevasse near Carmack's Bend.[26] Both vessels overturned in the torrent pouring through the break in the levee, and their crews were drowned to the last man. Despite occasional accidents, only a few rivermen working on flatboats were drowned, and the rare fatalities which did occur were usually the result of gross carelessness or intoxication. Significantly, Brown's lumber firm did not lose a single boatman or raftsman

[24] Andrew Brown, Jr., to Andrew Brown, September 5, 1845, Learned Collection; Andrew Brown Day Book (1843–48), 61; Andrew Brown Cash Book (1848–55), July 3, 1854.
[25] Andrew Brown, Jr., to Andrew Brown, April 11 and September 5, 1845, Learned Collection.
[26] Natchez Courier, April 26, 1859.

from this cause during more than three decades of rafting and flat-boating. The only drowning during the prewar years occurred when a Negro sawmill laborer, who in defiance of strict orders was playing on loose cypress logs floating in deep water behind the breakwater at the Natchez sawmill, fell in.[27]

While the work of lumber flatboatmen was not especially danger-ous, it was strenuous. The current of the Mississippi tended to force the primitive, unpowered craft ashore on the "convex side of every bend, and the whole course of the Mississippi . . . [was] only a series of bends," according to a correspondent of the Natchez *Courier*.[28] Hence, while negotiating every turn, boatmen had to pull hard at the sweeps in order to maintain the flatboat's position in mid-stream. The labor of holding a proper course was particularly onerous at times when the wind was blowing strongly toward that bank of the river where the current was swiftest. Not infrequently, "the utmost exertions of the half a dozen muscular men, who form the complement of flat-boat men," would not enable them "to counteract the force of both wind and current." [29] Under such adverse conditions experienced flat-boat captains moored their vessels until the wind moderated. River-men also tied their flatboats to trees along the riverbank during the night as the chance of grounding was too great to be risked. When-ever possible, the crews of flatboats lightened and shared their labors by lashing two of their vessels together, an arrangement which had the added inducement of bringing new faces and fresh tales into the social circle.

In Andrew Brown's lumber business, rafting and flatboating were handled largely by white rivermen during the 1820's and 1830's. The men he employed were chosen from the professional flatboatmen, "with their loose, coarse brown trowsers, red or blue shirts, the sleeves drawn up to the shoulders [and] . . . rough, determined looking faces and athletic limbs," who manned the great downriver fleets of the Mississippi.[30] He paid common crewmen from seventy-five cents to a dollar a day and "captains" of flatboats and foremen of rafting crews about twice as much. All employees were provided with meals and

---

[27] Key to Dott, August 13, 1850, Learned Collection.
[28] Natchez *Courier*, April 21, 1837.
[29] *Ibid.*
[30] *Ibid.*

transportation by steamboat back to the point where the voyage originated.[31]

While the organization still remained small, Andrew Brown or a
partner acted as flatboat master on those rare occasions when they
carried lumber to customers downstream from Natchez.[32] Andrew
Brown, Jr., relieved his father of this activity in 1840; but later when
his business in New Orleans became too demanding, he tried hiring
white flatboat captains for several years. The Browns, however, found
themselves unable to obtain men who were sufficiently capable and
reliable enough to be trusted with this heavy responsibility; so they
eventually placed Negro slaves whom they had personally trained
in charge of the boating and rafting operations, using white captains
only when they needed more crews than they normally employed.

Lack of seamanship (or, more properly, rivermanship) was not a
problem with respect to white flatboat captains. "Captain Pomp,"
William Strickland, and Isham D. Brown all worked for Brown as flatboat skippers during the 1840's; and each of them was thoroughly
capable of navigating two flatboats at a time from Natchez to New
Orleans. Pomp was loyal and honest, but "he trifles away a great deal
of time, & time is everything with us now," Andrew Brown, Jr., informed his father during 1845.[33] Pomp ran up excessive expenses by
unnecessarily prolonged trips and insisted upon using more crewmen
than Andrew, Jr., though desirable.[34] Isham D. Brown was an exceptionally skilled riverman, but Key, young Brown's successor in New
Orleans, learned by bitter experience that he was "disposed to drink
& spree," and was "not to be trusted with anything." [35] Key suggested
to Andrew Brown, Sr., that Isham Brown be transferred to the sawmill,
as he was a diligent worker; but, he wrote, "it will not do to have him
on a boat from which any person on the [German] Coast may infer
that he is in the employ of AB or AB & Co, and from that entrust him
as our agent." [36] Because Brown did not want Isham Brown in the sawmill crew, the riverman was discharged on August 16, 1851.[37] He then

[31] Andrew Brown, Jr., to Andrew Brown, August 5, 1845, Learned Collection;
Andrew Brown Ledger (1829–36), February 1, 1830; Andrew Brown Journal
(1843–48), 90.
[32] Andrew Brown Ledger (1829–36).
[33] Andrew Brown, Jr., to Andrew Brown, April 26, 1845. Learned Collection.
[34] Ibid., May 10, 1845.
[35] Key to Dott, July 9, 1850, Learned Collection.
[36] Ibid.
[37] Andrew Brown Receipt Book (1848–58), August 16, 1851.

took revenge on the company by stopping at various towns between Natchez and New Orleans to collect and pocket sums of money owed Andrew Brown of Natchez. As a result, Key ran an advertisement in the New Orleans *Times Picayune* warning his customers not to accept the riverman as an agent of the lumber firm.[38] Strickland, the ablest of the three, apparently left Brown's service of his own accord.[39]

Simon Gray, who belonged to Andrew Donnan, a coal dealer and blacksmith of Natchez, was the first of Brown's sawmill Negroes to be elevated to a position of responsibility.[40] Gray, a personable and intelligent mulatto, was hired to Andrew Brown, Sr., by his master sometime prior to 1835. When he went to work in the sawmill, the slave possessed no particular skills and was accordingly used by Brown as a common laborer.[41] He did not remain in this category for long, however, for by 1838 he was directing a rafting crew engaged in bringing logs down from the Yazoo River basin to the Brown sawmill at Natchez.[42] As head of a crew Gray was equipped with a pass signed by Brown which authorized him to travel free from interference by legal authorities anywhere he wished on the "Yazoo or any other river, under good conduct." [43] Brown at this time was also intrusting him with small sums of money for expenses of his crew and was even permitting him to purchase timber from Yazoo River logmen for use of the mill.[44] When Gray demonstrated his reliability and good judgment in these minor transactions, Brown allowed him to handle cash in large amounts. In one typical instance, the slave was given $800 to deliver to one of Brown's creditors, a task he carried out in routine fashion.[45]

When the Brown lumber company enlarged the scope of its operations during 1844, the resulting reorganization brought increased responsibility to Simon Gray. Before moving to New Orleans, Andrew

[38] New Orleans *Times Picayune*, September 2, 1851.
[39] Andrew Brown Journal (1843–48), 93.
[40] Harnett T. Kane, *Natchez on the Mississippi* (New York, 1947), 135. Refer also to John Hebron Moore, "Simon Gray, Riverman: A Slave Who Was Almost Free," *Mississippi Valley Historical Review*, XLIX (December, 1962), 472–84.
[41] Andrew Brown Journal (1835).
[42] Andrew Brown Journal (1836–40), 268; Andrew Brown Time Book (1838–40).
[43] Simon Gray Memorandum Book (1841).
[44] Andrew Brown Hands Ledger (1840–41), 13–14; Andrew Brown Journal (1840–43), 63, 73, and 88.
[45] Andrew Brown Journal (1843–48), 69.

Brown, Jr., the sales manager of the company, had been disposing of the cypress lumber which the Natchez market could not absorb by peddling it from flatboats at towns and plantations between Natchez and New Orleans. Gray, when not rafting logs to the mill, had often accompanied Brown as his assistant. In this way, the slave learned both the art of flatboating and the business of retailing lumber. In due course he became quite proficient in these dual aspects of marketing cypress lumber. Consequently, when Andrew Brown, Jr., found that he must devote his full time to the New Orleans branch of the firm, he recommended to his father that Gray be allowed to handle the job of transporting the lumber to market. Andrew Brown soon afterward promoted the hired slave to the rank of flatboat captain, a position he retained until the Civil War.[46]

The Negro captain quickly demonstrated that his employer's confidence in his seamanship was not misplaced. On his first voyage in command of a flatboat he brought his lumber-laden craft safely to its destination although it was leaking so badly that only the buoyancy of its cargo kept it afloat.[47] After a second trip in which Gray navigated two flatboats to New Orleans without mishap, the younger Brown wrote from New Orleans that "Simon managed the boats very well last time. He is a first-rate fellow & can be as careful as anyone when he likes." [48]

From 1845 until 1862 Simon Gray served as the Natchez lumber company's chief boatman. When the press of business required that two crews be used to supply the needs of the lumber yard in New Orleans, white men were employed temporarily as flatboat captains, but none of them ever succeeded in replacing the Negro. Andrew Brown continued to hold Gray in high regard despite occasional criticism of him by customers and New Orleans business associates.

As captain, Simon Gray exercised a degree of authority that is surprising to the modern student of slavery. His crews, usually numbering between ten and twenty men, were made up of both Negro slaves and white rivermen.[49] Some of the slaves were the property of the company, while others, like Gray himself, had been hired from their owners by the firm. The white crewmen, on the other hand,

[46] Andrew Brown, Jr., to Andrew Brown, May 24, 1845, Learned Collection.
[47] *Ibid.*, April 11, 1845.
[48] *Ibid.*, August 5, 1845.
[49] *Ibid.*, September 5, 1845, and December 11, 1847; Solomon to Andrew Brown, January 6, 1849, Learned Collection.

were employed by the Negro, who kept their records, paid their expenses, lent them money, and sometimes paid their wages.[50] Consequently, they looked upon Gray as their employer. Curiously enough, the flatboat captain appears to have been more popular with his white crewmen than with the slaves. The latter sometimes complained to Andrew Brown, Jr., that Gray's manner was unduly overbearing, but the whites did not.[51] Indeed, several of the white rivermen served under the Negro for a period of years. His unusual relationship with them was a subject of comment among the members of the firm. On one occasion, William I. Key reported from New Orleans that Gray had insisted on his paying the steamboat passage of some white rivermen from New Orleans to Natchez so that they could accompany him on his next trip. These crewmen Key described as the "meanest lot of *white men* . . . I ever saw." [52]

Gray's flatboat voyages were of two general kinds. The one he undertook most frequently was a simple delivery of lumber from the Natchez mill to the New Orleans lumber yard. On the New Orleans hauls, Gray's duties as captain were comparatively uncomplicated. At Natchez he supervised the loading of the cargoes into the flatboats, at the same time making a count of the number of lineal feet of lumber of each variety placed on board. On most of his trips, Gray handled two of these boats lashed together, employing a crew of twelve when weather and river conditions were favorable. Upon arriving in New Orleans, he moored his boats at the wharf and turned them and their cargo over to representatives of the lumber yard there. After delivering a cargo Gray returned to Natchez with his crew by steamboat to await the loading of another pair of flatboats. Ordinarily a trip from Natchez to New Orleans took him two weeks, but adverse weather and river currents could greatly prolong the voyage.[53]

Gray's other runs down the river were called "coasting trips," named for the German Coast district above the Crescent City. Because these often lasted from two to three weeks, Gray was compelled to exercise considerable initiative and independent judgment. The main object

[50] Key to Andrew Brown, February 18, 1850, Learned Collection; Simon Gray Memorandum Book (1854).

[51] Andrew Brown, Jr., to Andrew Brown, September 19, 1846, Learned Collection.

[52] Key to Andrew Brown, February 18, 1850, *ibid.*

[53] Gray's operations are revealed by the journals of Andrew Brown of Natchez and of Andrew Brown and Co. of New Orleans for the 1845–63 period.

of these ventures was to deliver orders of lumber to customers at riverside plantations. When space was available, however, extra lumber
was placed on the flatboat for Gray to sell at retail along the way. In
addition to making deliveries he also solicited orders for the mill,
quoted prices, extended credit to customers, and collected money owed
to the lumber company.[54] As a rule the Negro kept the necessary
records himself, but he occasionally hired a clerk when the bookkeeping became burdensome. His memoranda and reports submitted to the
company officials in New Orleans reveal that the Negro captain was
as literate as most white men of the laboring class and that he was
well versed in simple mathematics, having been taught to read and
write by Thomas Brown, Andrew Brown's nephew, during 1847.[55]

On lengthy retailing expeditions Gray was accustomed to submit-
ting reports about his progress by mail to the offices in New Orleans
and Natchez. The following letter, written from Plaquemine, Louisiana, on June 21, 1850, to Andrew Dott, Brown's sawmill manager in
Natchez, is typical:

> I now write you these few lines to let you know that I am a little better than
> I was when I left. I have got along quite well with the boat so far and have
> delivered *Mr. Moss* bill [of lumber] according to order and taken a draft for the
> same. I stoped the boat from leaking in the evening of the 19th of this month.
> This bill [order] of Mr Allens, it is to come with H. K. Moss next bill. I have
> not made any collections as yet but have the promis of some this morning. This
> letter that I send in your care I want to send to my wife, if you please.
>
> Nothing more at preasant. I remain your umble servent &c.[56]

The privileges which Brown accorded his Negro captain were not
approved by William I. Key, who objected particularly to Gray's being permitted to undertake retailing trips. As he was having continual
difficulty in keeping his yards stocked with lumber, he wanted to
abandon the German Coast trade altogether so that all of the Natchez
lumber could be sold in New Orleans. Key maintained that he could
obtain better prices for the cypress than Gray was obtaining from the
planters, and that he could collect accounts in the city more easily.[57]

[54] For examples of these activities, see J. C. Daugherty to Andrew Brown,
January 19, 1849; and Gourier and Auger to Andrew Brown, May 30, 1850,
both in Learned Collection.

[55] Alexander Brown, Jr., to Alexander Brown, December 30, 1846, *ibid.* Simon
Gray Memorandum Book (1849–50).

[56] Simon Gray to Dott, June 21, 1850; Gray to Andrew Brown, July 31, 1850,
both in Learned Collection.

[57] Key to Dott, May 9, 1850, *ibid.*

Furthermore, Key had grave doubts about Gray's honesty, which, however, were not shared by Andrew Brown. Although the Negro frequently brought the New Orleans office large amounts of cash which he had collected from his customers, Key nevertheless suspected him of dishonesty in small matters. These suspicions Key expressed in 1850: "That fellow Simon, there is no confidence can be placed in him. The very fact of his not wishing anyone with him that *will* act honestly is the very reason that we ought to have someone on every Boat that can keep a proper account of everything that occurs during the trip." [58] He also complained that Gray was ignoring his orders. Despite repeated instructions to the contrary, the Negro persisted in advancing part of their pay to his white crewmen before reaching New Orleans. Gray also was inclined to delay reporting to the office after arriving in town, and he sometimes would deliberately, Key thought, miss the steamboat which was supposed to return him and his crew to Natchez.[59]

In July, 1850, Key detected Gray in an act he considered to be highly dishonest. Someone had warned him that the boatman was planning to bring a lumber flatboat belonging to a competitor from Natchez to New Orleans without obtaining authorization from the company.[60] Alerted by this information, Key arranged to intercept the party on the river above the city. When they met, he discovered that Gray was indeed transporting the load of lumber in question, using crews belonging to Brown's firm. The manager of the lumber yard was convinced that Gray intended to keep the matter secret, and that the boatman had been bribed. Key then complained bitterly to Brown—without effect—that "this thing of leaving Simon his own master has been going on too long and must be put an end to." [61]

Instead of restricting Gray's movements because of Key's accusations, Brown accorded increased freedom to the Negro. In August, 1850, he purchased "Simon's family" from Joseph W. Allen for the sum of $500.[62] This Brown did only as an act of kindness for the Negro captain, for he made no subsequent use of the woman or her children. The Gray family thus united was domiciled by Brown in a rented house in Natchez, and the monthly rent was charged against the op-

[58] *Ibid.*, May 13, 1850.
[59] Key to Andrew Brown, February 18, 1850, Learned Collection.
[60] Key to Dott, July 13, 1850, *ibid.*
[61] *Ibid.*, July 18, 1850.
[62] Key to Andrew Brown, August 17, 1850, Learned Collection.

erating expenses of the firm. Further demonstrating his reliance upon the boatman, Brown sent Gray to Plaquemine, Louisiana, in 1852 to bring Dan Tucker, a slave whom Brown had purchased there, to Natchez.[63] This, of course, was a task ordinarily reserved for responsible white men.

In 1853 Simon Gray became free in all but the legal sense of the word. Until this time Brown's company had been paying Andrew Donnan seventy-five cents per day for his services.[64] In addition, Simon himself received a bonus of five dollars for each trip to New Orleans, plus a salary of eight dollars per month.[65] Although the records are obscure on this point, it appears likely that Donnan gave Gray his freedom without going to the trouble to have a special act of emancipation passed by the state legislature. Whether this was true or not, Donnan ceased to receive payment for Simon's hire, and the Negro's monthly wages were increased from eight to twenty dollars.[66] This latter sum was the wage which the lumber company was paying free white boatmen. In December, 1854, Key's assistant in New Orleans wrote that Simon Gray was leaving the city without "I am afraid, having made much progress in emancipation." [67]

Even though Simon Gray continued to remain a slave in the eyes of the law, Andrew Brown nevertheless permitted the Negro to take part in private business enterprises when his services were not required by the company. The first of these ventures occurred in August, 1855. At that time Gray purchased a flatboat in Natchez, filled it with a cargo of 1,700 barrels of sand, and floated it to New Orleans.[68] To help with the navigation of the flatboat, he hired Alfred, one of the slaves belonging to the sawmill.[69] In New Orleans, Key disposed of the load for Gray by selling the sand to builders. A second cargo delivered in October brought twenty-five cents per barrel. As was usual in such cases, the sale was made on credit with 6 per cent interest being charged against the purchasers. Gray eventually grossed

[63] Andrew Brown Cash Book (1848–55), April 8, 1852.
[64] Andrew Brown Journal (1848–53), 403; Andrew Brown Receipt Book (1848–53), March 23, 1853.
[65] Andrew Brown Journal (1848–53), 373.
[66] Andrew Brown Journal (1853–60), 63.
[67] Paul to Andrew Brown, December 6, 1854, Learned Collection.
[68] Key to Solomon, August 21, 1855; Paul to Andrew Brown, August 22, 1855, both in *ibid*. Gray in account with A. Brown, 1855, Andrew Brown Miscellaneous Financial Papers.
[69] Andrew Brown Journal (1853–60), 214.

$487.44 from his second sand speculation and, in addition, was able to dispose of his flatboat for $60. Out of his profits he had to pay the company for his and Alfred's time at the rate of one dollar per day each, and also had to settle with the owner of the sand bank from which he had obtained his commodity.[70]

These ventures were followed by many others over the next few years. On one undertaken in March, 1856, Simon grossed $440.00 and netted $225.75. Another undertaken the next month was less profitable, for it netted him only $144.50.[71] He continued in the business in spite of price fluctuations, and by June, 1856, had succeeded in accumulating more than five hundred dollars to his credit with the lumber company over and above the small sums he had withdrawn from time to time.[72]

Gray apparently used this money to buy a son, Washington Gray, who had not been included in the purchase of "Simon's family" mentioned earlier. In any case, Andrew Brown acquired "Simon's boy Washington" for five hundred dollars.[73] Subsequently, the mill paid Brown for the boy's services, but whether this money was then retained by him or given to Simon is not clear.[74] In all probability, however, Brown was again accommodating his flatboat captain by acting in his behalf to accomplish an end forbidden by the slave code.

During the years in which Simon Gray was transporting sand to New Orleans, he continued to handle lumber flatboats and log rafts for the company. He took part in an unusual episode in March, 1856, when a log raft moored at the Natchez mill broke loose and drifted downstream. Gray and a white employee were dispatched to overtake the raft and assume charge of it, but they failed to make contact. The runaway raft drifted past Baton Rouge and finally entered Bayou Lafourche.[75]

Meanwhile, William Key received word in New Orleans of the accident by telegraph. He hastened upriver on a steamboat in hopes of intercepting the raft, taking with him Jim Matthews, a slave who was Simon's counterpart in the rafting division of the company. Fail-

[70] Key to Solomon, October 20, 1855, Learned Collection.
[71] Gray's account of his sand trips to New Orleans, 1856, Andrew Brown Miscellaneous Financial Papers.
[72] Andrew Brown Journal (1853–60), 266.
[73] Paul to Solomon, June 14, 1856, Learned Collection; Andrew Brown Journal (1853–60), 273.
[74] Andrew Brown Cash Book (1855–64), 47.
[75] Paul to Solomon, March 11, 1856, Learned Collection.

ing to sight the raft below Baton Rouge, they returned to New Orleans where they found Gray and the white workmen waiting for them. The two men reported that they had traced the raft into Bayou Lafourche and had found it tied up at Jacob's wood yard. The owner of this establishment told them that a white man had sold the timber to him for $500 and then departed for New Orleans. When Gray convinced Jacobs that the timber was the property of Andrew Brown, he offered the Negro and his white companion a reward of $250 if they would recover his money for him. They promptly left in pursuit of the swindler and overtook him on the wharf in New Orleans. When Brown's men accused the culprit of swindling Jacobs, he readily admitted his guilt, and gave them $400 on the condition that they let him go free. When Gray returned the money to its rightful owner, Jacobs gave him $50 as his share of the reward. To close the matter, Jacobs bought the raft again, this time from the proper owner.[76]

After 1856 Simon Gray became increasingly involved in the Yazoo Valley operation of the company. In January, 1857, Brown intrusted the Negro with an urgent and delicate mission. He was instructed to buy as much plank as he could from a sawmill in Yazoo City operated by Mayfield, Fuget and Company. The results of the subsequent negotiations he reported to Brown as follows:

> I have closed the trade for the lumber at $16 per M [thousand]. There is about 3000 feet 1 inch plank; the balance [is] 1¼, 1½ & 2 inch. I was just in time to get it. Mr. Klein had sent a man up and he arrived there in one hour after I had closed the bargain. He offered $18 for the lot. I have thought it best to go to Greenwood and see about [buying] the boat [to transport the lumber] and drop it down [to Yazoo City], and then will either come or send to you for hands [to serve as crew].[77]

Gray's purchase consisted of 155,000 feet of cypress lumber, costing $2,473.98. At New Orleans, Key's assistant noted that it was "rather shabby stuff" but welcome in the emergency nonetheless.[78]

From this time until 1863, Simon Gray was largely employed in the Yazoo swamps. When there was sufficient water in the Yazoo River he transported cargoes of cypress lumber manufactured by the small sawmills under contract with Andrew Brown. At times when the

[76] Ibid.; Key to Solomon, March 15, 1856, Learned Collection.
[77] Gray to Andrew Brown, January 25, 1857, Learned Collection.
[78] Paul to Key, February 3, 1857, ibid.

stream was not navigable, he directed the activities of a crew working in the cypress brakes, deadening timber, rolling logs, building levees and dams, constructing cribs of logs, and in general performing all the host of tasks preparatory to rafting the logs to the sawmill at Natchez.[79]

During much of 1858 and 1859 Gray was afflicted with ill health. He visited Hot Springs, Arkansas, to take the baths on numerous occasions, and in the course of these treatments spent nearly a thousand dollars. Apparently he had fallen victim to the occupational diseases of the riverman, malaria and rheumatism. In addition, he was wearing an "elastic stocking" to relieve varicose veins.[80]

Despite these ailments and his advancing age, Gray was able gradually to resume his regular duties. During the summer and fall of 1860 he delivered numerous loads of lumber to New Orleans.[81] By then he was also able to devote some attention to his own business interests. In January, 1861, for example, Gray stopped his lumber flatboat at Baton Rouge and loaded on a sizeable quantity of cordwood which he purchased there for $3.00 a cord. Upon reaching New Orleans the boatman disposed of his firewood at a profit of $1.30 per cord. Key, as usual, was displeased with Gray's business methods and commented sourly that "Simon should bear a portion of the expenses" of the flatboat which carried his cordwood to New Orleans.[82]

After the capture of New Orleans in April, 1862, by the Federal army cut off the Natchez sawmill from its market in the Crescent City, Andrew Brown moved almost all of his slaves from Natchez to his timber lands in the Yazoo Basin for safekeeping. Gray, who had been working in the swamps for more than a year, was now joined by his wife and children, and they continued to live there until after the fall of Vicksburg.[83] This Union victory in July, 1863, evidently brought the Negro flatboat captain the freedom he desired, for his name disappears from the records of the lumber company after this

[79] Andrew Brown Journal (1853–60); Andrew Brown Day Book (1854–62).

[80] Andrew Brown Journal (1853–60), 399, 408, 553; Andrew Brown Cash Book (1855–64), 136, 140, 150, 172, and 184.

[81] Andrew Brown Cash Book (1855–64), 244; Andrew Brown Journal (1853–60), 623. Key to John Shanks, September 15, 1860; Paul to Shanks, November 20, 1860, both in Learned Collection.

[82] Key to Shanks, January 5, 1861, Learned Collection.

[83] Andrew Brown Journal (1861–70), 82–83, 167, 393; Manuel Sparling to Andrew Brown, March 30 and May 11, 1862, Learned Collection.

date. In 1865, Andrew Brown included a debt owed him by Simon among a list of uncollectable accounts.[84]

Almost every aspect of Simon Gray's career violates the modern conception of the lot of a slave in the lower South. Contrary to law and custom the Negro riverman was educated beyond the point reached by an ordinary white workingman. He was permitted to travel about almost as freely as he would had he not been a slave. He was paid a regular wage throughout most of his career, and he was able to live in privacy with his family apart from his fellows. More surprisingly, he frequently bought and sold as an agent of his employer and was able to exercise authority effectively over other employees of the company, both black and white. Gray even owned and made use of firearms with full consent of his employer.[85] In short, the restrictions of slavery rested lightly upon this Natchez Negro.

James Matthews, a mulatto like Simon Gray, was another slave who rose from the ranks of common laborers in the sawmill to a position of authority in Brown's organization. Unlike Gray, who was a hired slave, however, Matthews was the property of the lumber firm, apparently having been purchased soon after Brown's entry into the business in 1829.[86] He continued as a simple mill hand for several years, during 1835 working alongside Simon Gray, Jacob, who eventually became Brown's engine operator, Harrison, Randall, and Ned, who formed the nucleus of the sawmill crew over the next two decades.[87]

Although Matthews did not succeed in distinguishing himself as quickly as Gray, as early as 1844 he gained the reputation of being one of the more intelligent of the sawmill slaves. In that year Andrew Brown, Jr., chose Matthews and Alfred to remain behind in New Orleans to assist him in disposing of a boatload of cypress lumber after the remainder of the flatboat crew had returned to Natchez. When this work was completed, the younger Brown sent Matthews back to Natchez on a steamboat by himself, thereby demonstrating unusual confidence in the Negro.[88] The following spring, the Scottish lumber

[84] Andrew Brown Journal (1861–70), 269.
[85] L. Odell to Andrew Brown, January 12, 1858, Andrew Brown Miscellaneous Financial Papers.
[86] Andrew Brown Ledger (1829–36), December 19, 1829.
[87] Andrew Brown Journal (1835).
[88] Andrew Brown, Jr., to Andrew Brown, June 18 and November 30, 1844, Learned Collection.

dealer selected Matthews to work with him at the newly established lumber yard in the Crescent City because he wished "to have one of the Boys that understands assorting out the stuff [lumber]." [89] During December, 1845, Andrew, Jr., advised his father to hire several white rivermen to help Matthews and Ned bring the next lumber boat to New Orleans, as the remainder of their Negro boatmen were still engaged in transferring lumber to the yard from the last flatboat. A white captain would be in charge of the crew, for Matthews was not yet trusted to act in that capacity.[90]

Matthews emerged from the manual labor class during 1848. In August of that year he made his maiden voyage as "master" of a flatboat carrying lumber to New Orleans. On this trip, John and William Holloway, George Simms, Thomas Powell, Isaac Banks, Robert Cullen, and "Old Man Rose," all white rivermen, served under the Negro in addition to three slaves, Oliver, Harry, and Aleck. In accordance with his long-standing custom, Brown paid Matthews a bonus of five dollars as compensation for his increased responsibilities.[91]

Having proved on this trip that he was a competent riverman and that he could be trusted to carry out an assignment without the direct supervision of his employers, Matthews was placed in permanent charge of a crew of raftsmen who were engaged in rafting cypress timber from Old River to the sawmill at Natchez. This, of course, was a position which demanded an unusual degree of loyalty from the slave, because he would have numerous opportunities to escape to the North in the normal course of events. He and his crewmen would frequently be out from under the eyes of any of the white officials of the company for periods as long as a month, and the Negro, as foreman, would handle small sums of cash entrusted to him for the purpose of defraying minor expenses of his crew.[92] Despite the temptations offered by his new position, Matthews never abused the faith placed in him by Andrew Brown. Furthermore, he possessed the tact necessary for commanding both white and Negro workmen. Throughout his career white loggers and raftsmen accepted Matthew as foreman without complaint. During 1849, for example, John McDonald, who had been logging for Brown for several years, worked under

[89] *Ibid.*, March 8, 1845.
[90] *Ibid.*, December 13, 1845.
[91] Andrew Brown Time Book (1848–49), August 16, 1848.
[92] Andrew Brown Cash Book (1848–55).

Matthews for one whole season,[93] and in 1852, Hugh Coyle was specifically hired at the salary of twenty-five dollars a month with the understanding that he would serve in Matthews' crew.[94]

Despite his skill on the river, Jim Matthews had his share of mishaps. During July, 1850, "the greatest *old granny* that ever lived," as an outraged Key described him, allowed a raft to pass below the breakwater at Natchez.[95] Simon Gray managed somehow to overtake the runaway raft below the town, and the two Negro rivermen continued downriver with the timber to Baton Rouge. They landed the timber at that river port and, on their own responsibility, sold the logs to three partners "Frierson, W. W. McMain, & Elijah Peake, of Henderson & Peake," for the sum of $475.00.[96] Key was indignant about the sale as he did not want these competitors to gain the benefit of Brown's top quality timber for their new sawmill.[97] At no time did any of the white officials of Brown's lumber company ever express fear that Gray and Matthews would abscond with this large sum of money; nor did they, then or later.

During the decade of the 1850's, James Matthews was the chief raftsman of the Natchez lumber company, just as Gray was the principal boatman. Sometimes Matthews assisted Gray by taking a flatboat load of lumber to New Orleans, and Gray reciprocated by bringing down an occasional raft from Old River when no flatboats were ready for a trip to the lumber yard in the Crescent City. Yet Matthews failed to attain the status enjoyed by Gray after the boatman's quasi-emancipation in 1853. He was paid in cash for work performed on Sundays, and he received an allowance of five dollars a month from Brown; but he was never placed on a salary such as Gray received even earlier than 1853. The company, however, frequently purchased timbers or parts of rafts which he had salvaged from the river. As a result, Matthews earned much more money than most of the other slaves belonging to Brown or his lumber firm.[98]

During those infrequent periods when there was no rafting, flatboating, or mill work for the Negro to do, Brown hired Matthews out

[93] Andrew Brown Journal (1848–53), 44.
[94] Andrew Brown Time Book (1852), July 19, 1852.
[95] Key to Dott, July 9, 1850, Learned Collection.
[96] Andrew Brown Journal (1848–53), 181.
[97] Key to Dott, July 9, 1850, Learned Collection.
[98] Key to Solomon, October 20, 1855, *ibid.*; Andrew Brown Journal (1853–60), 38.

to steamboat captains. During 1855 and 1856, while the mill was closed and no rafts were coming down from the Yazoo because of low water, Matthews worked for a time on the Yazoo River steamboat *Wallace* and then on the *Natchez* which plied the Mississippi River between New Orleans and Vicksburg. Brown received twenty-five dollars a month from the *Wallace* for Matthews' services and thirty dollars from the *Natchez*. While Matthews was employed on these vessels, Brown depended upon him for information about river conditions and news of timber for sale.[99]

Like Simon Gray, James Matthews eventually lost all awe of his employers and upon occasion insisted on following his own course of action in spite of orders to the contrary. During December, 1857, for example, he and his men experienced considerable hardship while taking a flatboat to New Orleans. During very bad weather their boat struck a sunken wreck which knocked a hole in the hull, sinking the vessel as far as the lumber in the cargo would allow. As the rivermen had to work very strenuously during the remainder of the trip, Matthews determined to give his men a rest after delivering his "sunk" flatboat to the lumber yard. Key, however, instructed him to return immediately on the steamboat *Natchez* without taking any time out for sampling the various recreations that the city offered to Negro rivermen with money in their pockets. Being too shrewd to disobey directly, Matthews pretended to misunderstand the junior partner of the firm. Instead of boarding the *Natchez* as directed, Matthews loaded his men—Scott and John Clark—and equipment on the *Fanny Benhill*. By the time Key discovered what he had done, the *Natchez* had left the wharf; and the three Negroes were able to spend Saturday night in the city instead of returning directly to Natchez. Key, to his utter frustration, could do no more than write Solomon about Matthews' "damned contumaciousness in persisting to have his own way!" [100] The Negro raftsman also displayed religious scruples, probably acquired from Andrew Brown, Jr., against beginning a trip on Sunday, and he characteristically found excuses to delay his departure until the following day.[101] Regardless of his stubbornness, however, Matthews was respected by the white executives of the company.

[99] Andrew Brown to the steamboat *Natchez*, October 19, 1856; Paul to Solomon, October 27, 1855, both in Learned Collection.
[100] Key to Solomon, December 22, 1857, *ibid.*
[101] *Ibid.*, December 15, 1857.

"Jim arrived safe and looks the finest looking fellow in Orleans," as one reported to Natchez; "how would you like to own a dozen such?"[102]

During the final year of the 1850's Matthews was busily employed with rafting timber to the sawmill at Natchez from Brown's various logging camps in the Yazoo. Throughout the year he headed a mixed lot of approximately a dozen raftsmen which included both Negroes and whites, with the whites usually predominating. On one of these typical trips undertaken in June, Matthews brought a raft down from Old River containing forty-eight large timbers. The trip took five days, and the total expense for moving the logs was $100.75. Matthews' crew included eight white rivermen who were paid $1.25 per day, and two Negroes, John Clark and George Washington. Matthews himself was paid $1.50 and John Clark $1.00 as spending money. The cost of passage for the crew and their equipment aboard the steamboat *Grand Duke* on their way up to Old River was $22.00. The average cost of transportation per timber was $2.00; per sawlog, $0.45.[103]

On an earlier trip, Matthews' crew rafted fifty, forty-foot timbers from the logging operation carried out by the partnership of Andrew Brown and James J. Wheless. Preparations for rafting and the river trip took them sixteen days. On this venture Matthews had four white raftsmen under him in addition to the Negroes, Scott, Dan Tucker, Dan Hunter, Burwell, and Randall. The total transportation cost came to $109.30. As they worked through one Sunday, each of the Negroes was paid a dollar.[104]

After taking an enormous flatboat loaded with 243,766 feet of lumber to New Orleans in December, 1859, Matthews and his crew, including at least four whites, returned to the Yazoo to join the logging crews working there.[105] Throughout the year the "Timber Account" in Brown's ledger included entries for wages paid "Jim & Hands" ranging between two and four hundred and fifty dollars. From the size of the payroll it would appear that Matthews was still heading a mixed crew of five whites and five Negroes.[106]

During 1861 and early 1862, when the mill at Natchez had little need for timber, Matthews remained on Brown's Yazoo timberlands,

[102] Paul to Solomon, November 10, 1857, Learned Collection.
[103] Andrew Brown Timber Expense Book (1857–60), June 13, 1859.
[104] *Ibid.*, April 27, 1859.
[105] Andrew Brown & Co. Journal (1855–60), December 1, 1859.
[106] Andrew Brown Cash Book (1855–64), 222, 288.

logging mainly on the Black Bayou brake.[107] Then, in June, he was taken out of the swamps and hired out to the Natchez building contractor, Thomas Rose, for whom he worked nearly a year.[108] After the fall of Vicksburg, however, Matthews left Natchez to go to New Orleans. On August 29, 1863, Key learned that "Jim is soldiering."[109] With his enlistment in the Federal army, the Negro's lengthy connection with Brown and the lumber company finally came to an end.

The emancipation of the slaves belonging to Andrew Brown and of those belonging to the partnership of Brown and Key abruptly terminated a development which was showing considerable promise. Over a period of thirty-five years, Brown had pioneered, along with other lumber manufacturers, in admitting Negro slaves into their industry. He, more than the others, however, had painstakingly trained his Negroes so that they could perform ever more demanding tasks, rewarding them liberally when they showed unusual initiative. In making Simon Gray and James Matthews foremen of logging and rafting crews Brown broke new ground, for he was opening the doors of industrial advancement to slaves. Brown also made it clear that he was setting no limits to the heights to which his Negroes could aspire by permitting Simon to engage in commercial ventures of his own. Had the old Scot's experiment been allowed to continue for a few more years, it is entirely possible that Gray might have emerged as an official in the company. With the end of slavery, however, these Negroes lost their unusual opportunity to rise above the ranks of manual labor in this branch of industry in the Old Southwest. From mid-1863 onward, all positions of authority were reserved only for whites.

[107] *Ibid.*, 344, 352.
[108] *Ibid.*, 382.
[109] Paul to Key, August 29, 1863, Learned Collection.

6

Merchandising at New Orleans

DURING a reorganization of Andrew Brown's enterprises brought about by the death of his son, William I. Key joined the firm as a junior partner and manager of the New Orleans division. Key, originally from Crail and a nephew of Mrs. Andrew Brown, Sr., was one of many Scottish immigrants who had settled in Natchez during the 1820's and 1830's.[1] He worked for his uncle-in-law as a clerk in the sawmill for a brief while during 1840, along with Andrew, Jr., and their mutual friend A. J. Postlethwaite.[2] After he learned his way around the business community of the town, he left the lumber firm and established a mercantile house, William I. Key and Company, in partnership with Postlethwaite.[3] As Key retained intimate personal and business ties with the Browns during the 1840's, he was the natural successor to Andrew, Jr. Late in 1848 he became the owner of a one-fourth share in the firms of Andrew Brown of Natchez and Andrew Brown and Company, the manufacturing and merchandising division of Brown's reconstituted lumber firm.[4]

Brown apparently did not require that Key invest any of his capital in the new partnership; instead, he seems to have tendered the part ownership as an inducement to obtain Key's full-time services which were urgently needed in New Orleans. Whether this be true or not,

[1] Andrew Brown & Co. Journal (1855–60), 225. Unless cited otherwise all journals, cash books, etc., referred to in this chapter are located in the Rufus F. Learned Collection.

[2] Andrew Brown Journal (1840–43).

[3] Natchez *Courier*, June 1, 1846.

[4] Andrew Brown of Natchez Balance Sheet, October 31, 1850, Andrew Brown Miscellaneous Financial Papers.

Key did assume the management of the lumber yard during April, 1849.[5] In the meanwhile Henry S. Solomon, a carpenter who had managed the lumber yard during the illness of Andrew, Jr., continued in charge until relieved by Key.[6]

Key and his wife Agnes moved to New Orleans at the time of the California gold rush. Around the city rumors that great wealth was being amassed overnight were rife, and reports of inflated commodity prices on the West Coast whetted the appetites of commission merchants of the Crescent City. Lumber dealers, hearing that planking was selling at San Francisco for $400 per thousand lineal feet, planned an invasion of the California markets with yellow pine and cypress.[7]

Both Key and Solomon were naturally intrigued by the possibility of selling cypress for such fabulous prices, and they approached Andrew Brown with a suggestion that the company send a shipment of lumber to San Francisco. Somewhat to their surprise, the venturesome old Scot agreed at once to undertake the speculation, provided that a suitable vessel could be purchased for a reasonable price. When Key finished a detailed estimate of the probable cost of the project, he concluded that the partnership would have to invest approximately a hundred dollars per thousand feet in order to take its cypress lumber to market in California. He nevertheless recommended to Brown that they assume the risk because of the extraordinary prices that commodities of this kind were reported to be bringing. In determining to make the gamble, Key was by no means unique: during June, 1849, for example, a single New Orleans commission house shipped 400,000 feet of yellow pine and 100,000 feet of assorted dressed lumber to San Francisco.[8]

Before they completed their arrangements, however, Brown and Key decided to change the nature of the cargo. They learned that large numbers of prefabricated houses were being exported to the West Coast from England and the northern United States. Key calculated that he and his partner could use their limited cargo space more profitably by shipping knocked-down houses rather than less valuable bulk lumber, and his recommendation to Brown to this effect was vigorously endorsed by Henry Solomon. Soon afterward, the senior

[5] William I. Key to Andrew Dott, May 19, 1849, Learned Collection.
[6] Henry S. Solomon to Key, December 26, 1848; Solomon to Andrew Brown, August 29, 1848, both *ibid.*
[7] Key to Dott, June 9 and 19, 1849, *ibid.*
[8] *Ibid.*

partner came to New Orleans to confer with Key about the new plan. By coincidence, the steamboat *Belle of the West,* laden with fifty-five prefabricated houses of Cincinnati manufacture, arrived at the river port while the Natchez lumbermen was there. Through her captain, Brown was introduced to a carpenter in charge of the houses who showed them to him and answered all his questions. Becoming convinced that he could manufacture portable houses of much higher quality than the ones he had seen, Brown informed Key that he was ready to proceed with the scheme.[9]

With the aid of the "House of J. P. Whitney & Co." of New York, Key in December, 1849, succeeded in purchasing the *Desdemona,* an eight-year old vessel of 620 tons burden for the sum of $22,000. He then had the bark towed upriver to Natchez by the steamboat *Constitution.*[10] As soon as the *Desdemona* was moored at the wharf near the mill, Brown began loading her cargo aboard. Despite his efforts to expedite the bark's departure, many frustrating delays were encountered. Finally, the *Desdemona* left for New Orleans with her cargo complete in March, 1850, months too late to capitalize on the California boom.[11] As early as January, lumber prices at San Francisco had declined to two hundred dollars per thousand for the best grade of dressed white pine, with the same item in yellow pine bringing no more than $150. Scantling, joists, and dunnage, selling from $50 to $125, were going for less than the cost of transportation from the East Coast.[12] Thus the California adventure was doomed to failure even before the *Desdemona* put out to sea.

Loading difficulties and falling prices were merely two of the misfortunes which befell the Scottish partners. While crossing the bar at the mouth of the Mississippi River, the *Desdemona* grounded repeatedly, severely damaging her bottom. For several days afterward her pumps were able to cope with leaks, but then a storm off Bermuda opened her seams below the water line. Fearing that the vessel would go down, Captain Thomas E. Whitney changed course for New York, eventually arriving there with the pumps working at maximum capacity.[13]

[9] *Ibid.,* July 21, 1849.
[10] *Ibid.,* November 1, December 10 and 20, 1849.
[11] *Ibid.,* March 31, 1850.
[12] *Ibid.,* March 22, 1850.
[13] Solomon to Key, April 25, 1850; Thomas E. Whitney to Andrew Brown, April 29, 1850, both in Learned Collection.

Much time was lost in removing the cargo, repairing the hull in drydock, and then reloading the houses and lumber.[14] On June 30, 1850, the *Desdemona* resumed her voyage and completed her trip around the Horn without further incident.[15] Upon arriving at San Francisco, Solomon, who accompanied the ship as company representative, found that the bottom had dropped out of the lumber market. He had great difficulty disposing of his lumber and houses at any price, and his reports to Key revealed that his expenses were actually in excess of his gross sales over a period of seven months. In November, 1851, Key calculated that the company had already lost $40,000 on the California speculation, exclusive of the cost of the ship.[16]

Contrary to their original expectations, Brown and Key were unable to sell the *Desdemona* on the West Coast, and they were consequently forced to continue as shipowners much against their wills. Over the next five years they tried to reclaim some of their investment in the bark by hauling freight under charter, but they managed to do little more than meet expenses during this period.[17] Finally, to the great relief of both Key and Brown, the faithful but unwanted *Desdemona* was damaged beyond repair off Cardiff, Wales, in April, 1856.[18] J. P. Whitney and Company recovered $10,000 in insurance from Lloyd's of London on behalf of Andrew Brown and Company, thereby reducing the loss on the *Desdemona* to $21,457.40.[19] The total expense of the California adventure and its aftermath ultimately cost Brown and Key more than $60,000.[20]

While the lion's share of the task of providing a cargo for the *Desdemona* in 1850 had fallen upon Andrew Brown at Natchez, the much more unpleasant chore of settling the debts connected with the California speculation was assigned to Key. The cost of the project was charged against the New Orleans branch of the lumber firm, and the junior partner accordingly had to contend with a $40,000 deficit

[14] Solomon to Key, June 4, 1850, *ibid.*
[15] Key to Dott, July 13, 1850, *ibid.*
[16] Key to Andrew Brown, November 25, 1851, *ibid.*
[17] Key to Solomon, July 30, 1853, May 13, 1854, April 24, 1855, November 17 and 27, 1855; John F. Paul to Solomon, April 17 and October 27, 1855; Andrew Brown & Co. Journal (1855–60), 27, 58, 60–61, 71; all in Learned Collection.
[18] Key to Solomon, April 12, 1856, Learned Collection.
[19] Paul to Solomon, January 17, 1857, *ibid.*; Andrew Brown & Co. Journal (1855–60), 225, 421.
[20] Andrew Brown Journal (1853–60), 232; Andrew Brown & Co. Journal (1855–60), 80.

left over from the bout with "California fever" until the middle of the decade. Indeed, the fundamental soundness of Brown's lumber business is revealed by the two partners' impressive achievement of paying off the California indebtedness by the end of 1855. Thanks to the retail outlet in the Crescent City, the sawmill at Natchez was to sell between 1848 and 1853 from fifty to seventy thousand dollars worth of cypress lumber annually. In the 1849–52 period, the lumber manufacturing unit alone earned profits for the firm totaling more than $135,000. In fact, the sawmill cleared $30,000 during 1850, the year in which most of the bills for the California speculation fell due, which was a sum more than sufficient to defray the purchase price of the *Desdemona*. As a result of this extraordinary prosperity, Brown and Key were not seriously crippled by their ill-starred gamble.[21]

Instead of being discouraged by their misfortune, the two Scots characteristically responded to this reversal by increasing their investment in the lumber business in New Orleans. During 1852 Andrew Brown and Company erected a woodworking factory at No. 10, Front Street, which they operated as a subsidiary of the lumber yard under the title of the New Orleans Sash Factory.[22] By the time the doors of the new establishment were opened in February, 1853, the lot, buildings, machinery, and equipment had cost the partners $25,000, no inconsiderable amount judged by the standards of the fifties.[23]

Brown's decision to enter into the business of manufacturing wood products for the New Orleans building trade was not arrived at hastily as in the case of the California adventure. Instead it was based on several years experience with a smaller plant at Natchez. Soon after opening the New Orleans lumber yard in the early 1840's, it will be recalled, Andrew Brown, Jr., had discovered that contractors of the city were eager purchasers of dressed lumber; and he had made temporary arrangements from time to time with various woodworking shops to dress some of his cypress flooring. Being unable to obtain all of the services of this kind that he desired, the younger Brown had suggested to his father shortly before his death that a planing machine be installed at the sawmill. In this instance the elder Brown was easily persuaded, for he had recently learned that very large quantities

[21] Andrew Brown Journal (1843–48); *ibid.* (1848–53).
[22] New Orleans *Times Picayune*, February 26, 1853.
[23] Sash Factory Balance Sheet, December 31, 1856, Andrew Brown Miscellaneous Financial Papers.

of dressed cypress lumber would be required for the Louisiana state capitol then being constructed at Baton Rouge.[24] Therefore, during December, 1848, he purchased from John Hill and Thomas L. Jones for $1,650 a complete steam-powered planing shop located some distance from the sawmill at Natchez-under-the-Hill.[25]

On the advice of an engineer in charge of a factory belonging to Prague and Sherman, Brown hired Thomas Thorn, a skilled machinist, to repair and operate the newly-acquired establishment.[26] Thorn, who had been the proprietor of a similar shop in New Orleans, soon put the Natchez plant in good order and in a short time was able to supply Brown with all the dressed flooring and weatherboarding he needed to fill the contract he had acquired for the state house at Baton Rouge.[27] The shop was also equipped with a lathe, and Thorn was increasingly employed in making walnut and mahogany newel posts and balusters for customers in New Orleans.[28] Unfortunately, the bank of the Mississippi River caved in beneath the building during 1852, causing a loss amounting to more than $2,400; and the woodworking shop at Natchez was put out of operation before it had an opportunity to show a profit.[29]

Instead of replacing the shop at Natchez, Brown wisely decided to erect a much more elaborate factory near the lumber yard at New Orleans. This location placed the factory close to potential customers and allowed the sales force of the lumber yard to handle the merchandising of its products without additional expense to the parent firm. Key was more than willing to act as superintendent of the factory in exchange for a fourth interest, and he subsequently directed both the construction and operation of the new enterprise. Under his shrewd and energetic management, the sash, blind, and door factory prospered from the beginning, earning more than $20,000 within three years—almost enough to pay for factory site, building, and machinery.[30] Sales rose year by year despite a yellow fever epidemic in the

[24] David D. Avery to Andrew Brown, May 7, 1850, Learned Collection.
[25] Andrew Brown Journal (1848–53), 11; Andrew Brown Day Book (1848–51), December 29, 1848; Contract Between Andrew Brown and Thomas Jones, December 22, 1848, Andrew Brown Miscellaneous Papers.
[26] Key to Dott, June 23, 1849, Learned Collection.
[27] Solomon to Dott, January 29, 1850, *ibid.*
[28] Key to Andrew Brown, August 3, 1850, *ibid.*
[29] Andrew Brown Journal (1848–53), 428.
[30] Andrew Brown & Co. Journal (1855–60), 143.

summer of 1853, which temporarily suspended operations,[31] and a labor dispute over wages two years later.[32] In 1855 the New Orleans Sash Factory was specializing in mahogany products, and its balusters and newels made of this wood were in strong demand.[33] With justifiable satisfaction Key reported to Natchez that "all the stair builders here get their supplies from us" and that a flow of orders for building supplies was keeping the factory working at full capacity.[34] The New Orleans Sash Factory won most of the customers of the Mariposa Mills owned by Prague and Sherman. Key found them "trying to regain their lost custom" with the "renowned little sneaking Sherman as *Roper-in*." [35] While business was slack in the lumber industry during the 1855 building season, Key acknowledged gratefully that "income from the factory the past three months has helped me through many a hard day." [36]

During March, 1856, Key was compelled to deal with a strike while the factory was working overtime to keep up with orders. Approximately a dozen workmen out of the total complement of fifty employees threatened to resign unless their wages were raised. Key, a typical nineteenth century employer, without hesitation decided to "let the scamps clear out [rather] than accede to their demand & establish a bad precedent." In assuming this inflexible attitude toward his factory workers, Key risked nothing worse than a brief inconvenience, for there was no shortage of applicants for relatively highly paid factory work. He was able to replace the strikers without difficulty, and he had no further trouble with the cowed workmen in the plant. Indeed, Key, until the Civil War, was always able to hire skilled white workmen so readily that he never considered training Negroes to work on the machines, although he preferred to utilize slaves in the lumber yard instead of white workers.[37]

During the 1856 building season the New Orleans Sash Factory was unable to keep pace with the demand for its ready-made sashes,

[31] Key to Solomon, August 2 and 9, 1853, Learned Collection.
[32] *Ibid.*, January 20, 1855.
[33] *Ibid.*, May 8, 1855.
[34] *Ibid.*
[35] *Ibid.*, May 15, 1855.
[36] *Ibid.*, April 12 and June 16, 1855; New Orleans *Times Picayune*, May 23, 1855.
[37] Key to Solomon, March 4, 1856, Learned Collection.

blinds, doors, newells, and balusters.[38] Key, hounded by the problems brought on by too much success, cautioned Solomon at Natchez in June not to accept any additional contracts unless the customer was willing to wait several weeks for delivery.[39] A month later, to his great frustration, he was compelled to cease accepting orders altogether.[40] During the autumn, the busy sash factory exhausted the available stocks of cypress and white pine, and Key was driven to utilizing undesirable substitutes. "We have been using lumber that was not fit to put into anything," he explained to Solomon, "but better cannot be done. We must use that, or stop!" [41]

As a result of the extremely prosperous 1856 season, Brown and Key determined to increase the productive capacity of the sash factory. The main building was materially enlarged during the winter and spring in order "to give the operatives there more system," as Key's assistant John F. Paul, expressed it, with the construction work being done in such a manner as not to interrupt the operations of the plant.[42] The arrival of good weather brought a "perfect flood of orders for flooring" to the lumber yard, and the factory was similarly besieged by eager customers "from all sections of the country." In March, 1857, Key had a backlog of $10,000 worth of orders for custom-made doors, sashes, and blinds.[43]

After brick additions to the main factory building were finished, Key and Brown installed many new pieces of machinery. From Leeds and Company, the large New Orleans steam engine manufacturer, the partners obtained an unusually powerful engine. Complete with three boilers and the necessary fittings, it cost the company $6,200. The Leeds engine was erected in the sash factory by representatives of the manufacturer, and it subsequently served as the main power plant.[44] Among the woodworking equipment added at this time were two planing machines, a tenoning machine, two splitting saws, three mortising machines, and a surfacing machine.[45] By this time Andrew

[38] *Ibid.*, March 15 and 22, 1856; Paul to Solomon, April 15, 1856, Learned Collection.
[39] Key to Solomon, June 10, 1856, Learned Collection.
[40] Paul to Solomon, July 29, 1856, *ibid.*
[41] Key to Solomon, December 27, 1856, *ibid.*
[42] Paul to Solomon, January 17, 1857, *ibid.*
[43] Paul to Key, January 31, 1857; Key to Solomon, March 28, 1857, both *ibid.*
[44] Andrew Brown & Co. Journal (1855–60), 196; Paul to Key, January 6, 1866.
[45] Andrew Brown & Co. Journal (1855–60), 175–76, 191, 370; Andrew Brown & Co. Cash Book (1857–65), 27, 29, 39, 109, 155, 159.

Brown and Company had increased their investment in the sash factory to $47,000, with the machinery alone being valued at $16,000.[46]

As a result of the expansion program, the New Orleans Sash Factory became perhaps the biggest establishment of its type in the lower South. The William P. Russell and Company sash factory in Charleston, South Carolina, was described as one of the largest in the United States; yet its gross annual production of $30,000 was only about one-fourth as great as that of Brown's factory. Indeed, the combined annual production of six such plants in South Carolina was less than that of the New Orleans Sash Factory by $10,000. None of the contemporary factories in Alabama, Georgia, or Florida were comparable in size.[47]

During January, 1858, the sash factory lost its foreman, S. L. Williams, who died of tuberculosis. He was replaced by J. L. Martin at the same annual salary of $1,200 that Williams had received. Martin came to the sash factory with the best recommendations, and Paul informed Solomon at Natchez that "we hope to be able to do work in a very superior style" as a result of the change in shop management. In this instance the expectations of Key and Paul were fully realized. Martin proved to be an unusually competent factory manager, and he remained in charge of production until the Civil War ended the building boom in New Orleans and closed the sash factory.[48]

The history of the New Orleans Sash Factory in the last half of the 1850's was a remarkable success story. In this period the annual sale of doors, sashes, openings of various types, stair case material, and other building supplies manufactured by this plant increased from $25,000 to $129,000, a gain of more than 500 per cent. During 1855, the gross sales of the factory were less than a third as large as those of the lumber yard and no more than two thirds those of the sawmill. By the close of 1860, however, the sash factory was grossing 50 per cent more than the combined sales of the sawmill and the lumber yard and was accordingly responsible for most of the profits

[46] Andrew Brown & Co. Journal (1855–60), 140; Balance Sheet of A. Brown & Co., New Orleans, September 30, 1865, Andrew Brown Miscellaneous Financial Papers.

[47] Earnest M. Lander, Jr., "Charleston: Manufacturing Center of the Old South," *Journal of Southern History*, XXVI (August, 1960), 339; *U.S. Census* (1860): *Manufacturing*, 2–12, 57, 61, 73–74, 198–200, 553, 559.

[48] Paul to Solomon, January 9 and 19, 1858, Learned Collection; Andrew Brown & Co. Journal (1855–60), 422 and 498.

earned by Andrew Brown of Natchez and Andrew Brown and Company of New Orleans. It had, in fact, emerged at that date as the most important unit in the lumber business belonging to Brown and Key.[49]

Indeed, during the late 1850's the products of the factory were in such active demand that Key did not have to seek customers; they sometimes presented themselves at the factory in embarrassing numbers. And if Key ever lost any trade to rival sash factories in the city, the Mariposa Mill already mentioned, and the Perserverance Door, Blind, and Sash Factory, established during 1856 by George Purves, an architect and builder, the Scottish lumber dealer was unaware of it.[50] With considerable satisfaction he remarked during the summer of 1860 that "we get all of the very best work to make for the City trade . . . [because] when we have seasoned stuff, there is no factory in the country [which] turns out as good work as we do." [51]

Although it did not show such extraordinary profits during the 1850's as the sash factory, the lumber yard continued the development begun under the guidance of Andrew Brown, Jr. Despite such occasional temporary setbacks to the commerce of the great cotton port of the Old Southwest as overflows and epidemics of cholera and yellow fever, New Orleans grew rapidly during that era. The construction industry prospered along with the suppliers of building materials.[52]

Andrew Brown and Company, while only one of many retail lumber yards in the city, fell heir to perhaps more than its share of customers because of Key's policy of maintaining a large and varied stock of building materials.[53] Cypress lumber continued to be his basic commodity throughout the decade, of course, and the sawmill at Natchez was his principal supplier. Like Andrew Brown, Jr., Key never hesitated to purchase cypress lumber from other wholesalers whenever

[49] Andrew Brown & Co. Journal (1855–60).
[50] For references to those woodworking factories refer to: *De Bow's Review,* XXVII (1859), advertisement section; New Orleans *Times Picayune,* June 16, 1853; May 23, 1855; July 14, 1857; and May 2, 1858. Refer also to *U.S. Census* (*1860*): *Manufacturing,* 199.
[51] Key to John Shanks, August 2, 1860, Learned Collection.
[52] Andrew Brown Journal (1848–53); *ibid.* (1853–60); Andrew Brown & Co. Journal (1855–60).
[53] Key to Dott, May 21, 1850; Key to Solomon, April 15, 1854, January 13, 1855, and July 9, 1857, all in Learned Collection; New Orleans *Times Picayune,* May 2, 1852.

the price was favorable.[54] He also bought white pine from the upper Mississippi Valley, which New Orleans contractors used interchangeably with cypress.[55] In fact, Brown and Key regularly received by flatboat from Pittsburgh large shipments of white pine lumber cut to order by their old business associates McQuewan & Douglas.[56] On the other hand, Key seldom stocked Southern yellow pine because lumber yards like those of Simpson and Dorr, and Nicol and Pooley were connected with sawmills on the Gulf Coast of Mississippi, Alabama, and Florida and could obtain this commodity cheaper than Key.[57] With the passing of the years, Key ascertained that maintaining stocks of walnut, cherry, cedar, mahogany, and other fine woods used in finishing the interiors of expensive buildings was particularly profitable.[58] Moreover, contractors who dealt with the sash factory were inclined to purchase lumber from Andrew Brown and Company for the sake of convenience. Hence, the sash factory proved to be an important attraction for the lumber yard as well as a source of profit from its own operations.

Key, during the 1850's, like Andrew Brown, Jr., during the 1840's, was continually handicapped by his chronic inability to maintain an adequate supply of cypress lumber of the dimensions, quality, and degree of seasoning preferred by New Orleans contractors.[59] Working in his favor and against the interests of some of his larger competitors was the builders' common dislike of yellow pine because of its tendency to split and warp and its flammable qualities.[60] White pine from the North stood higher in the estimation of the building trade, but cypress was still acknowledged to be the most suitable building

[54] Andrew Brown & Co. Journal (1855–60), January 7–28, 1856; Andrew Brown & Co. Journal (1855–60), 170, 180–81, 213, and 371; Key to Dott, May 25, 1850.

[55] Key to Dott, March 5 and June 29, 1850; New Orleans *Times Picayune*, February 20, 1853.

[56] Andrew Brown & Co. Journal (1855–60), 73, 126, 191, 461, and 482; Andrew Brown & Co. Cash Book (1857–65), 11. Key to Solomon, December 15, 1855, June 21 and December 16, 1856, both in Learned Collection.

[57] Andrew Brown & Co. Journal (1855–60), 109, 213, 496; New Orleans *Times Picayune*, June 1, 1858, June 21 and July 2, 1859, and August 1, 1860; Key to Shanks, May 22, 1860; Key to Solomon, February 20, 1855, and December 6, 1856; Paul to Solomon, January 19, 1858, correspondence in Learned Collection.

[58] Key to Solomon, April 15, 1854, Learned Collection; New Orleans *Times Picayune*, November 8, 1853.

[59] Key to Dott, May 14, 1850; Key to Solomon, January 9, 1854, both in Learned Collection.

[60] Key to Dott, July 6, 1856, *ibid.*

material for the lower Mississippi Valley. Andrew Brown's sawmill at Natchez, the principal source of cypress planking for Key's lumber yard, usually was able to obtain cypress logs of high quality from the valley of the Yazoo River; its machinery was carefully serviced and was of the most modern type; and it possessed the advantages of superior management and a stable, well-trained labor force of Negro slaves. Because of these factors, Brown generally manufactured cypress lumber second to none in quality, and the reputation of the New Orleans lumber yard benefitted accordingly. On the other hand, Brown seldom was able to stack his lumber in the mill yard long enough for it to become properly dried. The lumber manufacturer often had to load his flatboats with planking carried directly from the saw.[61] In Key's view, this practice was most unfortunate, for dry lumber sold more readily and at higher prices than did green lumber.[62]

At the root of Key's supply problem was his success as a salesman. From the beginning of the decade until the sawmill was greatly enlarged in 1859 he was able to dispose of much more lumber than Brown could manufacture. During 1853 the senior partner shipped 1,400,000 feet to the New Orleans lumber yard; yet, Key had to buy additional stock elsewhere to meet the requirements of his customers. In order to make up the deficit, Brown bought cypress lumber in large quantities from sawmills on the Yazoo River, and his flatboat crews delivered it to the lumber yard. But with the passing of years Key was forced to turn increasingly to alternate sources for lumber as his business outgrew the capacity of the Natchez mill. He made such purchases as he could from flatboats reaching the city. In times of emergency, which became frequent after 1855, he had to buy heavily from other yards in New Orleans and from mills as far away as Pensacola. Yet, even by going to these lengths, Key was not always able to meet the minimum needs of the New Orleans Sash Factory.[63]

Uncertainties of Mississippi River transportation also complicated Key's problems. Both high and low water stages of the river could cut off his supply of lumber from Natchez. When the river was at flood stage, swift currents made flatboating lumber from Natchez to

[61] *Ibid.*, April 13, 1850; Key to Solomon, August 6, 1853, and December 27, 1856; Key to Andrew Brown, January 18, 1851, all in Learned Collection.

[62] Key to Solomon, March 4 and April 12, 1856; Key to Dott, April 13, 1850, both in Learned Collection.

[63] Refer to the journals of Andrew Brown of Natchez and Andrew Brown & Co.

New Orleans hazardous and sometimes impossible. Low water, occurring usually during the summer and fall months, also produced difficult conditions for flatboatmen. Weak currents, sandbars, and snags worked the crews very hard at sweeps and windlass, and subtropical heat and mosquitoes rendered them subject to a wide variety of diseases. At the destination, unloading the cargo became tedious and costly when the river level was down. Because of these difficulties, Key could never expect to receive a steady flow of lumber from Natchez throughout the building season, even when the mill was hard at work. At times he was forced to resort to hauling small quantities of lumber from Natchez by steamboat, paying rates that were regarded as prohibitively high by usual standards.[64]

Because the principal markets for Andrew Brown of Natchez as well as Andrew Brown and Company were in New Orleans, Key was saddled with most of the responsibility for settling the financial affairs of both branches of the partnership. Moreover, a greater part of the sales made by the sawmill at Natchez and the lumber yard in New Orleans were credit transactions, as were purchases of logs by Brown and lumber by Key. The New Orleans Sash Factory was the exception to the rule until 1857, disposing of its wares only for cash. After that date, when a new sash factory entered the market, the rapidly growing sales of the factory were handled in the same fashion as the products of the lumber yard. As a result, Key spent much of his working life collecting debts owed the company and seeking short-term loans from banks, commission houses, building contractors, and business acquaintances with which to meet maturing obligations. He and Brown preferred to invest most of their profits in slaves who were to work in the lumber yard, sawmill, and on the rafts and flatboats, rather than retain these funds for working capital as modern businessmen would advise. A penalty for this choice was a never-ending drain on the partnership treasury caused by interest payments on loans ranging from 8 to 10 per cent.[65]

[64] Key to Dott, July 21, 1849, and March 31, 1850; Key to John C. Brown, June 29 and September 2, 1850; Key to Solomon, March 21, 1857; Key to Shanks, September 22, 1860, all in Learned Collection. Refer also to the journals of Andrew Brown of Natchez.

[65] The financial arrangements of the manufacturing and merchandising divisions of the firm are recorded in the journals of Andrew Brown of Natchez, and Andrew Brown & Co. For sample references to the problem of financing, refer to Key to Dott, June 11, 1850; Key to Solomon, July 14, 1857; Paul to Key, January 9, 1866; Key to Shanks, November 24, 1860, all in Learned Collection.

During the 1850's, a period when wages of both skilled and unskilled white workers were on the upgrade, Brown and Key believed that they were pursuing the most economical course by purchasing slaves. Brown, himself, was so confident about the wisdom of their policy that he invested substantial additional funds of his own in Negroes which he hired to the mill at the going rate for whites. During this period of cotton prosperity the price of slaves rose so high that the increase in the value of the partnership's human assets undoubtedly offset some of the losses from interest charges on borrowed money. On the other hand, Key was about as hard pressed for funds during good times as in bad (in prosperous periods Brown spent huge sums lavishly for timber and slaves), and he could recognize one from the other only by balancing the books and watching the lumber move out of his yard. Under these conditions, it is not surprising that Key always appeared close to nervous collapse. Brown, who was relatively free from the fiscal annoyances of their lumber business, enjoyed better health and peace of mind, and lived to much more advanced age than his nephew.[66]

Regardless of the wear and tear imposed on Key's nerves by the frustrations of his profession, business in his New Orleans lumber yard was very good indeed during the 1850's, especially as the gross sales of the yard rose from $58,000 in 1855 to $77,000 in 1860. Even during the panic year of 1857–58, the building trade in New Orleans remained busy, and Andrew Brown and Company sold $61,000 worth of lumber. When the proceeds of the sash factory were included, the record of Andrew Brown and Company was even more impressive. Gross sales rose in an almost straight line from $83,000 in 1855 to $155,000 in 1859, and then bolted upward to $200,000 in 1860. Net profits moved in parallel fashion. From a low point of $7,000 in 1854, the profits of the New Orleans firm rose to $20,000 in 1858, and $32,000 in 1860.[67]

[66] Refer to the journals of the Natchez and New Orleans divisions of the company.

[67] Refer to the journals and balance sheets of the two divisions of the company.

7

Manufacturing Cypress Lumber

W HILE Key was fighting nervous breakdown and bringing in spectacular profits in New Orleans, Andrew Brown was concentrating on the relatively uncomplicated task of manufacturing cypress lumber and sending it downriver in the largest possible quantities. A succession of capable sawmill managers during the 1850's—Andrew Dott, Henry S. Solomon, John C. Brown, and John Shanks—virtually freed him from the daily routine of the mill. Under their supervision, the Natchez plant functioned so smoothly that Brown was able to take extended trips to the North without undue anxiety about affairs at Magnolia Vale. The lumberman as a rule contented himself with regular inspections of his organization during this period, intervening in person only when decisions involving substantial sums of money, such as purchasing slaves or machinery, were to be made. Indeed, Brown's principal service to the partnership during the 1850's, aside from planning the remodeling of the mill, was securing a supply of cypress timber for the company.

Because of Key's large retail lumber trade in New Orleans, Brown was able to work the sawmill throughout the year as a matter of policy, stopping the machinery only when compelled to do so by mechanical difficulties or shortages of timber. In fact, the saws were not brought to rest even once during the 1850's because of lack of sales, for the lumber yard was disposing of more cypress than the Natchez mill could cut. Yet, despite Brown's determination to keep the mill operating at full capacity, he and his managers were unable to avoid frequent halts. Wrought iron and cast iron machinery wore out quickly under the strain of continuous operation, and replacing damaged parts was difficult since very little machinery was standardized and spare parts were seldom obtainable locally. Consequently, most of Brown's replacement parts had to be fabricated on special order by foundries at Natchez or New Orleans.[1]

The boilers of the main power plant in the Natchez sawmill were particular sources of trouble before the days of welding. In this period, steam boilers were made of rolled sheet iron plate, curved to the proper shape, and fastened to a framework by iron rivets. Although both the materials and the workmanship which went into this equipment were of uncertain quality, there was no satisfactory method for testing the strength of finished products before they left the factory. Upon being put into operation, boilers were judged to be up to standard if they neither exploded nor leaked steam excessively. The best of iron boilers lost their strength with usage, and engineers measured the rate of deterioration by the increase in leakage of steam. If new rivets failed to make boilers steam-tight again, then replacements were considered necessary. At Brown's sawmill, steam engine boilers were repaired annually and replaced about every five years.

Brown's main engine of one hundred horsepower was supplied with steam by a battery of three large boilers, and replacing them required a considerable investment. The lumberman, thrifty businessman that he was, was always anxious to minimize his operating costs. Hence he customarily purchased used boilers to replace his burned-out units. During 1853, for example, Brown obtained three second-hand boilers from Leeds and Company of New Orleans for a thousand dollars, making his selection in person from a set of four boilers which Leeds was selling on commission. These boilers, which had originally powered a steam towboat, were of the double-flue variety, twenty-four feet long and forty-two inches in diameter. Although Leeds naturally was unwilling to guarantee the condition of the used boilers, Brown nevertheless was able to arrange for them to be renovated in Leeds's workshops at his own risk and expense. The machinery manufacturing company then installed the re-worked boilers in the sawmill at Natchez, using experts dispatched from New Orleans for that purpose. Leeds charged Brown five hundred dollars for repairs and installa-

[1] The journals of Andrew Brown of Natchez contain many references to repairs of machinery. Unless cited otherwise, all journals, cash books, etc., referred to in this chapter are located in the Rufus F. Learned Collection.

tion, bringing the total cost of the new equipment to fifteen hundred dollars.[2]

The money Brown saved by his decision not to buy new boilers was soon dissipated. A short time after the mill resumed operation, one of the re-worked boilers exploded, fortunately injuring none of the crew. Key made an exhaustive search of machine shops in New Orleans, but finally reported to the senior partner that a suitable replacement was not to be found in that city.[3] Brown thus was left with no option but to reconstruct the damaged boiler on the sawmill site with the aid of boilermakers from New Orleans, who were loaned to him by Leeds and Company. The second rebuilding of the old steamboat boiler was finally completed successfully after several months of hard labor.[4] In the meanwhile, the sawmill necessarily remained idle. As a result, a loss of lumber production arising from the accident was far more injurious to the firm than the actual cost of the repairs and, in fact, caused the Natchez division of the lumber firm to show a loss of $4,600 for 1853, a most unusual occurrence in the history of the sawmill.[5]

His unpleasant experience with re-worked boilers alerted Brown to the physical and financial hazards inherent in second-hand steam-powered machinery, and he resolved to purchase nothing except the best in future. With this principle in mind, Key and Brown, as already mentioned, equipped their New Orleans sash factory with the most modern power plant and woodworking machinery obtainable in the Crescent City; and Brown subsequently followed this same plan while remodeling and enlarging the Natchez sawmill during the late 1850's.

During the process of expanding the capacity of his plant in 1858 and 1859, Brown ordered most of his new sawmilling machinery from the Ottawa Iron Works, which was located in Ferrysburg, Ottawa County, Michigan.[6] This machinery manufacturing establishment was owned by William M. Ferry, Jr., who was supplying the lumber industry of the Great Lakes region with various models of high- and low-pressure steam engines, circular and muley sawmills of the latest type, and machines especially designed for sawing wooden siding for

[2] Andrew Brown Journal (1853–60), 21 and 35; William I. Key to Henry S. Solomon, August 20, 1853, Learned Collection.

[3] Key to Solomon, August 20, 1853, Learned Collection.

[4] Andrew Brown Journal (1853–60), 81.

[5] Ibid., 68.

[6] Allegan (Mich.) Journal, March 8, 1858.

houses. During 1858 Brown contracted with this firm for an "Automatic Log Mill" incorporating a circular saw which Ferry had recently invented and patented, paying the manufacturer eight hundred dollars for the unit and for the right to operate it. The Ottawa Iron Works delivered the Ferry mill at Natchez during April, 1859.[7] Ferry, who was anxious to ensure that the machinery was properly installed and adjusted, sent Manuel Sparling, one of his workmen, south to Natchez with the shipment. In accordance with an understanding with Ferry, Sparling was paid by Brown at the rate of two dollars a day while he was setting up the Ferry mill.[8] Brown was favorably impressed by the skill of the Northern workman and even more pleased with his wages, for he was paying another millwright from New Orleans three dollars a day for the same kind of work.[9] Sparling, instead of returning to Michigan when his job was completed, accepted Brown's offer of a permanent position in his organization at the higher Natchez rate and subsequently remained on his payroll until 1867.[10] A warm relationship also developed between the Michigan sawmill manufacturer and his satisfied Mississippi customer, and Ferry upon occasion recruited sawyers in Michigan to work in Brown's sawmill at Natchez.[11]

In the process of updating his sawmill, Brown installed two machines of St. Louis manufacture for making cypress shingles in addition to the Ferry circular sawmill. One of these was a "McGeorge's Excelsior Shingle Machine," which had an advertised capacity of sixty to eighty shingles a minute and which was selling at retail for $200.[12] The other machine, of Yerger patent, cost twice as much.[13] Finally, during October, 1859, Brown received delivery of a third machine for cutting siding planks from the Ottawa Iron Works, paying Ferry $360.50 for this last item of woodworking equipment.[14]

During this same period, Brown increased the capacity of the saw-

---

[7] William M. Ferry, Jr., to Andrew Brown, June 2, 1858, Learned Collection.
[8] *Ibid.*, May 14, 1859.
[9] Andrew Brown Journal (1853–60), 662.
[10] Andrew Brown Journal (1861–70), September 16, 1864, and July 30, 1870.
[11] Ferry to Andrew Brown, August 1, 1859, and March 8, 1860, Learned Collection.
[12] Mobile *Register*, January 14, 1860; E. Barbarous to Andrew Brown, April 8, 1859, Learned Collection.
[13] Andrew Brown Cash Book (1856–64), 154; Barbarous to Andrew Brown, April 8, 1859, Learned Collection.
[14] Andrew Brown Journal (1853–60), 552.

mill to forty thousand feet per day by replacing the gangsaws with four of the so-called muley type.[15] In this conversion each frame, which contained a gang of four mill saws working up and down between the saw gates like a window sash, was replaced by a single reciprocating mill saw of special pattern. The blade of the muley saw was thicker than the usual sash mill saws, and tapered slightly in cross section from the points of its teeth toward the base of the saw. Muley saws operated at much higher speeds than gangsaws, making from four to six hundred strokes per minute; and they were reputed to cut to closer dimensions than the more familiar type. Like a circular sawmill, the muley mill made a single high-speed cut with each forward motion of the carriage, but it possessed an advantage over the circular sawmill in that it could handle logs of much greater diameter than a mill equipped with a single circular saw.[16]

At this time Brown also replaced the boilers of his principal steam engine, which had been installed in 1853, to complete the renovation program. When the additions to the building were erected and the last of the new machinery bolted into place, the cost of the modernization of the establishment exceeded $15,000. With its increased capacity, Brown's sawmill became comparable to the largest class of sawmills serving the export lumber trade at such ports as Charleston, Savannah, and Mobile. Its theoretical daily capacity of forty thousand feet exceeded the thirty thousand feet capacity of the Fig Island mill at Savannah and the Starke mill at Mobile and almost equalled the outputs of the large and modern Vale Royal mill at Savannah and the Wappo mill at Charleston.[17]

Soon after finishing the remodeling of the sawmill, Brown discovered to his dismay that he had not eliminated his mechanical problems. During June, 1860, the center boiler of the main steam engine

[15] Ibid., 554; Testimony of R. F. Learned, August 26, 1886, Estate of Andrew Brown vs. U.S.A. (a copy is in the possession of Howard Peabody, Natchez, Mississippi).

[16] Bale, Woodworking Machinery, 54; Rodney C. Loehr, "Saving the Kerf: The Introduction of the Band Saw Mill," Agricultural History XXIII (1949), 168. An illustration of a muley sawmill and a nearly contemporary description is given in J. Richards, "Selections from a Treatise on the Construction and Operation of Woodworking Machines (1872)," Forest History, IX (January, 1966), 21–22.

[17] Andrew Brown Journal (1853–60), 554; Augusta (Ga.) Chronicle and Sentinel, October 11, 1859; Mobile Advertiser, April 19, 1857; Savannah Republican, February 19, May 15, and June 29, 1848, and January 29, 1852.

exploded with fearful effect, tearing a hole five feet long in the side of the cylinder and drenching a Negro fireman with scalding water. The unfortunate workman died in agony a few hours after the accident, thereby gaining the unhappy distinction of being the only fatal casualty in the sawmill proper during Brown's lengthy career in the lumber business.[18]

Although Brown was occasionally plagued by mechanical problems during the 1850's, his most serious losses of lumber production resulted from unfavorable river conditions. The most important incident of this nature happened during the winter and spring months of 1855–56 at a time when the Mississippi River was at an extremely low stage. During the spring of 1855, Brown had dispatched four large flatboats containing approximately 950,000 lineal feet of cypress lumber to the yard at New Orleans. In June, however, the water level subsided so far that he was unable to arrange for any more deliveries that year. Making matters even worse for the lumber business, the river failed to rise as usual during the following winter and spring, and Brown was consequently unable to make his next delivery until February, 1857. In the meanwhile, the sawmill at Natchez was forced to remain closed for lack of raw material because there was no practical method of transporting sawlogs over exposed mudbanks to the end of the logway.[19]

Because low water also halted rafting of logs from the Yazoo Valley during this year when there was no "float," Brown was unable to provide sufficient employment for his slaves either in the mill or in the swamps. Being a businessman of considerable ingenuity, the lumberman hired many of his Negroes to employers in other types of business and in this fashion enabled them at least to earn their keep. The captain of the steamboat *Natchez*, for example, contracted with Brown for the services of several of the sawmill Negroes, paying fifty-four dollars a month and board for the head raftsman, James Matthews, and forty dollars a month each for several other laborers. By contrast, white workmen were receiving fifty dollars a month on board the vessel.[20]

Brown's sawmill Negroes on the *Natchez* appeared to enjoy their

[18] Natchez *Courier*, June 26, 1860.
[19] Key to Solomon, May 26, 1855; F. H. West to Rufus F. Learned, June 23, 1881, both in Learned Collection.
[20] Key to Solomon, October 20, 1855, Learned Collection.

temporary change of occupation and took fullest advantage of their unusual opportunities for getting into mischief. Jacob, who ordinarily fired the boilers and operated the steam engine at the sawmill, on one occasion, while the vessel was docked at New Orleans unloading cotton, managed to slip away unobserved and lose himself in the crowd on the wharf. He then reveled in idleness for several days until Key finally caught up with him and "administered some wholesome medicine . . . that may be of service to the gentleman." Jacob, nevertheless, had the last laugh on Key. While loose in the city, the Natchez fireman "got bit by some of his private amours," as Key described it; and his resulting poor health kept him on light duties for a time.[21]

Excessively high water sometimes caused trouble at the mill also, although the effects were not nearly so crippling as those resulting from the low water of 1855–56. The flood of 1853 which destroyed Brown's planing shop provides a typical illustration. Brown, whose wife had died in early 1853, was away on a lengthy trip to the North to recover from his grief when the rising waters of the Mississippi washed away a section of the mill's breakwater. Key, upon learning of the disaster, reminded Solomon, who had been left in charge at Natchez, that the breakwater was "a very important safeguard to the stability & permanence of the whole sawmill property" and instructed him to assign top priority to making the essential repairs, even to stopping the mill and using the entire mill crew on the job if that became necessary. The competent Solomon, as usual, handled the emergency to the full satisfaction of the junior partner.[22]

A similar but more costly episode occurred during 1858. In May of that year the Mississippi River rose high enough to flood almost all of Natchez-under-the-Hill. According to the editor of the *Free Trader* "one square of Rear Levee Street, the one next to the side of the Hill, and the two squares of Silver Street is all the space that's left out of water." Passengers were able to board steamboats by way of a temporary "causeway thrown up from Ray's store to the Upper Wharf-boat, and platforms from the Lower Wharf-boat to Smyth and Reynolds." Brown's mill, being located on higher ground, was not inundated, but even more of his breakwater was washed away than in 1853.[23]

[21] *Ibid.*

[22] Key to Solomon, August 2 and 20, 1853; Andrew Brown Journal (1853–60), 82.

[23] Natchez *Free Trader*, May 25, 1858.

The damage to the breakwater caused by the flood of 1858 was so extensive that many months were required for rebuilding the missing portions. Some of the merchants owning property below the bluffs learned from the flood that Brown's jetty protected their lots as well as his sawmill, and they accordingly petitioned the Natchez city council for public assistance in repairing the breakwater. The editor of the Natchez *Courier* supported the petition, commenting that the breakwater "originally built at Mr. Brown's individual expense . . . has saved not merely 'Under the Hill' but probably much of the Bluff itself." In the opinion of the journalist the city was morally obligated to participate in "rebuilding and extending the Breakwater, which the flood of the last two years has so seriously damaged." [24] The frugal city authorities after investigation, however, declined to extend financial aid to Brown at the taxpayer's expense, believing no doubt that the sawmill owner would complete the task unassisted.[25] If so, they were not disappointed for Brown and Key did finish the repairs during 1860.[26]

The sawmill at Natchez, unlike the New Orleans lumber yard, enjoyed its longest period of uninterrupted prosperity between 1848 and 1853. Throughout this five-year interval Andrew Brown's annual gross sales of lumber exceeded $50,000. During the next five years the annual totals were well below this average, ranging between $20,-000 and $40,000. The lowest point for the decade came during 1856 while the mill was closed for many months by low water in the Mississippi. Eventually, prosperity returned during the closing years of the decade, and the annual gross sales at the Natchez mill ranged from $60,000 to $70,000 during 1859 and 1860, despite production delays occasioned by remodeling the building and machinery.[27]

An additional indication of the rate of activity at the Natchez sawmill is provided by records containing the cost of timber consumed annually. From a minimum of $10,000 in 1849, the yearly cost climbed to a peak of $27,000 in 1854. During the ensuing year no more than $9,000 worth of logs were manufactured into lumber because of the closure of the mill. With the mill working at full capacity again, from

[24] Natchez *Courier*, November 16, 1859.
[25] *Ibid.*, December 15, 1859.
[26] Andrew Brown Journal (1853–60), 543.
[27] The gross sales of the sawmill division are recorded in the journals of Andrew Brown of Natchez and in the balance sheets of Andrew Brown of Natchez, Andrew Brown Miscellaneous Financial Papers.

$12,000 to $14,000 worth of sawlogs were utilized each year during the 1856–58 period. Once more the total fell below $10,000 during 1859 as a result of remodeling in the mill, but rose the next year to nearly $40,000, an amount double that of any previous twelve months. The sharp increase at the beginning of the new decade obviously was due to the greatly enlarged capacity of the mill.[28]

Profits earned by the lumber manufacturing division of the partnership fluctuated in parallel fashion with both the gross sales of the sawmill and with the cost of timber consumed. During 1849 the sawmill produced net earnings of $36,000.[29] The top of the rising profit curve was reached during 1852 when the partnership of Brown and Key realized $45,000.[30] From 1853 through 1855, the mill averaged less than $3,000 a year as a result of a rash of mechanical difficulties, adverse river conditions, epidemics of disease, and depression in the building industry.[31] After this date, however, earnings improved gradually through 1857, when a plateau lasting through 1861 was established at the $20,000 level.[32]

During the latter half of the fifties, Brown decided for various reasons to contract with Yazoo River sawmills for cypress lumber, in this fashion supplementing his own output which had consistently fallen below requirements of the New Orleans lumber yard. In this period quite a large number of small portable circular sawmills were being operated along the Yazoo and the Big Black rivers. Their products were acceptable to builders in New Orleans, although of much poorer quality than lumber turned out by larger Mississippi River establishments. Some large mills near Yazoo City were exceptions to the rule as they were equipped with gangsaws, and could accordingly produce boards comparable to those sawed by Brown at Natchez.[33]

During 1854, when the Natchez plant was still closed down, Brown purchased a cargo of lumber from James Johnston & Company who owned a large sawmill at Point Industry across the river from Yazoo

[28] The figures for consumption of logs are included in the journals of Andrew Brown of Natchez.

[29] Andrew Brown Ledger (1848–53), 72.

[30] Balance sheet of Andrew Brown of Natchez, 1852, Andrew Brown Miscellaneous Financial Papers.

[31] Andrew Brown Journal (1853–60), 68, 232, and 298.

[32] Balance sheets of Andrew Brown of Natchez, 1858, 1859, 1860, and 1861, Andrew Brown Miscellaneous Financial Papers.

[33] For information on these Delta sawmills refer to Yazoo City *Yazoo Democrat*, July 2 and 16, 1851, July 27, 1853; Natchez *Courier*, August 17, 1858.

City. Key was dissatisfied with the quality of plank in this shipment and informed Johnston of it in no uncertain terms. When the Yazoo City sawmiller opened negotiations with Brown in regard to a second shipment of eighty thousand feet, he hastened to assure the Natchez lumberman that this lot of plank would be much superior to the last. "We are edging closer and having less sap on the plank. . . . the planks is well piled [stacked so that it can dry out] as it is sawed. . . . we think that this lumber is good enoughf not to have any [k]nocked of[f] in measurement." He offered to sell the shipment to Brown for $25 per thousand plus $50 for the flatboat on condition that "not so much [be k]nocked of[f] as Mr Kees did on the other." [34] Brown eventually accepted Johnston's offer, and in accordance with the usual custom the Yazoo lumberman thereupon availed himself of Brown's facilities in New Orleans to place orders for goods and services he needed with business firms in the city. Brown also accommodated Johnston by paying his bills, and then deducting the payments from the amount Brown owed him for lumber. A year later, he still owed Brown $7.45 when the accounts were balanced; and he wrote to promise payment of this small sum at the first opportunity.[35]

Although Brown would have liked to contract with Johnston for his entire lumber output, the latter chose to market his lumber in New Orleans where he had no difficulty in obtaining customers.[36] After enjoying the benefits of rising prices during the late 1850's, however, Johnston, like so many of his fellows, was overtaken by disaster. On July 30, 1860, his mill caught fire and burned to the ground along with all the lumber in the yard, totally wiping out Johnston's investment of $25,-000.[37]

Because the sawmill at Natchez had been closed by extraordinarily low water in the Mississippi during 1856, Brown had to buy cypress for the lumber yard at New Orleans wherever he could find suitable planking during the next season. In February, 1857, for example, he bought 155,000 feet from Isaac K. Mayfield, of Mayfield & Company, for $3,866.[38] Somewhat later he contracted to take all the

---

[34] James Johnston to Andrew Brown, May 14, 1854, Learned Collection.
[35] *Ibid.*, July 20, 1855.
[36] Key to Solomon, April 12, 1856, Learned Collection.
[37] New Orleans *Times Picayune*, August 1, 1860.
[38] Andrew Brown Journal (1853–60), 312.

lumber Mayfield produced in his Page circular sawmill at Hamrick's Landing on the Yazoo River.[39] On March 1, Brown made an additional purchase of a flatboat load from "M. Jules' Mill, Yazoo," for use in the New Orleans sash factory, paying $25 a thousand for the lumber.[40]

Mayfield apparently was delighted to resolve his outstanding financial and merchandising problems through his contract with Brown. He had been in such bad shape while negotiations with the Natchez lumberman were under way that he was unable to pay the freight on two circular saws (one 64 inches in diameter, the other 32) which he had ordered from George Page & Company of Baltimore.[41] He also had to put off various creditors in Vicksburg by persuading them that his contract with Brown would assure the payment of his bills.[42] Obviously relieved at being able to call on Brown for what he needed, Mayfield wrote for five hundred pounds of bacon and a barrel of lard oil on April 20, 1857, reporting joyously that "I am sawing as wide and pretty stuff as a forty-eight inch [circular] saw can make. I commenced to haul your lumber out to the river this morning and will be able to carry out 250,000 feet by the middle of next month." [43] Two weeks later, he wrote in the same exalted mood that he was "getting on with my mill finely," and that he expected to have sawed four hundred thousand feet by the time Brown got the first flatboat load of lumber. "I've hired a man who has been running a circular mill thirteen years," he concluded, humorously, "and I am satisfied (as his name is Brown & I sell to Brown) that I will have things done up (Brown) brown." [44] When Key examined the first shipment of Mayfield's lumber to reach New Orleans, however, he failed to show much enthusiasm. Instead, Key complained to Solomon that Mayfield's plank was hardly better than refuse.[45] Yet, despite his objections, Key had to admit that Mayfield's poor quality lumber was better than none in time of shortage; and he subsequently disposed of an additional three hundred thousand feet of Mayfield's plank, as well as seventy

---

[39] A. B. Reading to Andrew Brown, March 31, 1857, Learned Collection.
[40] Andrew Brown Journal (1855–60), 156.
[41] George Page & Co. to Isaac K. Mayfield, April 4, 1857; Isaac K. Mayfield to Andrew Brown, April 20, 1857, both in Learned Collection.
[42] Reading to Andrew Brown, March 31, 1857, Learned Collection.
[43] Mayfield to Andrew Brown, April 20, 1857, ibid.
[44] Ibid., May 7, 1857.
[45] Key to Solomon, May 23, 1857, Learned Collection.

thousand feet from two small Yazoo mills belonging to D. W. Hendricks and Purnel & Buck.[46]

Even though Brown's sawmill at Natchez was able to resume normal operations during the spring of 1857, his need for supplementary sources for cypress did not diminish. The last two years of the 1850's witnessed the development of a building boom affecting nearly all of the lower Mississippi Valley, and the lumber yards in New Orleans were hard pressed to supply the demand for building materials. Key felt the pinch like his competitors and accordingly purchased lumber of virtually all kinds at every opportunity. At his urging Brown enlarged the plant at Natchez and bought all the lumber procurable from the Yazoo sawmills. In April, 1858, for example, he obtained 155,000 feet from a mill belonging to William D. Whitney and another 78,000 feet from D. W. Hendricks.[47] During June, Brown received a second shipment from Hendricks totaling 233,000 feet for which he paid the sawmill operator $5,700.[48] Whitney and Hendricks formed a partnership during 1860 and contracted with Brown for the total output of their sawmills.[49] How much they sold to Brown and Key that year is not clear from the records, but they delivered one shipment of 202,000 feet at the wholesale price of $20 per thousand.[50]

As the antebellum period drew to a close, Andrew Brown looked to the future with apparently well-justified optimism. All the economic signs forecast increased prosperity for the lower Mississippi Valley. New Orleans, the metropolis of the southwestern cotton kingdom, was gaining in wealth and population, and the building trades were benefitting accordingly. By the end of 1859, Brown was prepared to share in the general prosperity as never before. Through his arrangements with sawmills in the Yazoo Valley and the modernization of his plant at Natchez he was in a position to supply building contractors with an almost unlimited supply of lumber. As in 1839, however, his expectations were to be frustrated by unforeseen and unavoidable events—depression in the first instance, disruption of the Union in the second.

[46] Andrew Brown Day Book (1856–58), 197 and 202; Andrew Brown Journal (1853–60), 339; Andrew Brown & Co. Journal (1855–60), 213.
[47] Andrew Brown Day Book (1856–58), 330.
[48] Andrew Brown & Co. Journal (1855–60), 284.
[49] D. W. Hendricks to Andrew Brown [no date], 1860, Learned Collection.
[50] Andrew Brown Journal (1853–60), 674. Refer also to C. Harris to Andrew Brown, September 3, 1860, Learned Collection.

8

Wage and Slave Labor
In Andrew Brown's Lumber Firm

BEFORE 1850 Andrew Brown and his son filled the executive post in their various enterprises themselves. Brown superintended the operations of the sawmill, procured timber, and handled the transportation of logs and lumber. As mentioned earlier, his son acted as sales manager for the parent company as well as general manager of the lumber outlet in New Orleans. Since neither of the Browns required much assistance in carrying out his administrative duties, they did not employ junior executives in either division. Instead, the younger lumberman even handled the task of bookkeeping for the New Orleans subsidiary in addition to selling, collecting, and borrowing money for both divisions of the company.

Because of the greater complexity of his assignment, Andrew Brown, Sr., was less able to dispense with white clerical employees than his son. As the business was organized during the 1840's and 1850's, a clerk was an essential cog in the machinery of the sawmill, for records had to be kept of cash and credit sales, expenditures, wages of employees, lumber shipments, timber used by the mill, and loans and repayments. Hence, a succession of sawmill clerks worked in the mill office after Brown enlarged the establishment during 1835. Brown gave close personal attention to the company's records, and his business success was due in part to his appreciation of the value of detailed bookkeeping.

Considering their work to be of vital importance, Brown naturally chose with great care the employees who would handle his money, and his long history as an employer testified that he was skilled at judging competence and character. Brown selected promising young men to serve as sawmill clerks, supervised their training himself, and paid them well. The schooling in the art of commerce they received while in the employ of the lumber company must have been thorough, for several of Brown's white collar workers subsequently became successful Natchez businessmen. To cite a few examples, Brown hired A. J. Postlethwaite, William I. Key, and Andrew Brown, Jr., at salaries of from $75 to $80 a month during the 1840's. Within the decade, Postlethwaite had become a Natchez dry goods merchant; Key, first a dry goods merchant and then a junior partner to Brown in the lumber business; and Andrew Brown, Jr., a spectacularly efficient assistant to his father.[1]

The list of Horatio Alger success stories originating in Brown's sawmill office, however, does not stop here. During 1850, John C. Brown, who was no relative of the sawmill owner, was hired as clerk at a salary of a thousand dollars a year.[2] After working for the lumber company for two years, he went into business for himself, eventually becoming the Natchez representative of the New Orleans cotton factors "Mandeville & McIlhenny."[3] Rufus Learned, a son of Brown's second wife, went into the sawmill during 1857 at $35 a month, rising as he learned the trade to the respectable salary of $75 a month by 1861.[4] As a result of the training he received during this period, Learned was able to go into the sawmill business for himself and later to assume the management of Brown's company in 1866.[5]

While Brown was becoming less active in the management of the sawmill during the early 1850's, Henry S. Solomon emerged at Natchez as his right hand man. Solomon, a carpenter from New Jersey in his twenties, was hired by Brown during the late 1840's.[6] He quickly revealed unusual capacity for leadership to his employer and was accordingly placed in charge of the New Orleans division of the business in the interval between the death of Andrew Brown, Jr., and the

---

[1] Andrew Brown Journal (1840–43), 54, 154–155, 167, 218; Andrew Brown Hands Ledger (1840–41), 2 and 4. Unless otherwise indicated all journals, ledgers, etc., cited in this chapter are located in the Rufus F. Learned Collection.

[2] William I. Key to Andrew Dott, July [?], 1850, Learned Collection; Andrew Brown Journal (1848–53), 313.

[3] Natchez *Courier,* April 3, 1857.

[4] Andrew Brown Journal (1853–60), 371, 553; *ibid.* (1861–70), 81.

[5] Andrew Brown Journal (1861–70), 372.

[6] Andrew Brown Journal (1849–53).

arrival of William I. Key.[7] While he was in New Orleans, it was Solomon who urged Brown and Key to undertake the shipment of lumber to California. After the owners of the company adopted his proposal, Solomon returned to Natchez and played a leading part in preparing a cargo of pre-fabricated houses. Although Andrew Dott, the ambitious sawmill clerk at Natchez at the time, wished to be placed in charge of the venture, Brown selected Solomon to accompany the *Desdemona* as the principal agent of the company.[8] Taking Thomas Seaton, and a few other local carpenters from Natchez with him on the vessel, Solomon made the long voyage to San Francisco. Once there, however, the carpenter from New Jersey was unable to sell his wares at a profit despite his best efforts; and he eventually returned to Natchez to report his failure.[9]

Nevertheless, neither Brown nor Key blamed Solomon for the unfortunate outcome of their speculation, and Brown named him bookkeeper and manager of the sawmill in April, 1853.[10] From that date, he was in almost complete charge of the manufacturing portion of the business until he was incapacitated by tuberculosis during 1859.[11] During these years Solomon was paid a hundred dollars a month, a salary which allowed the bachelor to live comfortably and still save money.[12] In fact, Solomon joined the ranks of Natchez slaveowners in 1857 by purchasing a Negro, Arthur Weldon, from George and Thomas Weldon, the building contractors.[13] Solomon was on such intimate terms with Brown that he spent his last months in the home of his employer, being cared for as though he were a member of the family. In many respects, Solomon filled a void in Brown's life left by the death of his son.[14]

When illness compelled Solomon to leave the sawmill, his place was taken by John Shanks at a salary of $80 per month. Shanks, about whom Key's assistant John Paul said, "but for a little wildness, he

[7] Henry S. Solomon to Andrew Brown, January 20 and March 17, 1849, Learned Collection.

[8] Key to Dott, May 19 and June 20, 1849; Soloman to Dott, January 25, 1850; Solomon to Key, April 25, 1850; Key to Andrew Brown, November 25, 1851, all correspondence in Learned Collection.

[9] Key to Solomon, July 16, 1853, Learned Collection.

[10] Andrew Brown Journal (1853–60), 25.

[11] Andrew Brown Journal (1853–60); Natchez *Courier*, March 10, 1860.

[12] Andrew Brown Journal (1853–60).

[13] *Ibid.*, 211.

[14] Natchez *Courier*, March 10, 1860.

would be a perfect man," had recently passed through a most painful experience.[15] On August 4, 1858, Shanks was assaulted by Osborne Hutchins on the wharfboat at Natchez-under-the-Hill and had received a severe beating. Fearing that his life was still in danger from Hutchins, Shanks returned to his residence and armed himself with a pistol. That evening, about dusk, Shanks encountered Hutchins again, this time in the City Hotel Saloon. Hutchins immediately knocked Shanks to the floor, injuring him painfully. When he was able to rise, Shanks drew his pistol and shot Hutchins who was returning once more to the attack. When Shanks learned that Hutchins had died of his wounds during the night, he surrendered himself to the sheriff immediately. He was bound over to the circuit court by the mayor of Natchez, in his capacity as magistrate, and released on $3,000 bond. The trial took place during the May, 1859, term of court, and the jury found Shanks "not guilty" after deliberating only fifteen minutes. As he left the courtroom a free man, Shanks was approached by the father of the victim, who praised him for his conduct in the affair! Soon afterward Shanks, now something of a local celebrity, was hired by Brown. He served quite effectively as sawmill clerk until the mill was closed down as a result of the depression engendered by the Civil War.[16]

Soon after taking charge of the New Orleans lumber yard during 1849, William Key hired a fellow Scot, John F. Paul, to assist him in the office. Paul had recently returned from Texas where he had served as an officer in the Mexican War. He quickly made himself useful to Key, "particularly in collecting invoices, bills, and [he] relieves me from a great deal of walking," Key reported to Natchez.[17] Over the next few years, the "Apostle," as he sometimes referred to himself, became a trusted intimate as well as assistant manager to Key, drawing a salary of $150 a month. In his employer's absence, Paul carried on the business, even raising loans on behalf of the partnership upon occasion. When Key departed from New Orleans to enter the Confederate army, he left Paul in complete charge of the affairs of the New Orleans division of the Brown and Key partnership. He remained in this position after the war until Brown liquidated all his assets in

[15] John F. Paul to Solomon, May 21, 1859.
[16] Andrew Brown Journal (1853–60); *ibid.* (1861–70); Natchez *Courier*, August 6, 1858, and May 19, 1859; Natchez *Free Trader*, August 6 and 10, 1858.
[17] Key to Dott, November 1, 1849, Learned Collection.

the Crescent City. Like his employers, Paul exemplified the better traits of the *emigré* Scot during the mid-nineteenth century. He was industrious, intelligent, loyal, and brimming over with humor and initiative.[18]

The only skilled workmen regularly employed in antebellum sawmills were sawyers, who ranked socially and financially with carpenters but who fell below machinists and enginewrights on the pay scale. Brown, during most of his career, employed two or more white sawyers at a time, paying his head sawyer as much as the sawmill clerk. During 1835, Brown's engineer and principal sawyer received $80 a month and board, with the latter item calculated at fifty cents a day.[19] This salary was increased to $85 a month during 1836.[20] During 1837, at a time when the building trades in Natchez were booming, Brown hired E. Jones as an engineer at $100 per month and Charles H. Pearsons as a sawyer at the same figure.[21] In Pearsons' case, at least, Brown did not pay for his employee's meals; instead he deducted the cost of board and washing from his account.[22]

With the onset of the depression in late 1839, a high rate of unemployment developed among carpenters and sawmill workers at Natchez, and the wages of sawyers were adversely affected. In June, 1840, Samuel Rose commenced work in Brown's sawmill at the salary of a thousand dollars a year.[23] On February 1, 1843, Rose's compensation was reduced to eight hundred dollars per annum, remaining at the figure until January 1, 1844, when it was restored to the original amount.[24] Francis Reid, a second sawyer, however, was paid at the rate of eight hundred dollars per annum, without room or board.[25] The downward pressure on wages continued to be felt during the mid-forties, and C. S. Ricks was hired on November 22, 1847, as a second sawyer at $60 per month and board (equivalent to $75 without board).[26] Even at this rate, a frugal workman could accumulate property, or so it would seem in the case of Ricks. During February, 1848,

[18] Many letters written by Paul are included in the Learned Collection for the period between 1849 and 1867.
[19] Andrew Brown Journal (1835), October 22, 1835.
[20] Andrew Brown Account Book (1836–40), May 9, 1837.
[21] *Ibid.*, January 21, 1837.
[22] *Ibid.*, February 7, 1837.
[23] Andrew Brown Hands Ledger (1840–41), 6.
[24] Andrew Brown Journal (1843–48), May 31, 1844.
[25] *Ibid.*, July 1, 1845.
[26] Andrew Brown Day Book (1843–48), 302.

this sawyer arranged for Andrew Brown, Jr., to buy a Negro named Anthony in New Orleans for him. Ricks subsequently allowed the Negro to work in the sawmill, with Brown paying for Anthony's services at a rate of fifteen dollars a month plus room and board.[27]

Josiah Rose, younger brother of the head sawyer, joined him in the sawmill during 1847 as an apprentice sawyer, receiving pay at the rate of thirty-three dollars a month. After eight months training the younger Rose received a five dollar a month raise. In November, 1849, he was promoted to the rank of second sawyer, from that time drawing seventy-five dollars a month without board until his death during 1851.[28]

Inasmuch as correspondence from the pen of Southern sawyers of the antebellum period is somewhat rare, the following letter of application addressed to Andrew Brown from Shreveport, Louisiana, on August 10, 1850, is of some historical interest:[29]

> I have taken the liberty of writing you a few lines to ascertain what prospect there is in Natchez for a young man to get into business who is capable of either taking charge of a saw mill or of running Page Patent, or Circuit Saws. I have had considerable experience first in running the saws, and since in keeping them in order, and attending and measuring logs & lumber &c. I have been connected with the Steam Mill of Messrs. Webster & Co. at this place since they started and I presume can remain here as long as I choose. But I am not satisfied with the manner in which business is carried on, nor do I like the Society or the place. If you have any use for me in either capacity, or if you know where I could get a situation by the year, you will confer a favor upon me by informing me, together with some representation of the mill and business and the probable wages &c.
>
> Yours Obt Servant
George Edgerton

Edgerton, however, was not hired by Brown.

Wages of sawyers in Brown's mill did not rise appreciably above the depressed level of the 1840's until the last half of the decade of the 1850's. Thomas L. Jones, from whom Brown bought the planing mill, for example, went to work for the Scot during November 1851, at a yearly salary of $1,100.[30] He was joined by a second sawyer,

[27] Andrew Brown, Jr., to Andrew Brown, February 12, 1848, Learned Collection; Andrew Brown Journal (1843–48), 245.
[28] Andrew Brown Day Book (1848–51), August 17, 1850; Andrew Brown Journal (1843–48), 245; Andrew Brown Receipt Book (1848–58), August 29, 1851.
[29] George Edgerton to Andrew Brown, August 10, 1850, Learned Collection.
[30] Andrew Brown Journal (1848–53), 373.

John Mays, who received the standard wage of sixty dollars a month and board.[31] During 1854, William Brownlee accepted a salary of only fifty-five dollars a month; he was raised, however, a year later to $76.66 per month. Having become a permanent and respected fixture in Brown's organization, Brownlee in 1858 was promoted to the position of head sawyer with a salary of a hundred dollars a month.[32]

As a result of the remodeling and expansion of the Natchez sawmill during 1859, Brown needed several more sawyers than he had formerly employed. He was unable to locate workmen of the skill that he required in the Natchez–New Orleans area, and he therefore sought assistance from William Ferry, the sawmill manufacturer of Ferrysburg, Michigan. Ferry soon accommodated Brown by hiring two experienced white pine sawyers, L. M. Kimball and M. C. Messenger, who agreed to go to Natchez provided their transportation there was paid. Surprisingly enough, the two Michigan sawyers accepted Brown's offer of two dollars a day, and board, which suggests that wages in the Great Lakes lumber industry were lagging behind those in Natchez. Ferry advanced the workmen their steamboat fare totaling $80.80, and lent them twenty dollars for expenses. Brown quickly refunded these sums to the manufacturer in his letter of appreciation.[33] Not long after the arrival of Messenger and Kimball, Brown requested that Ferry send him two additional sawyers. In March, 1860, George Smith and James A. Wilson signed an agreement to work for the Natchez sawmill operator at the same wages of sixty per month and board.[34] These four men worked in the mill until it closed down, in company with Edwin Burrows, William Sanderson, William Brownlee, and upon occasion, Manuel Sparling. The seven sawyers were drawing wages of $2.50 a day and board during late 1860 and 1861, while Sparling as head sawyer was receiving $115 a month and board.[35]

Although Brown followed a policy of training his Negroes to fill many roles in his lumber business, including the management of steam engines, he did not trust slaves at the controls of power saws. He

[31] Andrew Brown Journal (1851–55), May 13, 1852.
[32] Andrew Brown Journal (1851–55), December 31, 1854; *ibid.* (1853–60), 208 and 454.
[33] Andrew Brown Cash Book (1856–64), 199, 200, and 202.
[34] William M. Ferry, Jr., to Andrew Brown, March 8, 1860, Learned Collection.
[35] Andrew Brown Journal (1853–60), 670.

apparently did not regard them as capable of carrying out the very complicated instructions which were necessary to produce lumber of the various dimensions required, and there is no extant evidence to suggest that he ever considered training Negro sawyers. In all likelihood, it was the lack of education among the sawmill Negroes which brought Brown to this negative conclusion rather than any want of mechanical aptitude on their part. In any event, the lumberman definitely did not exclude slaves from this category of skilled labor because of a desire to reserve higher wages for whites. He had no color consciousness of this kind, and economics would have disposed him to use Negroes in a time of rising wages for skilled workmen, just as he replaced white boatmen with Negroes.

On November 16, 1852, the editor of the New Orleans *Times Picayune* remarked when reporting a strike by steamboat stevedores that "the cheapness of slave and the dearness of white labor strike the most unobservant stranger as a singular feature in our domestic economy. No where in the Union is the white man better paid for manual labor than in the South." [36] Although the newspaperman was hostile to efforts of white laborers to raise their wages, and therefore biased, he nevertheless was speaking the truth. White manual laborers in the lower Mississippi Valley were relatively scarce throughout the antebellum period because cotton prices were generally favorable, credit easy to obtain, and abundant land available to the would-be farmer. Moreover, except in periods of extreme depression, the supply of Negro slaves fell far short of the demand. Consequently, wage earners were in a comparatively favorable bargaining position. Between 1820 and 1860, white laborers were consistently able to obtain wages of a dollar a day or better, a rate which gave them a better purchasing power than unskilled Southern workers enjoyed in the period between the Civil War and World War II.[37]

Sawmill workers in the lower Mississippi Valley as a class were paid at least as well as the general run of manual laborers. In the pine forests of Louisiana, for example, owners of small sawmills paid their mill workers seventeen dollars a month, plus room and board. As board was usually calculated at fifteen dollars a month, and housing

[36] New Orleans *Times Picayune*, November 16, 1852.
[37] The journals of the Natchez sawmill contain many references to wages of white laborers.

worth at least four dollars, the pine sawmill crews were earning slightly in excess of the dollar a day norm.[38]

When he first began his career as a sawmill operator in 1829, Brown paid his white workers from $0.77 to $1.25 a day in cash and fifty cents a day for their board.[39] In the event that they wished to feed themselves, Brown allowed them fifty cents a day in lieu of board. The Scot did not provide housing for his white employees because his mill was located within easy walking distance of Natchez-under-the-Hill. Other mills less favorably located, however, had to provide quarters for their white workers.[40]

Brown maintained his wage scale for white laborers virtually without change through the booming mid-thirties and the depression of 1839–49. During 1838, for example, Jacob Rasp, John Riley, Phillip Apple, and John Norton were employed in the mill at thirty dollars a month and board.[41] David Buchanan, an experienced riverman, was working as a raftsman at the same figure, but Harrison Masters, a less-skilled raftsman, received only twenty dollars a month and board.[42] A. Fife, a shingle-maker, ranking one step above common labor, was paid $1.75 a day, while Sylvanus Osborn, a carpenter, was carried on the books at two dollars a day and board.[43] During 1849 Brown hired two nephews, Alexander and Andrew I. Brown, as common laborers, and paid them twenty-five dollars a month. After the young men became experienced workers he raised them to thirty-five dollars a month. While working for their uncle the young Browns from Illinois were treated like his other employees, except that they lived in his house while in Natchez.[44] During 1853 times were prosperous, and Brown was experiencing difficulty obtaining enough workers to man his mill. He therefore, raised the wages he was offering for white labor to $1.25 a day and board, a rate he maintained until the Civil War.[45] As always, he preferred Negro sawmill workers to whites, hir-

[38] De Bow's Review, XII (1852), 635.
[39] Andrew Brown Journal (1829–30).
[40] New Orleans Times Picayune, March 31, 1850.
[41] Andrew Brown Time Book (1838–40), January, March 19, and April 28, 1838.
[42] Ibid., April 20, 1838.
[43] Andrew Brown Account Book (1836–40), May 12, 1837; Andrew Brown Time Book (1838–40), April 25 and May 15, 1838.
[44] Andrew Brown Journal (1848–1853), 35.
[45] Andrew Brown Time Book (1853–54), December 13, 1853.

ing whites only to supplement his basic crew of slaves, yet he was never able to dispense with whites entirely.

As Andrew Brown, Jr., discovered soon after opening his lumber yard in New Orleans, white manual laborers were able to command higher wages in New Orleans than in Natchez. During 1845, for example, he learned to his disgust that common workmen were receiving $1.50 a day in the Crescent City, while similar hands were being paid only a dollar a day at his father's sawmill. The differential, however, was less than he realized, inasmuch as the New Orleans workmen were not furnished board in addition to their wages. The following year, he wrote Andrew Brown, Sr., that "everyone has gone to Texas, almost, & men cannot be hired under 14 [fourteen bits, or $1.75] per day, which is normal." [46] Because of the wage level which he considered to be excessive, Andrew, Jr., adopted a policy of running his yard with the help of Negroes brought down from Natchez. When Key succeeded him as manager of the New Orleans division of the company, he too relied as a matter of policy upon Negro rather than white labor, where the lumber yard was concerned. On rare occasions when Key was unable to bring in enough Negro workers to deal with an emergency, he did resort to hiring whites. During the spring of 1857 such a situation developed, and Key informed Solomon at Natchez "that we are now hiring hands at $2 per day to get through our work." [47]

Despite their relatively high wages, common white laborers of New Orleans were unable to maintain as high a standard of living as Natchez workers, in the opinion of Key. During the yellow fever epidemic which afflicted New Orleans during the summer of 1853, the lumber dealer wrote: "I almost dread the coming of our lumber boat. I cannot forsee how it is to be discharged. Hands are not to be [had] that we can work, & what we may get will not be able to do half the work we have been used to exact. . . . I pity the poor & hardworking laborer in times like the present. They have neither the capacity nor the means of getting the attention that the disease so urgently needs. Our Factory hands are nearly all down. . . . Two of our best hands have died since Saturday, Teddy D. Noyes & Grimes." [48]

From surviving records of the lumber company at Natchez, it is unmistakably clear that Andrew Brown from the beginning of his

[46] Andrew Brown, Jr., to Andrew Brown, June 6, 1846, Learned Collection.
[47] Key to Solomon, May 28, 1857, *ibid.*
[48] *Ibid.*, August 2, 1853.

career as a lumberman intended to use slaves in his sawmilling operation in preference to whites. During 1829 and 1830, Brown employed eight slaves in the sawmill, two of whom belonged to the partnership of Brown and Dart and six of whom were hired by the partners from their owners. As Brown was paying from $0.77 to $1.00 a day for both whites and slaves, he obviously was not motivated by an impulse to use hired slaves as a cheap substitute for whites. This conclusion is supported by the purchase of "Boneypart" on September 25, 1829, for the sum of four hundred dollars, no trifling amount to Brown and Charles Dart at this starting point in their careers as lumbermen. James Matthews was one of the Negroes hired by Brown at this early date, and he and "Boneypart" continued to be trusted workers in the lumber business for many years, outlasting all of the white employees on Brown's payroll at this time.[49]

When his financial condition permitted, Brown invested surplus funds in slaves, both on his own account and on behalf of the company. During 1835, the year in which he first enlarged the original sawmill, the Scottish architect acquired five men and one woman, including Charles who was to serve in the mill until his death many years later.[50] Even during the depths of the depression, in 1842, Brown purchased David when William Lancashire offered him for sale in a package with two horses and a cart for the bargain price of $400.[51] In 1846, as previously mentioned, he obtained title to Spencer, a skilled blacksmith who was twenty-four years old, for the relatively high price of $1020. Even the frugal Andrew Brown, Jr., regarded buying Spencer, who was "warranted sound & healthy in body and mind and a slave for life & title good against the claims of all persons whatever," [52] as a sound investment, "for blacksmith work done for the mill each year is $300 & upwards, besides what has heretofore been done at the mill." [53]

After purchasing Daniel for six hundred dollars on the last day of December, 1847,[54] Andrew Brown, Jr., informed his father regretfully that their purchases of lots needed to expand the lumber yard

[49] Andrew Brown Journal (1829–30).
[50] Andrew Brown Journal (1835), August 31 and December 17, 1835.
[51] Andrew Brown Journal (1840–43), 167.
[52] Noland D. James to Andrew Brown & Son, May 15, 1846, Learned Collection.
[53] Andrew Brown, Jr., to Andrew Brown, May 1, 1846, ibid.
[54] Andrew Brown Journal (1843–48), 197.

had been interferring with their program of acquiring slaves.[55] On February 12, 1848, however, the younger Brown bought George and Aleck for the company for eight hundred dollars each, in addition to paying seven hundred fifty dollars for Anthony on behalf of Brown's sawyer, C. S. Ricks.[56] His father purchased two Negro girls, Judy and Julia, for house servants about this time, paying four hundred dollars for each one.[57] Finally, during October and November, 1848, the company bought three more Negro men, William, Henry, and Dan Hunter for eighteen hundred dollars.[58] At this point, the death of Andrew Brown, Jr., and the subsequent reorganization of the company put a temporary end to the acquisition of slaves for the sawmill.

In 1851, the partnership of Brown and Key resumed the long-standing policy of investing surplus funds in slaves, as did Andrew Brown himself. Between them, the Scottish lumbermen purchased at least thirty-five Negro men to serve in the sawmill and in the lumber yard at New Orleans, as well as on boating and rafting crews. The company acquired John Key, Garland, and Jo Mac, during 1851,[59] and Tom Turner, Henry, Lewis, John Anderson, Will Selby, Jack Flournoy, Roland Napier, Mack, Henry, John Taylor, Wyatt, and Gale during 1858–60.[60] Andrew Brown invested his own funds in purchases of William Hamilton, Dan Tucker, Isham Seaton, "Big" George Washington, and Abraham, during 1851 and 1852.[61] The following year he acquired Gallon Weekly (whose original owner apparently possessed an active if perverted sense of humor), "Little" George Rochester, Joe, and Scott Bowers. During 1854, he added Burrell, Jacob Pugh, Frank, and Dan Young. Key purchased Bob, Pat, Horace, Tom, Reuben, and Jim Cherry, on behalf of the company during 1856 to work in the New Orleans lumber yard; and Brown bought Washington Gray to accommodate his father, Simon Gray.[62] As the surviving records are

[55] Andrew Brown, Jr., to Andrew Brown, February 5, 1848, Learned Collection.
[56] *Ibid.*, February 12, 1848.
[57] A. B. Bacon to Andrew Brown, January 30, 1849, Learned Collection; Andrew Brown Day Book (1848–51), December 1, 1849.
[58] Andrew Brown Journal (1843–48), October, 1848; *ibid.* (1848–53), 4.
[59] Andrew Brown Pocket Day Book (1851), June 19, and July 4, 1851.
[60] Andrew Brown Day Book (1858–62), 96, 105, 123, 124, 213, 232, 252; Andrew Brown Journal (1853–60), 492, 555, and 589.
[61] Andrew Brown Journal (1848–53), 351, 397, and 419; *ibid.* (1851–55), November, 1852.
[62] Andrew Brown Journal (1851–53), May 10, June 1 and 19, 1854; Andrew Brown Cash Book (1856–63), August 28, 1856.

incomplete, it is probable that Brown owned several Negroes purchased during the thirties, in addition to those named above.[63]

In spite of his best efforts in that direction, Brown never attained his goal of manning the various divisions of the lumber company with Negroes belonging to his partner and himself. Throughout his antebellum career, he had to make extensive use of slaves hired from various residents of the Natchez area. Furthermore, several hired slaves like Simon Gray and John Clark were key members of Brown's labor force. During the 1830's and 1840's, those Negroes who were hired from owners not connected with the company, outnumbered the slaves belonging to members of the firm. During 1842, for example, Brown employed Scott, paying F. C. Vennigerholz $15 per month for his services.[64] From W. W. Wilkins he obtained six Negroes at wages of $18 a month and board; from Mrs. A. Lyons, another at the same rate; and from C. A. LaCoste, two more at $16.[65]

When hired Negroes proved themselves to be especially good workmen, Brown made a practice of purchasing them as soon as he could persuade their owners to sell. Scott Bowers was one of several who belonged in this category. He was employed by Brown from 1842 to 1853, when Vennigerholz finally agreed to sell him to the company.[66] On the other hand, Charles A. LaCoste persistently refused to part with George and Moses, apparently preferring the steady income he was receiving in the form of wages to their value in cash. These two men worked from 1842 until the death of Moses in 1853.

By an ironic quirk of fate, LaCoste became disturbed in 1850 by the news that Charles Kingman, one of Brown's sawmill slaves, had been drowned. Fearing for the safety of his own Negroes, he wrote Brown as follows:

The recent loss of hands, by drowning, which you have sustained at the mill . . . prompt me, once more, to recall to your mind the imperative conditions upon which I have hired to you the boys *George & Moses* viz: *that they are to be employed on shore, and not in any work on the River*, either in rafting or floating logs to or from the mill. This condition I must insist upon your conforming to strickly, for the safety of the boys is an object of much greater solicitude to me than the amount of hire which I get from their labor. If you have any objection

[63] Andrew Brown & Co. Journal (1855–60), 22, 111; Andrew Brown & Co. Cash Book (1857–65), 185.
[64] Andrew Brown Day Book (1843–48), December 27, 1843.
[65] Andrew Brown Journal (1840–43), 186.
[66] *Ibid.* (1853–60), 35.

to the condition, I shall be at all times ready to relieve you of the boys and seek other employment for them.[67]

Upon receiving Brown's assurance that his slaves would be used only in the sawmill and sawmill yard, LaCoste left them with the lumber company. Three years later, however, Moses died of natural causes.[68]

Hugh L. Jones regularly hired out some of his slaves to Brown during the 1850's. One of them, John Clark, entered the sawmill as a hired hand during 1849 and remained there until the saws were stopped by the Civil War. He was employed on rafts and flatboats and in cutting timber, as well as as a regular mill worker. Jones received fifteen dollars a month from Brown for Clark, and he never agreed to sell the experienced Negro to Brown.[69]

Brown's sawmill crews varied in size and composition in accordance with the shifting production rate of the enterprise. During March, 1849, when the mill was producing lumber on a seven-day schedule, the names of thirty-one manual laborers were listed on the payroll. Five of the men drawing daily wages were white; they were John Cruse, Thomas Ager, Peter Griffin, George Sims, and William Holloway. Cruse, Sims, and Holloway ordinarily were occupied with bringing timber down to the mill from Old River, but at this time the raftsmen were employed in the mill. Of the Negro mill hands, eight were hired by Brown on a semi-permanent basis, with their owners receiving monthly payments for their services. Four others had been recently added to the crew to assist during the rush period, and they accordingly were drawing daily wages. The remaining sixteen Negroes fell into three categories; those belonging to Andrew Brown personally, those owned by the firm, and a few hired on a virtually permanent basis so that they were indistinguishable from the first two groups. Although gaps in the records made it impossible to determine ownership of several Negroes, Brown and the firm between them owned about a dozen slaves at this time.[70]

Under normal operating conditions during the 1840's Brown employed considerably fewer men around the mill than he did in later years. In November of 1848, for instance, he was using only eleven

[67] Charles A. LaCoste to Andrew Brown, August 12, 1850, Learned Collection.
[68] Andrew Brown Journal (1851–55), February, 1853.
[69] Andrew Brown Cash Book (1855–64), 220; Andrew Brown Day Book (1855–58), 171; Andrew Brown Journal (1853–60), 117, 163, and 594; Paul to Key, April 15, 1864, Learned Collection.
[70] Andrew Brown Time Book (1848–50), March 12, 1849.

hands, none of whom were white. Other Negroes were working in the lumber yard at New Orleans and on flatboats and rafts. Brown at the time was using six slaves who belonged to A. Davis in addition to nine other Negro hired hands. George, "Little" Randall, Ben, Harrison, Gallant, and Aleck, who belonged to Brown or the company, were serving in the mill. Simon and Jim Matthews were working on the river with mixed crews.[71]

In January, 1854, Brown utilized seven white "Mill and Yard Hands." Among them, a blacksmith was receiving two dollars a day; one manual laborer, $1.25; and the others $1.00. Twenty-seven Negroes, including James Matthews, were in the mill. Apparently, all of them belonged to Brown or the firm except four who were hired on a monthly basis.[72]

Beginning in 1853, annual entries appeared in the journals of the lumber manufacturing division listing the slaves belonging to Andrew Brown who were hired by the firm for work in the mill. In that year he received fifteen dollars a month for each of nine Negro men.[73] During the following year, the number of his slaves increased to twelve, although the wage rate remained the same. As a result of deaths from various causes, the number of Brown's slaves employed in the mill decreased to nine during 1856, but the average wage of these surviving Negroes was raised to twenty dollars a month. In 1858, wages in the general area were rising because of prosperity in the cotton economy; and Brown accordingly increased the wages of his nine slaves to twenty-five dollars a month, where they remained until the mill was closed down.[74]

The purchases of slaves undertaken by Brown and his various partners during the 1840's and 1850's were offset to a degree by a fairly high mortality rate among Negroes associated with the sawmill. Between 1844 and 1861, a total of seventeen Negroes died from different causes, including hired slaves as well as those belonging to Brown and the firm. Of these, two were children of Brown's female house servants, and another was an elderly woman. Most of the fourteen men who perished while working for Brown fell prey to illness; nine died from yellow fever, cholera, pneumonia, and other diseases. Of

[71] Ibid., November 27, 1848.
[72] Ibid. (1853–54), January 14, 1854.
[73] Andrew Brown Journal (1853–60), 84.
[74] Ibid. 162, 229, 295, 371, 453, and 670; Andrew Brown Journal (1861–70), 15.

the remainder, one was shot to death, two were drowned, one was killed by a boiler explosion in the mill, and one died as the result of a kick by a mule in the New Orleans lumber yard. Only two could properly be classified as industrial casualties, as the drownings resulted from carelessness of the men involved rather than the hazards of their occupation. In order to set this mortality list in proper proportion, it should be compared with that of Brown's own family, whose members enjoyed all the advantages that money could provide. During the same years, the family consisted of Andrew Brown and his first and second wives, his son Andrew, Jr., and his daughters Mary and Elizabeth. Out of these six persons, Andrew, Jr., and Mrs. Elizabeth Brown died of disease, as did John H. Foggo, the husband of Mary Brown, in 1865. Thus the death rate among the slaves, while high, was no greater than among the whites.[75]

Developments which followed after the death of Brown's slave, Jacob Pugh, revealed interesting sidelights on the Scot's attitude toward his slaves and also on the protection that slaves received from both civil and criminal law. During Tuesday night, October 20, 1856, Samuel A. Cox, an overseer, was passing through a residential area in Natchez when he observed that a drunken Negro was creating a commotion on the veranda of a nearby house. In accordance with a custom of the time, Cox placed the Negro, Jacob Pugh, under arrest for disturbing the peace, tied his arms behind him, and set out to conduct his captive to the police station. Enroute to the "Guard House," however, the Negro managed to wrench himself away from his captor, kicked him severely, and then fled with his arms still bound with a rope. Recovering somewhat from the kick he had received, but still excited, Cox drew a revolver and fired over the head of the fugitive. When the Negro failed to stop, Cox shot a second time, killing him almost instantly.[76]

Cox was arrested the following morning and brought before the coroner. A coroner's jury returned a bill of manslaughter against the

[75] Andrew Brown Cash Book (1848–55), March 11, 1850; Andrew Brown Journal (1843–48), December 14, 1844; *ibid.* (1848–53), 194; *ibid.* (1851–55), January, 1852; *ibid.* (1853–60), 6, 51, 79, 483, and 675; Solomon to Andrew Brown, January 30, 1849; Key to Solomon, January 9 and February 20, 1855, both letters in Learned Collection; Andrew Brown Cash Book (1848–55), April 15 and December 21, 1854; February 8, 1855; Andrew Brown Receipts (1850–56), May 20, July 10, and October 21, 1856; Natchez *Courier*, October 19, 1858.
[76] Natchez *Courier*, October 22, 1856.

unfortunate overseer, binding him over to the circuit court, and allowing him to go free on bail of three thousand dollars.[77] Andrew Brown, the owner of the Negro, Jacob Pugh, was furiously angry at Cox for slaying his slave; and he employed the attorney, William T. Martin, for a fee of $150, to assist in the prosecution of the overseer.[78]

Cox was brought to trial during the May term of the circuit court of Adams County, and the jury found him guilty of manslaughter in the fourth degree, after deliberating throughout the night. His offense as defined by the statutes of the state was "the involuntary killing of another by any weapon, or by any means neither cruel nor unusual, in the heat of passion." The jury apparently agreed that shooting the fleeing Negro was not necessary to bring about his apprehension since his arms were tied. In any event, Cox was given the maximum sentence for this crime, two years imprisonment in the state penitentiary.[79] According to the editor of the Natchez *Courier*, public opinion supported the actions of the judge and jury, despite widespread sympathy for the plight of Cox. In the popular view, Cox had been acting correctly when he arrested Pugh, but he had exceeded the allowable limits by shooting the slave.[80]

Cox's punishment for killing Pugh, however, did not end with his imprisonment. A still vengeful Andrew Brown brought suit against Cox for trespass and was awarded damages of $1,500. As the usual annual wage for overseers was $600, Cox was thus penalized by two years' imprisonment (with the accompanying loss of income for this length of time) and by an additional loss of two years' income in the form of damages. With this example before them, other whites were surely alerted to the risk involved in killing slaves under any circumstances whatsoever.[81]

From these events it is clear that slaves, as persons, were protected from violence by criminal law as were whites. Unlike the latter, however, Negroes enjoyed additional legal protection because they were valuable property. In all likelihood, the probability of being sued successfully for damages in the event they attacked a slave must have functioned as a much more potent deterrent upon whites than the

[77] *Ibid.*, October 23, 1856.
[78] Andrew Brown Day Book (1856–58), 296.
[79] "The State vs. S. A. Cox," Natchez *Courier*, May 14, 1857.
[80] Natchez *Courier*, May 19, 1857.
[81] "Circuit Court of Adams County—Third Day, May Term," Natchez *Courier*, May 6, 1858; Andrew Brown Journal (1853–60), 449.

criminal law itself. It is significant that whites killed one another with little regard for the criminal code during the antebellum years, but they very seldom killed Negroes even in the heat of anger. This, therefore, was the powerful protection against the ire of hostile whites which slaves lost when they gained their freedom. Indeed removal of the civil penalty exposed them to the savagery of the postwar lynch mobs. Freedom undoubtedly was sweeter for Negroes than slavery, but it was not nearly so safe.

The lives of Negro sawmill workers in Andrew Brown's enterprises were very different from those of field hands on cotton plantations. The principal difference was that Brown's industrial slaves were not regimented to the degree prevalent on cotton plantations. When their stint in the mill was completed, sawmill workers were allowed to pursue their distractions in Natchez as their fancies dictated. Aside from a curious item of $5 paid for "Scot's marriage fee," the extant correspondence and business records contain no hint that Brown concerned himself either with their social diversions or their morality— or their lack of it.[82] His Negroes frequently found themselves in jail as a result of their boisterous off-hour activities, but he paid their fines and dropped the matter there. In much the same spirit as a contemporary ship captain, Brown occasionally ordered slaves to be whipped, almost always, however, for infractions involving their jobs. His Negroes were rarely exposed to the "untanned cowhide" for other kinds of misbehavior. In fact, Brown usually did not punish runaways after they were apprehended and returned to Natchez, having the wisdom to perceive that flogging would only cause the culprits to desert again more readily when the opportunity presented itself to them.

Brown was also far in advance of his contemporaries in regard to his method of working slave labor. Instead of relying upon punishment as others did, he used incentives to obtain the cooperation of the Negroes. Moreover, he was ahead of his time in preferring to reward his workers with money rather than goods or leisure. From 1829 onward, he paid slaves a dollar a day for "extra" work done at night or on Sundays or holidays. Furthermore, whenever they were called upon to perform unusual tasks, they were rewarded with money. He also encouraged his Negroes to watch the river in front of the mill for loose logs and other salvageable pieces of flotsam by paying them

[82] Andrew Brown Cash Book (1848–55), August 3, 1853.

at the same rate as paid to whites. The Negroes often received from five to ten dollars for a log they had secured, which they were permitted to spend for whiskey or whatever else took their fancies. As a result of Brown's enlightened treatment, the Negroes in his employ were well-trained and relatively self-reliant. In the words of his nephew Alexander, "It is false about Negroes having no ambition. A great many of them [in the sawmill] work after hours and make as much as gets them a good soot of clothes to poot on Sundays." [83] Key violently disagreed with Brown's method of handling slaves and expressed himself to Solomon as follows: "I don't believe in giving Niggers money—the more they get the worse they are. God knows these Niggers are bad enough now!" [84] His uncle-in-law, however, went blandly on his way, completely disregarding Key's objections.

Brown's records also demonstrated that he maintained a consistent though unsentimental interest in the material welfare of Negroes in his employ. He fed them well in a commercial boarding house and provided them with clothing of good quality. In fact, the expense of clothing the slaves was a significant item in the total cost of operating the sawmill. Between January 1, 1841, and March 1, 1843, for example, Brown paid $1,151.43 to William I. Key and Company for purchase of Negro clothing and shoes.[85] The types of clothing issued to the slaves are revealed by a purchase Brown made on October 24, 1840, consisting of 36 pairs of pants at $2 each, 26 flannel shirts at $1.50, and 18 "Roundebout" jackets at $2.25.[86] During May, 1853, Key dispatched "per *Princess* . . . a package of summer clothing for the boys at the mill: 4 doz. pairs cottonade pants & 4 doz. shirts. I suppose that will be sufficient to give all of them 2 pair each." [87] During December, 1855, he reported that he was shipping "1 doz. pairs of Lowell Pants for the Boys, 2 doz. Blue flannel shirts of the largest size & 1 doz. each stripe & check, also of the largest & best [quality]." [88]

As would be expected from Brown's general attitude toward slaves, the Negroes in his employ received the best of medical treatment in Natchez or New Orleans. A bill presented to Brown by Dr. William L. Jones in December, 1854, showed that the Natchez physician often

[83] Alexander Brown, Jr., to Alexander Brown, December 30, 1846.
[84] Key to Solomon, November 10, 1855, Learned Collection.
[85] Andrew Brown Journal (1840–43), 218.
[86] *Ibid.*, 20.
[87] Key to Solomon, May 17, 1853, Learned Collection.
[88] *Ibid.*, December 18, 1855.

was called upon to treat sawmill slaves. Between September 9 and 20, for example, he made twenty calls on slaves in Brown's charge, for which he received a fee of two dollars a visit. During this interval Dr. Jones treated Scott, Morris, George, Sarah, Abraham, Josephine, Jim Matthews, John, "Boney", and an infant named Henry.[89] The lumberman apparently set no limit upon the amount he was willing to expend on one of his sick slaves. During 1856, for example, he paid no less than two hundred dollars for medical services rendered to his slave, Dan Young, who failed to recover in spite of the treatments he received.[90]

With the temptation of New Orleans so conveniently close, Key experienced considerable difficulty in keeping his lumber yard slaves in good working condition. With some bitterness he related to Solomon in 1855 that: "Two of the infernal Niggers in the yard got into a fight some days ago & one of them bit the finger of the other so badly that it had to be taken off to save the hand. Mortification had set in and was spreading up the back of his hand. . . . Doct. Bem had been dressing it for several days," Key continued, "but the devilish Nigger either could not or wouldn't keep the dressing on it. I had him moved from the house to the Touro Infirmary on Sunday morning. The operation was performed by Doct. Hunt. They can't tell yet how it may be, but so far it has the appearance of doing well."[91]

In June of that same year, Key reported another case of illness to Solomon, as follows: "One of our darkies [is] very sick, and I am fearful his case is a bad one. I had three of them sick with diarrhea last week & all got well but this one, & he, the damned infernal skunk, before he was well needs must gorge himself with fish or some other mess, and of course never said a word about being worse until the disease which is more of dysentery than anything else has got such a hold of him that it will be a hard matter to get him over it."[92]

During September, 1860, Key, for once, was able to submit an optimistic medical report. "That boy Bob," he wrote, "is very much better. Close attention and a good Doctor has saved his life."[93]

Although Brown generally received exceptionally good cooperation

[89] Dr. William L. Jones to Andrew Brown, December, 1854, Learned Collection.
[90] Andrew Brown & Co. Journal (1855–60), 111.
[91] Key to Solomon, August 28, 1855, Learned Collection.
[92] *Ibid.*, June 2, 1855.
[93] Paul to John Shanks, September 25, 1860, Learned Collection.

from the slaves in his employ, he was not altogether free from disciplinary problems. As Negroes who worked on rafts and flatboats enjoyed even wider latitude than sawmill laborers, they quite naturally succumbed to temptations more frequently than the others. The rivermen took every opportunity to go ashore at riverside towns, and, having money, they apparently had little difficulty in obtaining whiskey on such occasions. If they imbibed too freely, as they were prone to do, local authorities usually threw them into jail. In such cases, Simon, Jim Matthews, or other heads of crews would have to pay standard five dollar fines in order to free them. Incidents of this kind happened so frequently that they were seldom subject of comment by the white employees of the lumber company.

Jacob, who had belonged to Brown for more than twenty years, was especially adept at jumping ship. During September, 1855, for example, he took French leave from the steamboat *Natchez* while enroute from New Orleans to Natchez. Having no pass, he was picked up by the authorities in the Fourth District of New Orleans and lodged in the "Calaboose . . . with $9.25 to pay." [94] In October, "he left the boat last Saturday and has been loafing about on his own hook since. I caught him last night and administered some wholesome medicine to him that may be of service to the gentleman," wrote Key.[95] Only a month later Key reported to Solomon with exasperation that Jacob had approached the captain of a steamboat on which he was returning to Natchez with a request for a three dollar loan even before the vessel left the wharf. He explained to Captain Lutken not too convincingly that he needed the money to buy medicine because he was suffering from small pox. Lutken, who was no fool, refused Jacob's plea and instructed the Negro to return with his ailments to Key at the lumber yard. The slave departed forthwith but for neither the lumber yard nor the hospital. After catching and putting Jacob aboard a Natchez-bound steamboat for a second time, Key explained to Solomon that "he has been practicing the same game every week for a chance to dodge . . . . I think," he concluded wrathfully, "that you had better administer the same dose of medicine to Jake that Bill Hamilton got . . . and the sooner you give him a dressing the better." [96] Needless to relate, however, Brown permitted no such punishment

[94] Key to Solomon, September 8, 1855, *ibid.*
[95] *Ibid.*, October 20, 1855.
[96] *Ibid.*, November 24, 1855.

at Natchez for the Negro boatman who had worked for him since 1835.

On rare occasions Brown's Negroes were charged with theft. During 1835, in the first case of this kind, Aleck was caught stealing food from the kitchen of a nearby residence, and received a sound thrashing. Twenty years later Harrison committed a similar crime, and Brown had to pay fifty dollars to the Negro's victim in order to keep him out of the hands of the law. Big George Washington was involved in a similar episode, and Lewis stole a boat while escaping in 1862; but this completed an unimpressive total. Brown no longer punished his slaves himself during the 1850's, preferring to pay the white raftsman H. Coyle five dollars each for whipping them.[97]

Clues as to the real opinion of slaves about the "Peculiar Institution" are scattered through the ledgers and correspondence files of the Natchez lumber firm. Although slavery under Brown's administration was characterized by benevolent paternalism, some of his slaves were not reconciled to its restrictions by the kindness of the Scottish slaveowner. A few of them persisted in running away whenever they got the chance. To be sure many of these flights were more in the nature of schoolboys playing hookey than serious personal protests against involuntary servitude. Furthermore, there was no single instance of a physical assault upon a white by a slave in the history of the lumber firm. On the other hand, a few of the Negroes employed by Brown were extremely discontented with their lot, and made no attempt to disguise their state of mind.

Dan Hunter, who was purchased by Andrew Brown & Son during 1848, was rebellious throughout his years in the Natchez sawmill. He ran away for the first time during 1849, and was not apprehended until William Key offered a reward and alerted the police in New Orleans. Hunter made a second attempt to escape during 1854, but was quickly arrested and jailed. He tried and failed again in January, 1856. On January 15, Key informed Solomon that "we have found that Scoundrel Dan Hunter in the Parish Prison where he had been for a week. . . . He didn't give his own name, called himself Henry, & said he belonged to a man 3 miles above Natchez. I will keep him where he is until the *Natchez* is in, & in the meantime [will] have some wholesome medicine administered to him, which I hope will cure him of

[97] Andrew Brown Journal (1835), August 23, 1835; *ibid.* (1853–60), 277; *ibid.* (1861–70), 137; Andrew Brown Cash Book (1855–64), January 26, 1856.

city life." [98] Undeterred by the flogging administered at Key's orders, he ran away again with the same results in January, 1857. During 1860 the Negro succeeded in avoiding the local police and reached Texas before being captured. Brown dispatched James Nichols to bring Hunter back, which he did at a cost of $150. Undiscouraged by his many failures to secure his freedom, Hunter fled again in the spring of 1861, only to be caught, jailed, and returned in the custody of F. H. West, a white workman in Brown's employ. On this last occasion, his jail fees totaled $26.50 and West's expenses $5.50. After this he was watched so closely that he did not gain his freedom until after the fall of Vicksburg. No one knowing Dan Hunter could possibly have maintained an illusion that he was indifferent to his condition as a slave.[99]

John Key, although not as persistent as Dan Hunter, did not yield to him in his dislike for slavery. During 1850 Key was hired to Brown by his owner Hugh L. Jones for sawmill work. He ran away in December of that year, only to be captured and returned to the mill. Instead of punishing the fugitive, Jones gave him the customary "Christmas" bonus of a dollar in cash, which all Brown's sawmill hands received. Despite his discontent, Key was such a good worker that Brown purchased him at the price of $1,025 during June, 1851. The lumberman soon had reason to regret his bargain, for the rebellious Negro made his escape to Memphis. He was jailed there on September 27, and remained in custody until January 5, 1852, because he steadfastly refused to identify himself or his owner. In so doing, he chose to submit to incarceration rather than to return to the comparative freedom of slavery in Brown's sawmill. In another attempt, Key managed to reach the town of Raymond before capture. After being returned to Natchez, he tried to escape a third time in the space of a year. On this final adventure he managed to reach the Yazoo Valley, only to end up in the Issaquena County jail. To return him to Natchez after one of these flights cost Brown $101; another, $85; and the third $43.25. Although the records of the lumber company are silent on Key's subsequent career, the absence of his name from the various

[98] Key to Solomon, January 15, 1856, Learned Collection.
[99] Andrew Brown Journal (1843–48), 258; ibid. (1848–53), 81; ibid. (1861–70), 36; Andrew Brown Cash Book (1855–64), 56, 236, and 302; Andrew Brown Pocket Cash Book (1854), September 12, 1854; ibid. (1856), October 18, 1856. Andrew Brown to steamboat Natchez, October 19, 1856; Key to Dott, [1849 ?]; Key to Solomon, March 15, 1856, correspondence in Learned Collection.

lists of slaves suggests that the incorrigible runaway was sold by the company.[100]

William Thompson earned the distinction of being the only one of the many slaves employed by the Natchez lumber company who actually succeeded in making his way to freedom before the Civil War.[101] Brown purchased Thompson from R. H. Elam during 1851 for the sum of one thousand dollars. Although the Negro was assigned a responsible job with unusual privileges in the engine room of the sawmill, he was discontented with his lot. He ran away during 1854, but was captured and returned to the mill. During the following year, however, Thompson made use of his skill with the pen to forge a pass for himself. Armed with this document and a ready wit and tongue, the rebellious fireman made his way up the Mississippi to freedom in the North. Rumors that the fugitive had been seen in New Orleans or on various steamboats continued to plague officials of the lumber firm until a letter from Thompson to his friend James Matthews revealed that he was in Canada.[102]

The letter from this remarkable Negro is worthy of attention:[103]

London [Canada]
May 14, 1855

James Mathews, Sir,

I take up my Pen most Respectfully for to write to you hoping that this will find you and your family in good health as this leaves me in at Present, thanks be to God [for] all His Mercies to me. Sir, since I have left Employ [with the Andrew Brown sawmill at Natchez] I have been on the Great Western Railroad driving an Engine. I give my best Respects to Mrs. Marton and family, Andrew Bron and family, and all my Enquiren [inquiring] friends. Sir, I now state to you the Reates of this Country. This is a good Wheat country, and Oats and everything [is] in proportion, unless [except] Corn, and you [in Mississippi] can beat this Country growing Corn. Wheat is 2 dollars pr bushel, Oats 4 shilling

---

[100] Andrew Brown Cash Book (1848–55), December 13, 1850, January 1, and February 9, 1852; Andrew Brown Journal (1848–53), 234 and 283; Andrew Brown Pocket Cash Book (1851–52), July 15, 1851, January 1, 1852; "John Key's Runaway Exps.," Andrew Brown Receipts (1850–56); E. W. Shelby to James Nicols, February 18, 1852; W. H. Eaves to Andrew Brown, January 5, 1852, correspondence in Learned Collection.

[101] See John Hebron Moore (ed.), "A Letter from a Fugitive Slave," *Journal of Mississippi History*, XXIV (April, 1962), 99–101.

[102] Andrew Brown Day Book (1848–51), July, 1851; Andrew Brown Journal (1853–60), 99, 118. Key to Solomon, March 18 and June 10, 1856, Learned Collection.

[103] William Thompson to James Matthews, May 14, 1855, Learned Collection.

pr bushell, Pork 4 dollars pr 100 lbs. Butter is 20 ct. pr lbs. and everything else is dear in proportion.

When you write direct your letter to E. M. Jones, New Lon[don], Canada, West, for William Thompson.

No more at present, But I Remain your true friend

William Thompson

When you write let me know if you got anny word from my Mother since i lift there.

The combination of joy in his freedom mingled with concern and affection for Andrew Brown and his friends among the sawmill workers is most revealing about the attitude of William Thompson. Obviously lacking in animosity toward his former owner, the Negro was motivated solely by his determination to obtain liberty for himself. In short, he made a gallant flight to Canada in precisely the same spirit that brought many thousands of white immigrants to the New World.

9

End of an Era

THE lumber enterprises belonging to Andrew Brown and William Key were almost destroyed by secession and the ensuing Civil War. Indeed, the partnership survived the conflict as much because of good fortune as because of astute management. Clouds had begun to gather on their economic horizon soon after the beginning of the sixties. Having gained momentum during the preceding five years, the boom in the building trades finally reached its peak in the late spring of 1860. Beginning in June, the demand for lumber started to slacken as the confidence of the business community was shaken by the rumblings of secession. Although during that summer much construction was still in progress in the towns along the Mississippi River, few additional projects were initiated during the final six months of the antebellum period.[1]

The fading of prosperity in the lower Mississippi Valley was obscured by a general shortage of lumber carried over from the brisk building season of 1859.[2] Key had been unable to accumulate an adequate stock of building materials in his New Orleans lumber yard during the shipping season of 1859–60. He had, in fact, been able to provide the minimum lumber requirements for his woodworking factory during the fall and spring only by resorting to buying whatever in the way of lumber was to be had in the markets of New Orleans, Mobile, and Pensacola.[3] Consequently, he attributed an unusual absence of customers during the summer months to the unattractive con-

---

[1] William I. Key to John Shanks, June 19, 1860, Learned Collection.
[2] *Ibid.*, August 7, 1860.
[3] *Ibid.*, August 25, 1860.

dition of his stockpile,[4] a view that gained substantiation from a continuing demand for the products of his woodworking plant.[5]

Key began to shed his illusions about the general health of the southwestern economy toward the end of August, 1860. When an eagerly anticipated shipment of lumber arrived at this time, the dealer expected to be mobbed by his former customers. This, however, did not occur.[6] For several weeks afterward he clung to the belief that New Orleans building contractors had temporarily transferred their trade from him to other suppliers, and he still hoped to attract them back with a good assortment of lumber in his yards.[7] On August 25, however, Key noted with growing concern that "cotton is coming in fast, but there are no buyers here yet." [8] Within a month the lumber dealer was compelled to admit that the city was in the clutches of a full-fledged depression which would "deter a great many from building." [9] In his view of that date, the depression was caused by forebodings over the coming presidential election, with all its potentialities for trouble. Because of fears of political upheaval "our capitalists & monetary institutions . . . seem to be moving with great caution & uncertainty. . . . The purse strings now so firmly grasped by nervous hands," Key concluded, will only be loosed again if the "outcome of the contest . . . is favorable to the Union Party & the South, or in other words, Anti-Lincoln." [10]

As a prophet, Key was proven to be partially correct. The election of a Republican did nothing to lift the stagnation of business in New Orleans.[11] Instead, many business houses in the city closed their doors within a month after the election.[12] "A. B. & Co. are all right so far," Key reported to his partner at Natchez shortly before Christmas, "but how long I may be able to say so, I cannot predict." [13]

The New Orleans Sash Factory did not feel the collapse of the construction boom as early as the lumber yard.[14] Orders for doors,

[4] Ibid.
[5] Ibid., August 2, 1860.
[6] Ibid., August 21, 1860.
[7] Ibid.
[8] Ibid., August 25, 1860.
[9] Ibid., October 9, 1860.
[10] Ibid., October 9, 20, and 27, 1860.
[11] Ibid., November 13, 1860.
[12] Ibid., December 15, 1860.
[13] Ibid.
[14] Ibid., June 19, 1860.

windows and other products of the plant continued to be received' throughout the summer.[15] Furthermore, disease reduced the number of workers in the factory during August and diminished the rate of production, thereby stretching out the business in hand.[16] The inflow of new orders began to decline noticeably during October, however, and by December the factory was "only running half time." [17] All the remaining contracts were filled before Christmas, and the establishment was closed for an extended but unwelcome holiday.[18]

Although the lumber yard and sash factory experienced a very serious loss of trade during the second half of 1860, the year taken as a whole was by no means disastrous. Thanks to large returns from the manufacture of doors, windows, mantels, newells, and other fixtures, the combined profit of the lumber yard and factory for the year was $32,000, of which Brown received three-fourths and Key, the remainder.[19] Surveying the record of the New Orleans subsidiaries, Key observed that "we really have no business to complain, I mean comparatively with others. . . . Many of our wholesale merchants are not actually selling enough to pay their incidental expenses." [20]

The dearth of trade brought on by the disruption of the Union did not disappear during the spring of 1861. Nor did the subsequent outbreak of hostilities prove stimulating to commerce in the lower Mississippi Valley. The construction industry remained at a standstill in all the cotton ports along the river, and lumber manufacturers and merchants had no demand for their products. Consequently the net profits of the sash factory and lumber yard in New Orleans fell to a mere $2,000 during 1861.[21] The sawmill at Natchez fared even worse during the first year of war. Brown shipped only a single flatboat load of lumber to the yard in New Orleans and sold no more than 700,000 feet to local customers. Hoping that the depression would be of short duration, Brown continued to operate his mill. As a result the yards at the mill were bulging with 1,828,000 feet of cypress at the end of the year. When the ledgers of the manufacturing

[15] *Ibid.*, October 9, 1860.
[16] *Ibid.*, August 28, 1860.
[17] *Ibid.*, October 9, and December 1, 1860.
[18] *Ibid.*, December 11, 1860.
[19] Andrew Brown and Company Journal (1855–60), 426. Unless otherwise noted all journals, ledgers, etc., cited in this chapter are located in the Learned Collection.
[20] Key to Shanks, December 11, 1860, Learned Collection.
[21] Refer to the journals and balance sheets of these divisions of the company.

division were balanced as of December 31, 1861, they showed a profit of $20,423.53 for the year's operations, but this was largely illusory. Actually unsold lumber stockpiled at the mill represented this sum and a good deal more besides.[22]

With the huge inventory of lumber stacked in the yards to dry—two-thirds of the output of the mill for twelve months—Brown saw no reason for increasing the carryover by running the sawmill during 1862. He hired out some of the Negroes to various local businessmen and dispatched the remainder of the sawmill labor force to take part in his several logging enterprises in the Yazoo Valley. He sold only a small trickle of lumber locally during 1862, earning barely enough cash to meet his current bills.[23]

On April 29, 1862, the city of New Orleans surrendered to a Federal fleet which had forced its way past the Confederate defenses on the river after six days of battle.[24] Key, having left some months previously to accept a commission as captain in the Confederate quartermaster corps, was not present to witness the occupation of the city. Only Paul, who had experienced enough soldiering during the Mexican War, remained behind to attend to the affairs of the company.[25]

Key had found little to occupy his time during the latter part of his stay in New Orleans, and Paul found still less to do upon taking over his new post. After running sporadically when occasional orders were received, the sash factory closed down permanently soon after the fall of the city.[26] The lumber yard was almost as dead. On April 22, 1862, Paul reported to Key who was then at Natchez that "still no business doing nor yet any prospect. . . . We collect a little money now and again and pay but little out." [27] At that time Paul had about sixteen thousand feet of flooring and refuse in the yard, for which he was asking $15 per thousand. He found no customers, however, even at that low price. Having no work for them, he hired out the slaves belonging to Andrew Brown and Company to Simpson & Dorr, the Florida yellow pine dealers.[28]

[22] Andrew Brown Journal (1861–70), 85.
[23] Ibid., 139.
[24] James G. Randall and David Donald, *The Civil War and Reconstruction* (2nd. ed.; Boston, 1961), 446.
[25] John F. Paul to Key, April 22, 1862, Learned Collection.
[26] Key to Rufus F. Learned, July 20, 1861; Paul to Key, April 19, 1862, both *ibid.*
[27] Paul to Key, April 22, 1862, *ibid.*
[28] *Ibid.*

Where the lumber yard was concerned, the arrival of the Federal military forces in New Orleans neither helped nor hindered. To be sure, the slaves belonging to the company were freed as a result of the Federal occupation, but that was hardly a serious matter by that time. As Paul remarked during February 1863, "there are no slaves here now . . . but 'tis perhaps as well, having no work for them to do. They were only an expense." [29]

While Paul continued his life of unaccustomed idleness in the New Orleans lumber yard during early 1863, conditions improved temporarily at Magnolia Vale. With the preliminaries to the siege of Vicksburg in progress, the Confederate military at Natchez began to draw upon Brown's vast supply of lumber and timber, despite the old Whig's well-known Unionist sympathies. First, the Confederate authorities compelled him to sell several thousand dollars worth of lumber to them during March, 1863, for the river stronghold downriver at Port Hudson.[30] Then in the same month Southern troops building a boom across the Yazoo River at Snyder's Bluff as an obstacle to Federal gunboats confiscated their materials from Brown. In all the lumberman supplied the Confederates with 673 cypress timbers from his Baker brake.[31]

During the months of war preceding the fall of Vicksburg, Brown had pursued his logging operations in the Yazoo Valley at a faster pace than usual. Hindman during 1860, it will be recalled, had begun felling timber on lands in the Yazoo belonging to Brown.[32] Under the terms of his contract with Brown, Hindman employed and paid his own crews while Brown provided the timberlands as his share of the partnership. Shortly after the logging boss started work in Baker brake No. 2, Brown dispatched the Northern mechanic Manuel Sparling to conduct similar logging operations in another brake on Black Bayou which also belonged to Brown. Along with Sparling went Simon Gray, the Negro riverman, who had gained considerable experience working in the woods with Wheless, and twenty of the sawmill slaves. As Sparling and most of the Negroes were unfamiliar

---

[29] *Ibid.*, February [?], 1863.
[30] Andrew Brown Journal (1861–70), 162.
[31] Andrew Brown Cash Book (1856–64), 381–82.
[32] Andrew Brown Journal (1853–60), 669; Andrew Brown Journal (1861–70), 84.

with the logging phase of the lumber business, the white foreman and his crew fell for a time under Hindman's overall direction.[33]

On October 20, 1861, Brown received a report on Hindman's progress in the woodsman's own version of the English language. At that date he had "about twelve hundred tears of timber redy to float when i get the dam dun and if the watter is not two hy i will finish cutting and cleaning up the balence of the timber." [34]

Because the mill was not in operation, Brown dispatched the remainder of his Negroes to join Sparling's crew, which was working in a remote portion of the Yazoo swamplands. In accordance with Brown's instructions Sparling erected cabins for the Negroes and a storehouse for supplies. He then set the slaves to cutting fence rails and clearing cane from about forty acres of deadened timber where corn could be cultivated for the consumption of the logging crews. While waiting for his first harvest Sparling was inconvenienced by the necessity of buying corn from neighboring farmers which he had to haul for seven miles to the nearest gristmill. As the roads were extremely bad through the swamplands, the new foreman had to employ two yokes of oxen to pull a wagon loaded with a mere five hundred pounds.[35]

Hindman's crew of whites and Sparling's Negroes both continued to work in the swamps throughout 1862. During March of that year Sparling reported to his employer at Natchez that Hindman and his men were moving from seventy-five to a hundred cypress trees a day from the brake into the float road. The Northern mechanic-turned-wood-boss noted with approval that Hindman's white loggers were handling this phase of the operation with great skill. He had to report regretfully, however, that his sawmill Negroes were not yet competent at felling timber.[36]

If the slaves had not become skilled woodsmen, they had learned to take advantage of a conflict of authority between the two timber bosses. Complying with Brown's orders, Sparling had temporarily assigned a dozen Negroes to assist Hindman's white loggers. Although they worked without friction alongside the white loggers and lived amicably at their camp, the slaves devised a clever scheme by which

[33] Manuel Sparling to Andrew Brown, April 30, 1860, Learned Collection; Andrew Brown Journal (1861–70), 82.

[34] William I. Hindman to Andrew Brown, October 20, 1861, Learned Collection.

[35] Sparling to Andrew Brown, March 21, 1862, ibid.

[36] Ibid., March 30, 1862.

they were able to obtain issues of tobacco from both foremen, telling each, of course, that the other had withheld the rations due them. Hindman, having little experience with slave labor, was completely taken in by the Negroes' tale and after hearing their complaints rode his horse over to Sparling's camp in a fearful rage. Sparling later reported to Brown in obvious agitation that he had barely managed to avoid a fight with the angry and dangerous woodsman.[37]

Although Sparling succeeded in keeping his crew of slaves at work in the Yazoo Valley during Grant's siege of Vicksburg, the Negroes deserted the logging camps immediately after the fall of the city. Sparling then returned to Natchez carrying the ill tidings to Brown. As a result of this emancipation of his slaves, Brown and his partner lost human property valued at approximately ten thousand dollars.[38]

A few months earlier, tragedy had struck the small crew of Negroes which Brown retained at Natchez. Five slaves, including two who had formerly belonged to the New Orleans lumber yard, tried to make their way to the Federal lines. When these unfortunates encountered a Confederate patrol, they were taken into custody. With freedom so close Alfred rashly attempted to escape from his captors, only to be shot down and killed by the soldiers. Brown, who recently had spent much money and energy in avenging the slaying of another slave in similar circumstances, would undoubtedly have preferred to allow the Negroes to escape rather than have them recaptured in this fashion. Despite his emotions, however, he had to pay the costs involved in apprehending the runaways to the amount of $281. Inasmuch as the slaves were freed soon afterward, his loss was total.[39]

Thus it was that Brown's experiment with industrial slavery, begun in hope and undertaken with kindness and intelligence, came to a close in near bankruptcy, bitterness, and bloodshed. During his three decades as a slaveowning lumberman, however, Brown had proved conclusively that Negro workmen could hold their own with whites in commercial and industrial enterprises provided that they received proper training and that a respectable proportion of the slave population was capable of filling positions of responsibility and authority, if they were given a chance.

[37] *Ibid.*
[38] Andrew Brown Journal (1861–70), 143.
[39] Andrew Brown Cash Book (1856–64), 394; Andrew Brown Journal (1861–70), 170.

The loss of his slaves was only the beginning of Brown's misfortunes during the war. Immediately after the fall of Vicksburg, Federal troops occupied Natchez, and one of their first acts was to requisition Brown's entire stockpile of lumber, measuring nearly two million feet, for the use of the army and a "Contrabrand Camp." Brown reckoned the value of lumber confiscated by the military at $62,000.[40] When this loss was added to the value of more than twenty slaves belonging to the partnership and $36,000 invested in Confederate securities, the blow to the two Scots was staggering. About all that remained to them was the sawmill, some timber and timberland in the Yazoo, and the closed-down sash factory in New Orleans.[41]

Worse, however, was still to come. During January, 1864, the U.S. quartermaster seized the sawmill itself, requiring Brown and Key, who had been paroled as a prisoner of war after the fall of Vicksburg, to operate the establishment under military orders.[42] In taking on this employment, Captain Key of the Confederate quartermaster corps exposed himself to more than a little risk. As he had not been discharged from the Confederate army, he became liable to arrest as a deserter in the event he fell into the hands of the Confederate authorities. Key, however, was reasonably safe so long as he remained in occupied Natchez and did not venture into the no-man's-land of the Yazoo swamps where guerrillas were operating. Key's new position struck his former assistant Paul as comic rather than potentially tragic. On February 19, 1864, Paul wrote from New Orleans: "So you are employed on the mill, a Scotch Yank! Lord preserve us. The depravity of human nature is dreadful. What is your rank? Do you wear your badge of office front or rear . . .? I have been telling your friends that you were learning to be a pilot between Natchez & Vicksburg, in place of which I found you a sawyer's clerk—is there any stealing attached to the office? If so, count me in. . . ."[43] Whatever his shortcomings in regard to patriotism may have been as seen from the Confederate viewpoint, Key was no coward. He made several trips into the Yazoo Valley after timber during April and May, 1864, giving no

[40] Andrew Brown Journal (1861–70), 162.
[41] Ibid., 186.
[42] Ibid., 142 and 193.
[43] Paul to Key, February 19, 1864, Learned Collection.

heed to warnings about the danger from guerrillas working for the Rebels or bandits working for themselves.[44]

When the Federals moved into Natchez, Brown allowed his logging operations to lapse. Not needing any timber for the mill and being unable to maintain a logging crew in the Yazoo swamplands, he was reduced to asking Nelson Fulton to take charge of his timber and timberlands. Fulton, who was logging on his own account in the same swamps as Brown, agreed to guard his logs against timber thieves and to raft them to Old River along with his own.[45]

During December, John A. Klein, who had been one of the big Yazoo sawmill operators and timber dealers, wrote Brown that "I fear from the prospects before us the total ruin of our once prosperous and happy people. . . . I am trying to save something from my *wreck*," he concluded despondently; "I had a competency—but it is gone." Klein at this time owned about eight hundred tiers of 50- and 60-foot cypress timber in Old River, which he was hoping to sell to the U.S. government for three dollars a log. The agent with whom he was negotiating planned to carry his rafts to Natchez, if the deal was consumated, to be sawn into plank at Brown's sawmill. When he ultimately brought the timber to the landing however, the mill was no longer in Brown's possession.[46]

The Federal military authorities retained control of Brown's sawmill for less than six months before returning the establishment to the owners. Fortunately, Brown and Key had many friends from prewar days in the upper Mississippi Valley, and through such connections these erstwhile Southern Whigs were able to approach the appropriate officers in the Union army. Brown was able to prove that he had never been a secessionist and that both he and Key were loyal U.S. citizens.[47]

With relatively little difficulty they were also able to persuade the general in command to issue orders that their sawmill be returned to them. The lumbermen gained this important concession with such ease that they were encouraged to press their run of luck even further.

[44] *Ibid.*, April 30 and May 7, 1864. Refer also to Nelson Fulton to Andrew Brown, February 20, 1864.

[45] Fulton to Andrew Brown, February 20, 1864, Learned Collection.

[46] John A. Klein to Andrew Brown, December 29, 1863, *ibid.*

[47] Andrew Brown Journal (1861–70), 193.

They prepared claims for damages arising from usage of their mill by the army, and also for lumber confiscated during 1863, and determined to seek a contract to supply additional lumber for the army.[48]

In the first stage of his commercial offensive against the Federals, Key called at the office of the quartermaster department in Vicksburg. There he was informed that his case would have to be presented to higher authority at Louisville, Kentucky. He also was told that he would have to negotiate with the quartermaster at St. Louis as an essential preliminary before approaching Louisville. With the aid of Lieutenant Henry Nirdiken, who had been an intimate of Brown and Key while serving as a quartermaster officer at Natchez, Key obtained credentials authorizing him to travel to St. Louis, Louisville, and Huntsville, Alabama.[49]

Key presented his claim to the colonel in charge at St. Louis, arguing that the damages he and Brown were requesting were hardly sufficient to cover the cost of repairing the machinery of the mill. That officer readily agreed that damages in some amount were due the lumbermen, but balked at the figure asked. Key, shrewdly sensing that the quartermaster's objections were routine tactics, decided to press for the full amount. On May 26 he wrote to the senior partner that he was determined not to sign a lumber contract with the U.S. quartermaster department unless their damage claim was allowed in full. "However desirable it may be to get the Saw Mill out of their hands," he informed Brown, "it is equally desirable to get paid for the use they have made of it. . . . If we fail in getting possession of it now," he concluded, "I am convinced that we will have no more control of it so long as Natchez is occupied." [50]

Upon appealing to the authorities at Louisville, Key finally achieved his objectives. The quartermaster department returned title of the sawmill to Brown and Key and issued vouchers totaling $10,513.20 in payment for usage of the mill from January 1, 1864. When the vouchers were cashed, Key received $9,514.45 in greenbacks after paying the usual discount. While in the North he also succeeded in obtaining a badly needed contract to supply lumber to the army. The large sum of cash obtained in this fashion from the U.S. government plus a guarantee of a lucrative business for the immediate future was

[48] Ibid.
[49] Key to Andrew Brown, May 17, 1864, Learned Collection.
[50] Ibid., May 26, 1864.

sufficient to tide the partnership over a period which otherwise would have witnessed their bankruptcy.[51]

Key enjoyed no such success in his efforts to collect for the lumber taken by the army in the summer of 1863. During the process of moving headquarters from Natchez, the quartermaster department had displaced all records relating to the building materials in question. Consequently Key and Brown were unable to document their claim. Furthermore the Federal authorities in Washington were understandably reluctant to pay more than $60,000 to citizens who had lived within the Confederacy. As a result of these factors the debt was not collected by the owners of the lumber business.[52]

Nevertheless, the almost $10,000 in cash which Key had obtained was enough to finance the resumption of lumber manufacturing. Brown instituted extensive repairs of machinery in the sawmill almost immediately after learning the good news from his partner. Leeds and Company supplied him with the necessary materials for putting the machinery in good working order and employed three boilermakers in New Orleans to assist the lumberman with the more difficult tasks. The work progressed rapidly, being greased with that most valuable lubricant, U.S. greenbacks; and by June 18, 1864, Brown's mill was producing cypress lumber once again. As most of the repairs were completed, the boilermakers took passage back to New Orleans on July 2.[53]

Paul, who had learned in recent years to anticipate the worst, was pleased to learn that the sawmill was at work again but inquired pessimistically, "What if, after all your repairs upon the Mill, your friends should take a fancy to the machine?" In this instance, however, Paul's fears were without cause. The Federals in Natchez had no appetite for the business of lumber manufacturing.[54]

Paul, unlike Brown and Key, was apprehensive that Confederate sympathizers might take reprisals against the two Scots. On June 18, 1864, for example, he wrote, "The greatest danger I now forsee is Fire. There are people in these degenerate days who seem to think destruction the only thing to end the war." [55] He accordingly urged

[51] Andrew Brown Journal (1861–70), 193.
[52] *Ibid.*
[53] Paul to Key, June 18 and 28, 1864, Learned Collection; Andrew Brown Journal (1861–70), 199.
[54] Paul to Key, June 28, 1864, Learned Collection.
[55] *Ibid.*, June 18, 1864.

Key to be diligent in guarding the sawmill against incendiaries. "A good vigilant *white* watchman would be worth his weight in gold," he concluded, "[but] *do not trust a Negro!*" [56] During 1864, Paul was pleased to learn that Key had obtained a military guard for the sawmill. "It will relieve you very much," he wrote, "if you only get [on] the soft side of them." [57] In this matter, too, Paul was needlessly fearful. At no time did the Confederate military, guerrillas, or civilian sympathizers cause trouble for Brown or Key after they regained possession of their sawmill.

As manager of the business affairs of Brown and Key in New Orleans, Paul spent 1863 and early 1864 "doing nothing with every prospect of continuing at the same business." [58] Out of desperation he joined with James Davidson and Middlemiss Davidson in an importing venture in which they brought goods from New York for resale in New Orleans. The first two shipments they received during March, 1864, were of lumber, one of which they disposed of easily. The other, however, met with buyer resistance, ending up in the practically empty lumber yard. "It reminded me of old times to see even three small piles . . . ," he wrote wistfully to Key.[59] Three months later Paul was doing "no business of any kind." [60]

During November, 1864, Paul opened up a small lumber yard of his own while still retaining responsibility for the remnants of the business of Andrew Brown and William Key. Although he was selling nothing on their behalf, he handled debts owed to the older lumber firm, on one hand, and obligations owed by them on the other. His stock of merchandise on opening day consisted of 128,000 feet of cypress, spruce, white pine, and yellow pine.[61] Prevailing prices for lumber on the New Orleans market at this time were $100 a thousand for the best grade of cypress and white pine boards; $75 for top quality spruce, second grade cypress, and white and yellow pine. Yellow pine flooring, however, was in exceptionally strong demand at from $90 to $130 per thousand. These high prices were not the result of local consumption but, rather, reflected inflation and an abnormally high cost of transporting lumber to the Crescent City. Paul reported

[56] *Ibid.*
[57] *Ibid.*, October 22, 1864.
[58] *Ibid.*, September 12, 1863, March 16, 1864, and June 14, 1864.
[59] *Ibid.*, March 16, 1864.
[60] *Ibid.*, June 14, 1864.
[61] *Ibid.*, November 12, 1864.

to Key that all dealers were anxious to unload their stocks and that they would accept almost any offer if cash was involved.[62] He had rented one of the yards belonging to Brown and Key to a New Yorker who had recently set up business in New Orleans, reporting to Natchez that "the rent is very low, but better than lying idle." [63]

The end of the conflict brought no significant revival in the construction and lumber businesses in New Orleans. During July, 1865, for example, Paul noted that "there is no demand . . . for any . . . kind of lumber here at present." [64] Two months later he advised Rufus Learned, who was then employed in the sawmill at Natchez and who was laying plans for marrying Elizabeth Brown, to "look . . . for hard times for the next four years. If I were you I would not get married until 1869. I know 'tis a long time lost, but where is the provender for all the little mouths that may spring up?" [65]

The autumn of 1865 brought a temporary though small-scale upsurge in the construction industry based upon long neglected repairs. After many months of slack demand the mills were poorly prepared to replace stocks of the lumber yards on short notice with properly seasoned lumber. As a result, Paul commented: "What Planning [*sic*] Mills there are running are dressing flooring & ceiling just fresh and green from the saw mills. It is said there are large quantities of Yellow Pine lumber at the mills over the Lake, but there is no transportation for it. All the small vessels finding more profitable employment on charters bringing Cotton out of the small streams." [66]

Under the distressed postwar conditions prevalent in the New Orleans area, an aging Andrew Brown and an ailing William Key had no incentive to reopen their New Orleans branch.[67] Instead they dismantled their woodworking factory, sold the machinery, and disposed of their real estate holdings. Prewar financial matters, however, remained to be settled; and Paul was kept busy with lawsuits for many months after the close of hostilities. Thus a large and very promising New Orleans industrial establishment became a casualty of the Civil War.[68]

[62] *Ibid.*, November 18, 1864.
[63] *Ibid.*, April 13, 1864.
[64] Paul to Learned, July 1, 1865, Learned Collection.
[65] *Ibid.*, September 5, 1865.
[66] *Ibid.*, October 24, 1865.
[67] *Ibid.*, July 1, 1865.
[68] Paul to Key, January 2, 1866, Learned Collection.

Although Brown and Key were unconcerned with their New Orleans division while they were resuming production of lumber on their
own account at Natchez, they could not similarly ignore the problem
of timber. Obtaining sawlogs with which to supply their renovated
plant became an urgent matter for them in the autumn of 1865. For
a time Brown was able to purchase the small amounts of logs he
needed from passing raftsmen. These purchases were adequate to
supplement a stock of 250 logs which he had obtained from the U.S.
government during February, 1865.[69]

Looking ahead to the time when he would again need a regular
supply of logs, Brown took steps to revive his prewar logging operations in the Yazoo Delta. With the assistance of his friend Lieutenant
Nirdiken at Vicksburg, he was able to obtain passes during February,
1865. These documents authorized Nelson Fulton and William Jones,
as his agents, to proceed up the Yazoo in skiffs with their crews to
raft timber down to Natchez for "Brown and Key of Natches." Nirdiken included that particular stipulation in the set of credentials, "so
that, if the Q.M. should propose interferring, it would show quite
plainly that the Timber was brought out expressly for us," a statement
which implied that he was financially involved with his lumbermen
friends.[70] The Federal lieutenant was by no means averse to petty
grafting, as he revealed in a letter to Key. A "cotton shark" had recently offered him a thousand dollars to procure a pass through the Federal lines; but, he reported without embarrassment to Key, "I have
not spoken to the General in relation to this & *don't think* I will, for Mr.
Main might get me into trouble." [71]

Through Nirdiken, Brown also contracted with John King to bring
out timber for the Natchez mill.[72] This logman brought a raft to Old
River on August 12, 1865, containing 93 tiers of his own sawlogs and
55 tiers of Andrew Brown's. The Natchez company paid him $1,430
for his timber plus $337 for "secureing, splicing and running" Brown's
own logs.[73] Of greater significance to the firm, however, was a contract with John A. Klein, of Klein & Tucker of Vicksburg, signed
during November, 1865, by which the timber dealers was to supply the

[69] Andrew Brown Journal (1861–70), 215 and 217.
[70] Henry Nirdiken to Key, December 30, 1864, Learned Collection.
[71] *Ibid.*, January 2, 1865.
[72] *Ibid.*
[73] Andrew Brown Timber Book (1865–67), August 9, 1865.

lumber manufacturers with all the logs his crews could bring out of the Yazoo that season. At the time of the transaction, Brown gave Klein three thousand dollars in cash as a part payment for 439 cypress timbers and promised the remainder of the price of $5,897.50 during the following February.[74] On December 2 Brown negotiated a second purchase of 2,412 logs from Klein for the sum of $8,100. These, plus additional lots bought during January and February, 1866, sufficed to keep the mill in operation until Brown and Key were able to resume logging in their brakes with crews of their own headed by Sparling and Hindman.[75]

Brown re-employed Manuel Sparling during June, 1864, and the mechanic spent the next few months repairing machinery for a salary of $100 a month and board.[76] Joseph Smithlin, an expert sawyer, was placed in charge of the sawmill as engineer with the relatively high salary of $150 a month and board.[77] Inasmuch as the former slaves of the company had been emancipated and were no longer available, Brown had to recruit a white labor force for the mill. Although he experienced no difficulty in hiring all the men he needed while there was still much unemployment in Natchez, their wages nevertheless represented an unaccustomed and unpleasant outlay of cash. Between August, 1864, and March 31, 1866, for example, Brown's sawmill workers received nearly $19,000 from the company.[78] During this same period, by contrast, timber consumed in the mill cost Brown and Key only $14,000.[79] Furthermore Brown had to furnish his postwar wage hands with provisions and supplies on credit, thereby inaugurating a commissary system at the Natchez sawmill.[80]

Their contract with the U.S. quartermaster department gave Brown and Key a monopoly on the military trade at Natchez during the remainder of 1864 and 1865. This was salvation for the company inasmuch as the lumber requirements of the civilian population were limited under the occupation. At this time when cash sales to local carpenters were bringing in no more than five hundred dollars a month, the army purchased a monthly average of seven thousand

[74] *Ibid.*, December 2, 1865.
[75] *Ibid.*, January and February, 1866.
[76] Andrew Brown Journal (1861–70), 200.
[77] *Ibid.*
[78] *Ibid.*, 293.
[79] *Ibid.*
[80] *Ibid.*, 225.

dollars. Because of this trade, Key reported jubilantly during November, 1864, that the mill was showing a profit and that his major problem was obtaining sufficient timber to fill his orders.[81] In reply Paul commented sourly from New Orleans: "You seem to be doing a flourishing business, but from the number of hands you are working I doubt if the profits will be large." [82] He himself was selling almost no lumber from his New Orleans yard and complained that "these new trade regulations amount to entire prohibition." [83]

Brown, by making an adjustment to the usual capitalistic system of manufacturing, once more displayed his tenacity and his remarkable flexibility of mind. After spending more than thirty years in developing a specialized form of slavery suitable for the cypress lumber industry, during which time he had preferred Negro workers to whites, he was able at an advanced age to adapt his system of management to white wage earners when altered conditions demanded the substitution. In so doing, he laid the foundation for another successful lumber business which his son-in-law, Rufus F. Learned, was able to exploit with profit during the difficult years of the late nineteenth century.[84]

[81] Paul to Key, November 1, 1864, Learned Collection. Refer also to *ibid.*, December 24, 1864.

[82] *Ibid.*, November 18, 1864.

[83] *Ibid.*, November 20, 1864.

[84] Rufus F. Learned resumed his earlier association with the sawmill belonging to his stepfather upon his release from the Confederate army in April, 1865. Because Brown was almost incapacitated by his age of seventy-five years and because his junior partner Key, who was already suffering from tuberculosis, was preoccupied with negotiations with the Federal government, Learned was employed during May, 1865, as manager of the sawmill. On January 1, 1868, Learned married Elizabeth Brown, the younger daughter of his stepfather. When Key died of tuberculosis during April of that year, Brown's new son-in-law took his place in the firm as junior partner. After the old Scot's death on January 28, 1871, the Learneds purchased the interests of the other heirs and thus became sole owners of the lumber firm. Andrew Brown Journal (1861–70); Robert H. Stewart to the Estate of Andrew Brown, February 7, 1871; *Lumber World Review*, January 10, 1920.

Essay on Sources

A satisfactory history of the American lumber industry has not yet been written. James Elliott Defebaugh, *History of the Lumber Industry of America* (2 vols.; Chicago, 1907), the most ambitious attempt at a survey to date, is amateurish, outdated, and, despite its title, mainly restricted to the Northern states. The work nevertheless contains a wealth of useful historical source material. Stanley F. Horn, *This Fascinating Lumber Business* (New York, 1943), is less valuable as a history than as a description of the industry during the 1940's.

During the last three decades, the historiography of lumbering in the Northern states has been enriched by several valuable monographs. Outstanding among the studies of the industry in various states are Robert F. Fries, *Empire in Pine: the Story of Lumbering in Wisconsin* (Madison, 1951); Agnes M. Larson, *A History of the White Pine Industry in Minnesota* (Minneapolis, 1949); and Richard G. Wood, *A History of Lumbering in Maine, 1820–1861* (Oronto, Maine, 1935). William G. Rector, *Log Transportation in the Lakes States Lumber Industry, 1840–1918* (Glendale, Calif., 1953), is a regional study of a particular phase of the lumber industry. Paul W. Gates, *Wisconsin Pine Lands of Cornell University: A Study of Land Policy and Absentee Ownership* (Ithaca, 1943), is an admirable study in depth of the problem of land ownership. Two excellent histories of Northern lumber firms are Ralph W. Hidy, Frank Earnest Hill, and Allan Nevins, *Timber and Men: The Weyerhaeuser Story* (New York, 1963), and Arthur R. Reynolds, *Daniel Shaw Lumber Company: A Case Study of the Wisconsin Lumbering Frontier* (New York, 1957).

Outstanding among the biographies of lumbermen and foresters are James A. Cronin, *Herman Von Shrenk, The Man Who Was Timber: A Biography* (Chicago, 1959); Richard N. Current, *Pine Logs and Politics: A Life of Philetus Sawyer, 1816–1900* (Madison, Wis.,

1950); Anita Shafer Goodstein, *Biography of a Businessman: Henry W. Sage, 1814–1897* (Ithaca, 1962); Martin Deming Lewis, *Lumberman from Flint: The Michigan Career of Henry H. Crapo* (Detroit, 1958); N. Nelson McGeary, *Gifford Pinchot: Forester-Politician* (Princeton, N.J., 1960); George T. Morgan, Jr., *William B. Greeley, A Practical Forester* (St. Paul, Minn., 1961); and Andrew Denny Rogers, *Bernard Eduard Fernow, A Story of North American Forestry* (Princeton, N.J., 1951).

There is no history of lumbering in the Southern region, and only one state history has appeared in print to date: Nollie W. Hickman, *Mississippi Harvest: Lumbering in the Longleaf Pine Belt, 1840–1915* (University, Miss., 1962). Based upon very extensive research in the records of lumber companies, this work is a reliable history of the longleaf pine industry of the state. The author, however, did not choose to cover the hardwood industry of northern Mississippi or the cypress industry of the Mississippi Valley.

In Charles C. Crittenden, *Commerce of North Carolina, 1763–1789* (New Haven, 1936), the author briefly discusses the colonial lumber trade of that colony, including information on logging and sawmilling as well as the foreign commerce in wood products.

The best source of information on the development of the modern cypress lumber industry is Rachael Edna Norgress, "History of the Cypress Lumber Industry in Louisiana," *Louisiana Historical Quarterly,* XXX (1947). Other articles of value are Paul Wallace Gates, "Federal Land Policy in the South, 1866–1888," *Journal of Southern History,* VI (August, 1940); John Hebron Moore, "William H. Mason, Southern Industrialist," *Journal of Southern History,* XXVII (May, 1961); James W. Silver, "The Hardwood Producers Come of Age," *Journal of Southern History,* XXIII (November, 1957); and "Paul Bunyan Comes to Mississippi," *Journal of Mississippi History,* XIX (April, 1957).

Although no single work covers the lumber industry in the lower Mississippi Valley during the Colonial era, N. M. Miller Surrey, *Commerce of Louisiana During the French Régime, 1699–1763* (New York, 1916), places proper emphasis upon the place of lumbering in the economy of the colony. Based upon exceptionally thorough research, this monograph remains definitive despite its age. Valuable information about the trade in lumber between the mainland and Caribbean possessions of France is contained in Clarence P. Gould, "Trade Between the Windward Islands and the Continental Colonies of the French Empire, 1638–1763," *Mississippi Valley Historical Review,* XXV (March, 1939). Clinton Newton Howard, *British Development of West Florida, 1763–1769* (Berkeley, Calif., 1947); and

Cecil Johnson, *British West Florida, 1763–1783* (New Haven, 1943), both touch upon lumbering in the British portion of the Mississippi Valley. Unfortunately, comparable studies for the Spanish period are conspicuous by their absence. The relationship between economics and diplomacy of the powers interested in the Mississippi Valley, however, are explored in Arthur Preston Whitaker, *Spanish American Frontier 1783–1795* (New York, 1927); and *Mississippi Question, 1795–1803: A Study in Trade, Politics, and Diplomacy* (New York, 1934). Two histories of Louisiana published during the nineteenth century remain useful because of the contemporary documents which they contain: Charles Gayarré, *History of Louisiana* (3 vols.; New York, 1854); and François-Xavier Martin, *History of Louisiana from the Earliest Period* (New Orleans, 1882).

Valuable collections of published documents relating to the economy of the lower Mississippi Valley during the Colonial period are Dunbar Rowland (ed.), *Mississippi Provincial Archives: French Dominion* (3 vols.; Jackson, Miss., 1927-32); and Lawrence Kinnaird (ed.), *Spain in the Mississippi Valley, 1765–1794* (3 vols.; Washington, D.C., 1946–49). Less comprehensive, but still useful are B. F. French, *Historical Memoirs of Louisiana from the First Settlement of the Colony to the Departure of Governor O'Reilly in 1770* (3 vols.; New York, 1853); James Alexander Robertson (ed. and trans.), *Louisiana Under the Rule of Spain, France, and the United States, 1785–1807* (2 vols.; Cleveland, Ohio, 1911); and Eron Rowland, *Life, Letters and Papers of William Dunbar* (Jackson, Miss., 1930).

Among the contemporary travel accounts which contain observations of the cypress lumber industry are François Marie Perrin du Lac, *Travels Through the Two Louisianas* (London, 1807); Le Page du Pratz, *History of Louisiana* (London, 1774); Seymour Feiler (ed. and trans.), *Jean-Bernard Bossu's Travels in the Interior of North America, 1751–1762* (Norman, Okla., 1962); and Thomas Hutchins, *Historical Narrative and Topographical Description of Louisiana and West Florida* (Philadelphia, 1784).

Early secondary descriptions of the Mississippi Valley cypress lumber industry are contained in Simon L. P. de Cubieres, *Memoire Sur le Cypres de la Louisiane* (Versailles, 1809); and Benjamin L. C. Wailes, *Report on the Agriculture and Geology of Mississippi* (Jackson, Miss., 1854).

Some of the legal problems encountered by the lumber industry of the lower Mississippi Valley at the time the United States took possession of the region are discussed in Vernon Carstensen (ed.), *Public Lands: Studies in the History of the Public Domain* (Madison, Wis., 1963). Pertinent original sources are published in *American*

State Papers: Public Lands (8 vols.; Washington, D.C., 1832–61); and in Clarence Edwin Carter (ed.), *Territorial Papers of the United States* (18 vols.; Washington, D.C., 1934——). The development of a national policy in regard to publicly owned timber lands, including those of the Mississippi Valley, are discussed in J. P. Kinney, *Essentials of American Timber Law* (New York, 1917); and *Development of Forest Law in America* (New York, 1917); Bernard E. Fernow, *A Brief History of Forestry in Europe and the United States and Other Countries* (Toronto, 1913); and Benjamin Horace Hibbard, *History of the Public Land Policies* (New York, 1924).

The policies of states in regard to disposing of cypress timber lands in the lower Mississippi Valley are described in Robert W. Harrison, *Alluvial Empire: A Study of State and Local Efforts toward Land Development in the Alluvial Valley of the Lower Mississippi River* (Little Rock, Ark., 1961). The sale of swamplands by the state of Mississippi is discussed in Hickman, *Mississippi Harvest*; and in John William Wade, "Lands of the Liquidating Levee Board through Litigation and Legislation," Mississippi Historical Society *Publications*, IX (1906).

The antebellum cypress lumber industry of the lower Mississippi has attracted no attention from modern historians. Scattered references, however, are found in J. F. H. Claiborne, *Mississippi as a Province, Territory and State* (Jackson, Miss., 1880); as well as Wailes, *Mississippi*. Some information on the subject is contained in the U.S. censuses for 1810–60, but more is to be gleaned from contemporary travel accounts. Among the best of the latter are Thomas Ashe, *Travels in America, Performed in 1806* (London, 1808); Samuel R. Brown, *Western Gazetteer* (Auburn, N. Y., 1817); and Donald C. Peattie (ed.), *Audubon's America: The Narratives and Experiences of John James Audubon* (Boston, 1940).

Among printed materials, contemporary periodicals and newspapers are the most fruitful sources of information about the domestic lumber trade of the Mississippi Basin prior to the Civil War. *De Bow's Review* contains many articles of value on the Southern lumber industry in general, and the trade of New Orleans in particular, and in addition published many advertisements by manufacturers of machinery used in lumbering. The Mobile *Register* (1820–60) is a mine of statistics and general information about domestic and overseas commerce in lumber originating in that port. Much of the traffic between the Pensacola lumber manufacturing region and New Orleans passed through Mobile en route, and a good part of the lumber shipped from mills located around Mobile Bay was carried in schooners to the Crescent City. As a result, much data on this coastal shipping trade was regularly published in the Mobile newspaper. The river and seaborne commerce in lumber was so small in comparison to cotton trade that it almost escaped notice by the New Orleans press, as a general rule. Lumber prices, for example, were quoted regularly by the Mobile *Register,* but seldom appeared in the list of commodity prices published in New Orleans. Nevertheless, the *Times Picayune* (1837–60) and the *Courier* (1810–60) are indispensable sources for the antebellum period. In addition to occasional news items, these papers carried many advertisements for sawmills, lumber yards, and other facets of the lumber trade. At Natchez, the *Free Trader* (1835–60) and the *Courier* (1833–60) provided quite adequate sources of the Brown lumber enterprises. The *Ariel* (1825–29), the *Natchez* (1830–32), *Mississippi Republican* (1813–18), *Mississippi Gazette* (1818–33), the *Chronicle* (1808–10), and *Mississippi Statesman* (1826–27) provide information about the lumber industry during the first three decades of the century.

Details of lumbering along the Yazoo River may be found in the Vicksburg *Register* (1829–39), the Vicksburg *Whig* (1839–60), Vicksburg *Sentinel* (1838–60), Yazoo City *Whig* (1839–55), Yazoo City *States Rights and Democratic Union* (1839), Yazoo City *American Banner* (1855–56), Yazoo City *Democrat* (1844–54), and the Greenwood (Miss.) *Reporter* (1845).

Because of the custom of republishing clippings from other newspapers, such journals as the Jackson *Mississippian* (1834–60); Jackson *Southern Reformer* (1843–46); Jackson *Southron* (1840–50); Raymond (Miss.) *Hinds County Gazette* (1849–60); and the Woodville (Miss.) *Republican* (1823–48) were surprisingly informative. Newspapers published in the lesser river ports provided scattered items about the local lumber trade. Among the more useful in this category were the Vidalia (La.) *Concordia Intelligencer* (1843–52); the Baton Rouge *Republic* (1822); Grand Gulf (Miss.) *Advertiser* (1835–39); and the Rodney (Miss.) *Telegraph* (1837–40).

In the British Museum there are several bound volumes containing a remarkable assortment of American newspapers for the year 1858. By examining the advertising sections of these papers, I found it possible to determine what kinds of sawmilling machinery were being offered for sale in all parts of the United States in the late antebellum period. Reliable secondary accounts of woodworking machinery of the early nineteenth century are contained in M. Powis Bale, *Woodworking Machinery: Its Rise, Progress, and Construction, with Hints on the Management of Saw Mills and the Economical Conversion of Timber* (London, 1922); and Bryan Latham, *Timber, Its Development and Distribution: A Historical Survey* (London, 1957).

The reports from English consuls stationed at Mobile and New Orleans, which are in the Public Records Office in London, were most disappointing. While the letters from consular agents at Mobile are rich in information about the overseas trade in lumber from that port, their counterparts at New Orleans ignored the industry altogether. Similarly, American customs officials reported regularly on the export trade of Mobile, but made only scattered references to lumbering with respect to New Orleans. These reports are reproduced on microfilm in the National Archives, *Corres. of Treasury Sec. With Customs Collectors, 1789–1833, New Orleans, La. Oct. 11, 1803–April 11, 1833* (Washington, 1956), Microcopy No. 178, Roll No. 16; and *Ltrs. Rec. by Sec. of Treasury from Customs Collectors, 1833–69, New Orleans, July 1, 1834–December 26, 1836* (Washington, 1956), Microcopy No. 174, Roll No. 9.

References to Andrew Brown and his firm are contained in: *Biographical and Historical Memoirs of Mississippi* (2 vols.; Chicago, 1891): Harnett T. Kane, *Natchez on the Mississippi* (New York, 1947); John Hebron Moore, "Simon Gray, Riverman: A Slave Who Was Almost Free," *Mississippi Valley Historical Review*, XLIX (December, 1962); and "A Letter from a Fugitive Slave," *Journal of Mississippi History*, XXIV (April, 1962); *Lumber World Review* (Chicago), January 10, 1920; *Southern Lumberman* (Nashville), December 15, 1931; and in Andrew L. Brown, "Browns of Fife and Their Descendents in America, 1770–1953: A Family History Prepared from the Best Available Sources" (unpublished manuscript, 1953).

The Stephen Duncan Papers in the Department of Archives and Manuscripts, Louisiana State University, yielded no information about Brown. No documents of the period during which Duncan and Brown were associates had been preserved.

In preparing this study, I have drawn most of the information about Brown and his business enterprises from the Rufus F. Learned Collection in the Lumber Archives of the University of Mississippi. This collection, comprising approximately one hundred cubic feet of documents, is made up of files of correspondence, bound volumes of journals, ledgers, and account, time, and memorandum books of many types. The files of correspondence are nearly complete for the 1840–65 period, except for the years 1851–53, which rats and insects destroyed. Fortunately, however, Andrew Brown's incoming correspondence remained largely intact for these years. Most of his early papers, other than the bound ledgers and journals, apparently perished when his house was hit by the tornado of 1840. The bound business records, however, are complete for the entire period.

A trip to England and Scotland in search of information about Brown's career before coming to America was largely fruitless. The public records of the village of Crail, Scotland, for the eighteenth and early nineteenth centuries have not been preserved. The crumbling tombstones in the churchyard of the old Presbyterian church, however, reveal that the Browns were persons of consequence during the 1700's and that for several generations they had intermarried with the Keys.

Index

Abraham, 135, 143

Adams County (Miss.) board of police: contracts with Brown for construction of a bridge, 26

Adams County (Miss.) circuit court: convicts killer of one of Brown's slaves, 140

Agricultural Bank of Mississippi, 30

Alabama: timber resources of, 73–74

Alabama and Tennessee railroad: timber transported by, 73

Aleck, 93, 135, 138, 145

Alfred, 92, 155

Allen, Charles H., 61, 67–68

Allen, James A., 61, 65, 67, 76

Allen, Joseph W.: sells Simon Gray's family to Brown, 87

Altamaha River, sawmills on, 20

Anthony, 129, 135

Arkansas River: rafts of timber from, 57

Audubon, John J.: describes loggers in the Mississippi Valley, 74

Axemen, 63–64

Baker cypress brake, 153

Ball, William B., 66

Bank of Louisiana, 13

Bank of the State of Mississippi, 30

Baton Rouge, La.: construction of state capitol building at, 103; runaway raft passes, 89–90; sawmills at, 15, 47, 69, 78, 94; very early steam sawmill at, 15

Bayou Lafourche: runaway raft lodges in, 89–90

Bayou Sara, La.: planters purchase steam engines from Kentucky, 16; sawmill at, 75

Beard, C., 32

Bellechasse and Delarue sawmill, 17

Bellevue Cotton Press: buys lumber, 31–32; sold by Mississippi Shipping Co., in 1840, 37

Bibb County, Ala., yellow pine timber from, 73

Big Black River: loggers on, 61, 65, 67–68; sawmills on, 120

Biloxi: family of Andrew Brown, Jr., takes refuge from yellow fever epidemic in, 58; first French settlement in Louisiana at, 3; sawmills near, 11

Bingaman, Adam L., 35

Black Bayou cypress brake, 97

Bobbs sawmill in New Orleans, 78

Bogue Phalia: logging on, 64

Bouligny, La., sawmill at, 68

Boulton and Watt low-pressure steam engine, 15

Bowers, Scott, 95, 96, 135, 136, 143

Breakwater of Brown's sawmill at Natchez: construction of, 23; damaged by floods, 118; rafts of timber delivered at, 32; rebuilding of, 119; sawmill slave drowned near, 81

Brown, Alexander, Jr. (nephew of Andrew Brown): comments on piety of Andrew Brown, Jr., 51; describes home of Andrew Brown, Jr., 51; relates that Brown's sawmill slaves earn cash by working after hours,